ANHEDONIA
LINE AND POEM

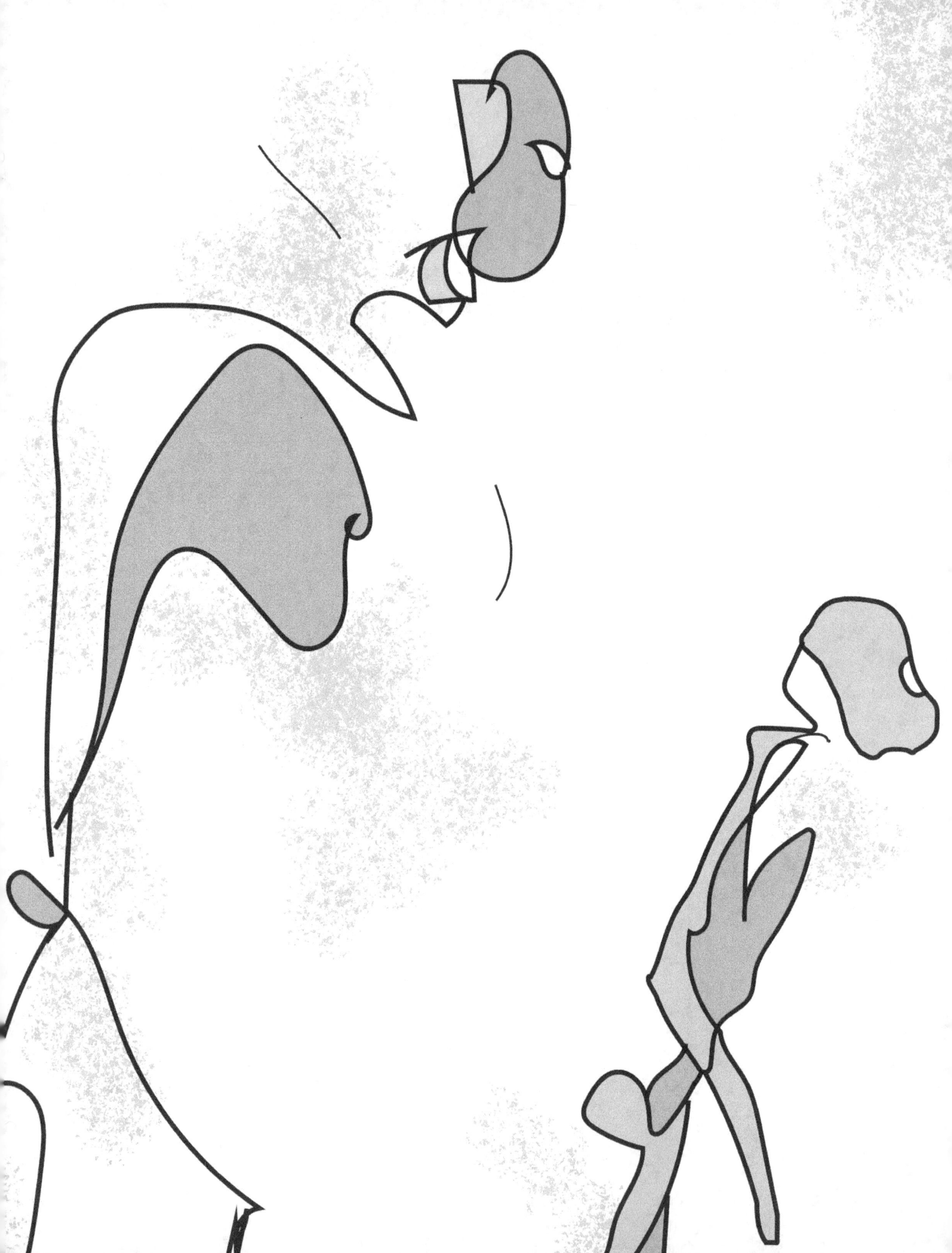

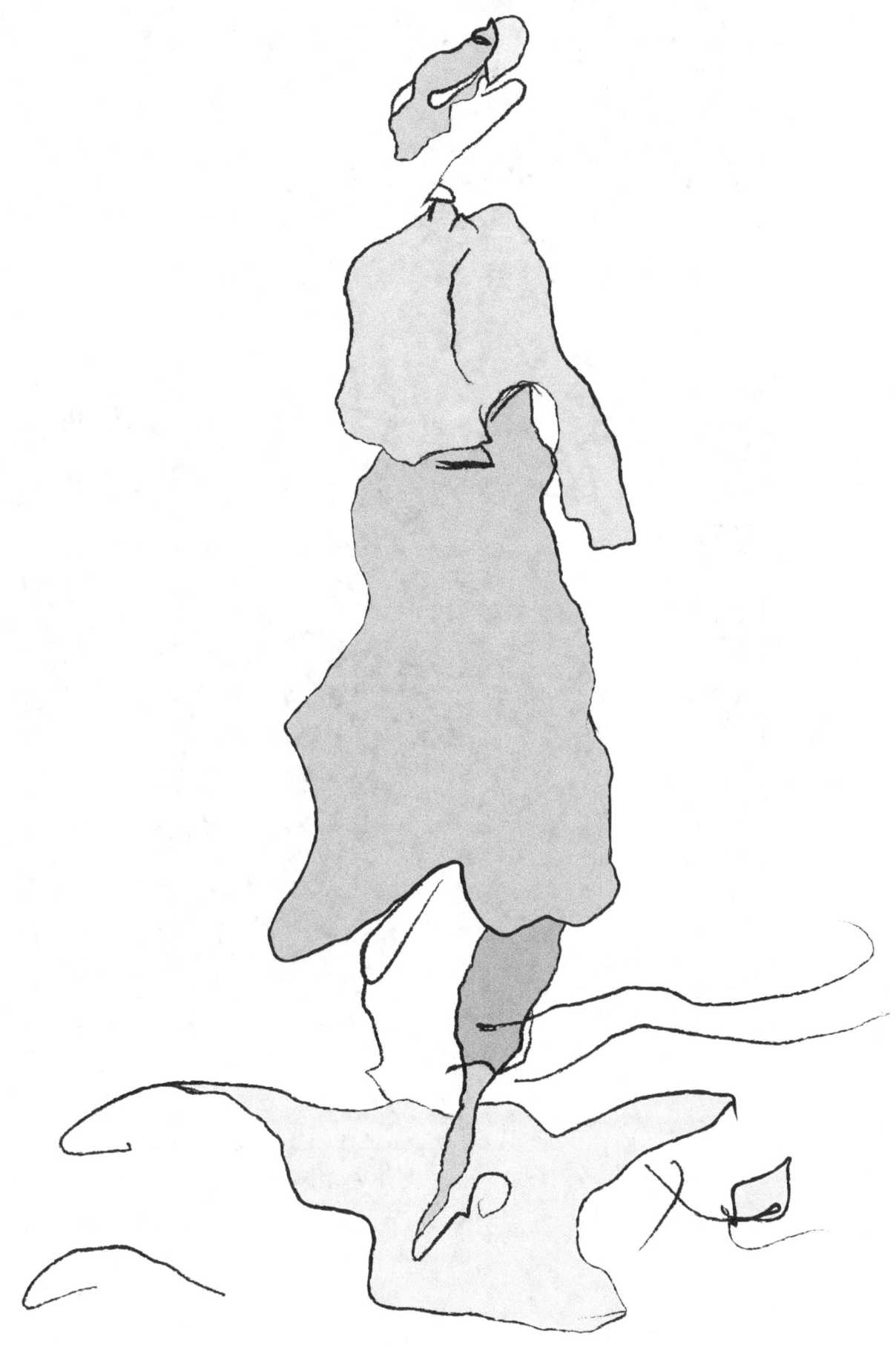

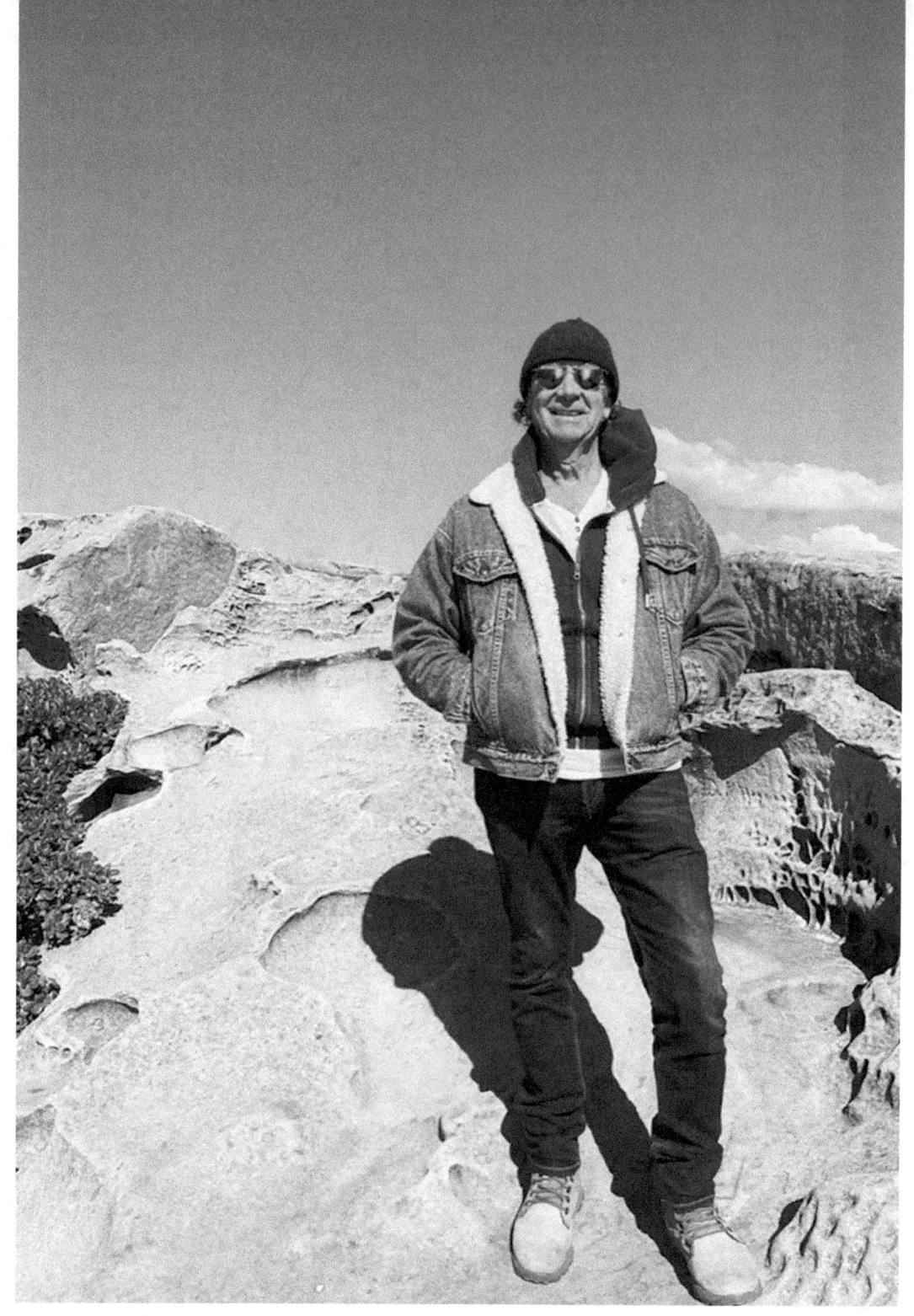

Bruce Blanshard
Born in Melbourne, Australia.
Award-winning Creative Director,
author, designer, painter, and editor.

ALSO BY THE AUTHOR

FICTION
The Gifting Tree
Cutter. Art Of Blood

LINE AND POETRY
Inkstone
Naked Hanoi
Anhedonia

NON FICTION
Unfu*k Yourselves

AS DESIGNER
Firmament Without Roof Cover
Seeds Of Night And Day
Out Of The Dark
Grass Cutting In A Temple Garden
A Ciel Overt
Night Picture Of Rain Sound
Cutter. Art Of Blood
Honey In The Blood
Quieter Histories
Poems From The Alley
Send The Raven
Unfu*k Yourselves
Fly Me To The Moon
Dance Me To The Stars

AS EDITOR
Honey In The Blood
Night Picture Of Rain Sound

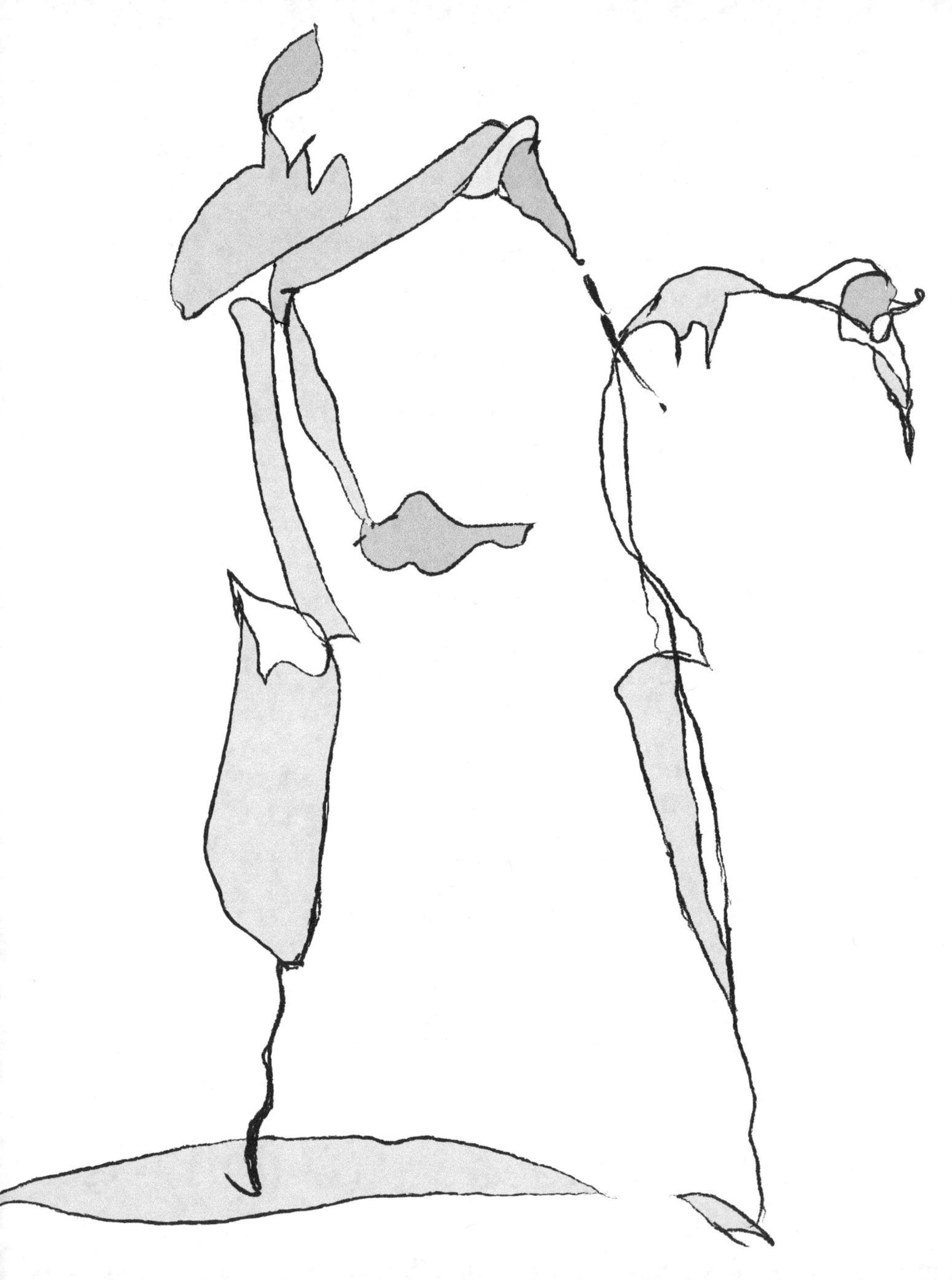

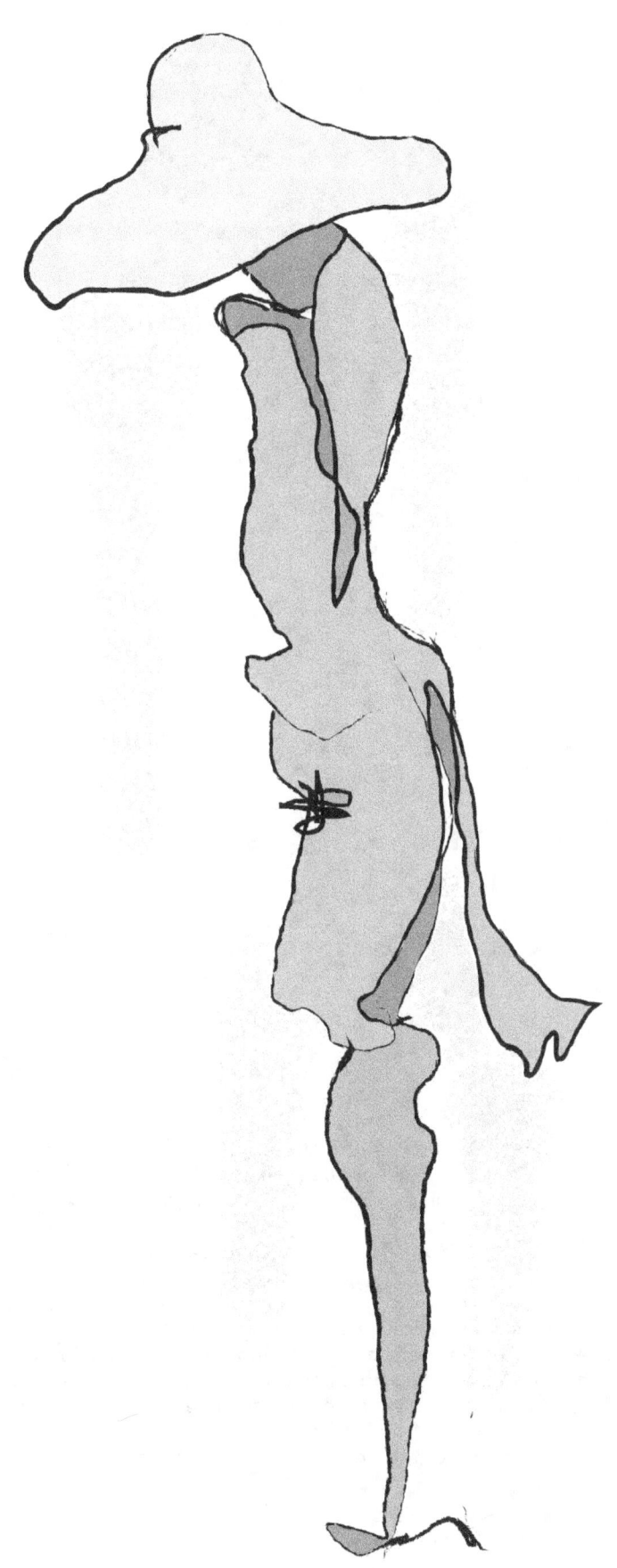

Published 2023 by Page Addie Press. United Kingdom. Australia
Anhedonia. Line and Poem
Copyright© All rights reserved, Bruce Blanshard

ISBN:978-1-7397780-5-7 paperback

No paragraph, photograph or part of this publication may be reproduced, stored in or introduced to a retrieval system, or transmitted, in any form (electronic, mechanical, photocopying, recording or otherwise) without the prior permission of the publisher or in accordance with the provisions of the Copyright Designs and Patents Act 1988. This book is sold subject to the condition that it shall not, be lent, re-sold, hired out, or circulated without the publisher's prior consent in any form of binding or cover other than the one in which it is published.

A CIP record for this book is available from the British Library,

BRUCE BLANSHARD

ANHEDONIA

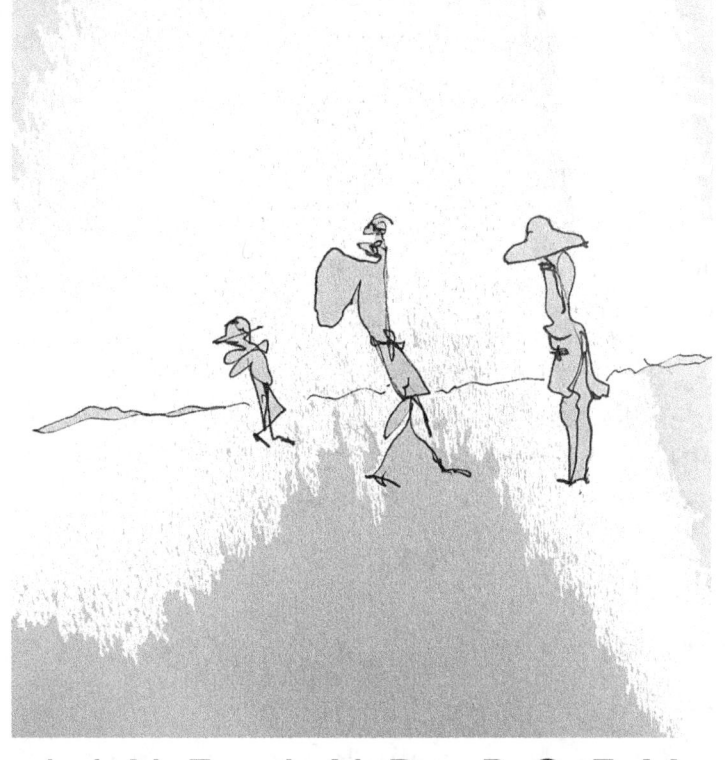

LINE AND POEM

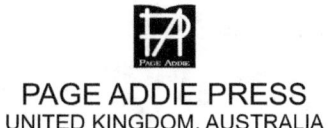

PAGE ADDIE PRESS
UNITED KINGDOM. AUSTRALIA

CONTENT

WALKER 12
LABYRINTH 14
SANDSTONE 16
BLUE SEA 18
MAGNETIC BEACH 21
CLOUDY 22
GULL 24
SUNSET STRIP 27
SAFE PASSAGE 28
LIVE MARKET 30
BACKDOOR 33
SEASHORE 35
FIFTY SHADE 37
DUNE GRASS 38
AUTUMN LIGHT 41
SHADOW PRINTS 43
BROKEN LADDER 44
SILVER RING 47
ANHEDONIA 48
BRICK WORK 51
STRANDS 52
TIN PAN BLUES 54
WAIST DEEP 57
HEADLAND 58
SIRIUS 60
AT SEA 62
SHADOW LIFE 65
EVENING LIGHT 67
OYSTER BAY 69
SPECKLED EGGS 70
SAND HILL 73
SHALLOWS 74

SHADE	76
RAGGED	79
SWEET CAFFEINE	81
BIRDING	84
TIPPING POINT	87
FLIP FLOP	88
SUNRISE	90
IRON BELL	92
STEVE (R.I.P.)	95
PARK	96
FLOOD WATERS	98
STREET CORNER	100
CONCRETE	102
CRYING PATH	104
CHANGE OF LIGHT	107
AMNESTY	108
GROUND ZERO	111
KEEP OF ROCK	112
NIGHT WORK	115
TRACKED	117
MONSOON	119
HOLIDAY	120
BLIND MAN BLIND WOMAN	123
BANYAN TREE	125
STUDIO	126
SEA BIRDS	129
SNAPSHOT	130
DESERT LAW	133
OPEN ROAD	135
TORA BAY	137
CHAIRMAN	139
BLACK SAND	140
TALARIA	142
HEARTLINE	144
SAPPHIRE BEACH	147

WALKER

Yellow sand underfoot
Aureate at blue verge of sea
Sun flares and disappears.

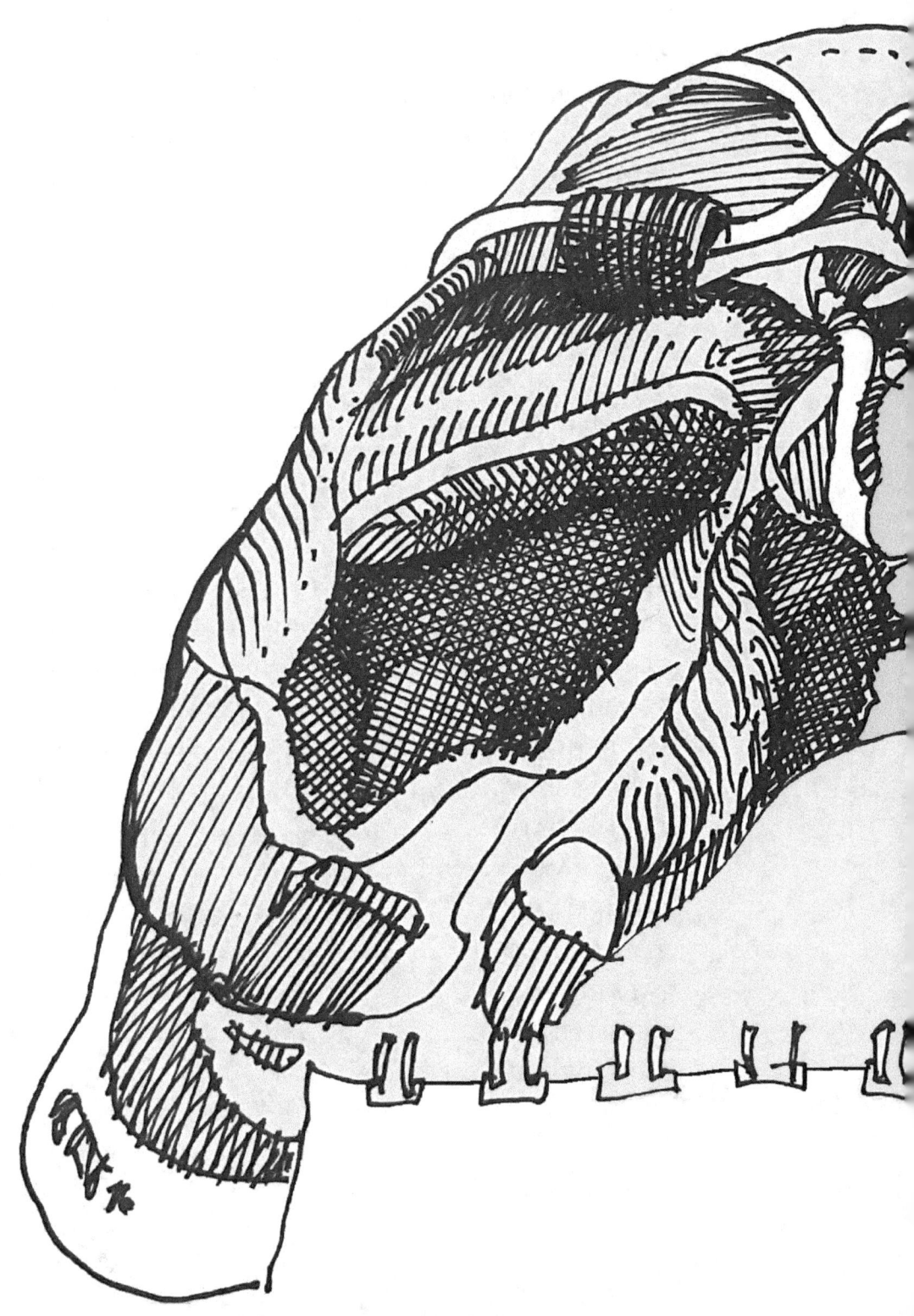

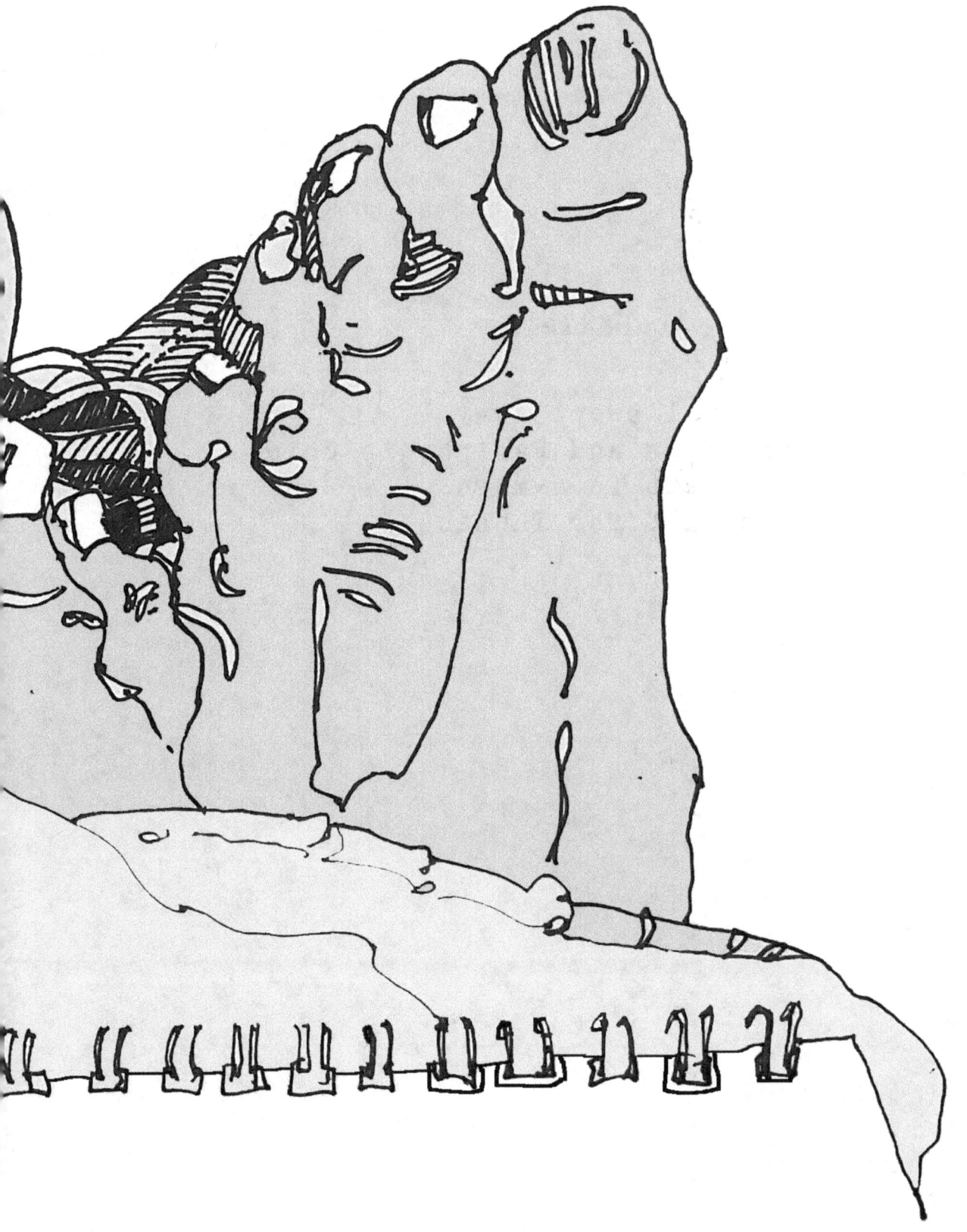

LABYRINTH

All swept away
Reborn in Minos and Pasiphae's union
Left in a maze
In wait for Theseus.

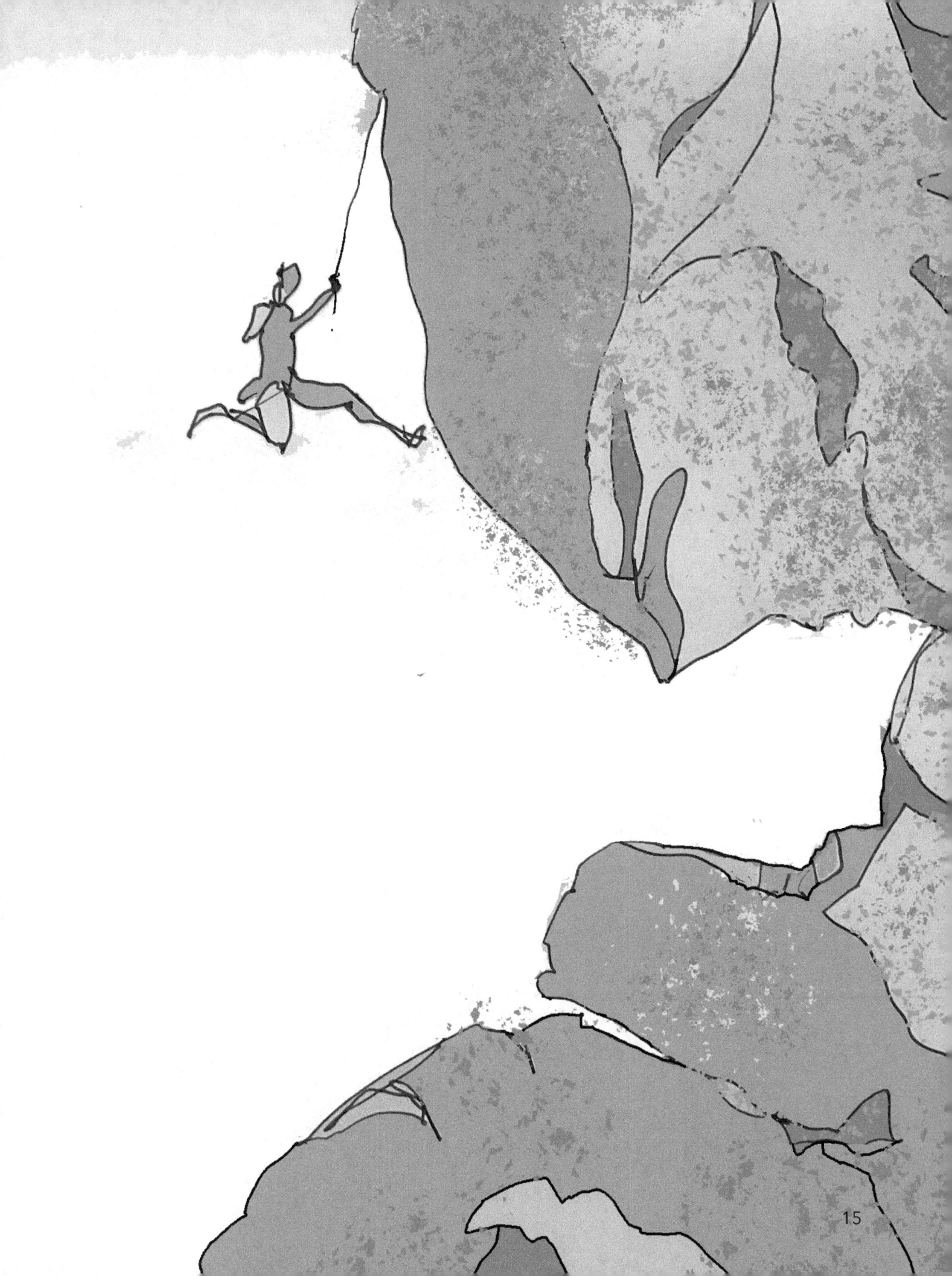

SANDSTONE

White gulls face
The after-breeze
Feathers arrowed
At the edge
Close against
The infinite breast.

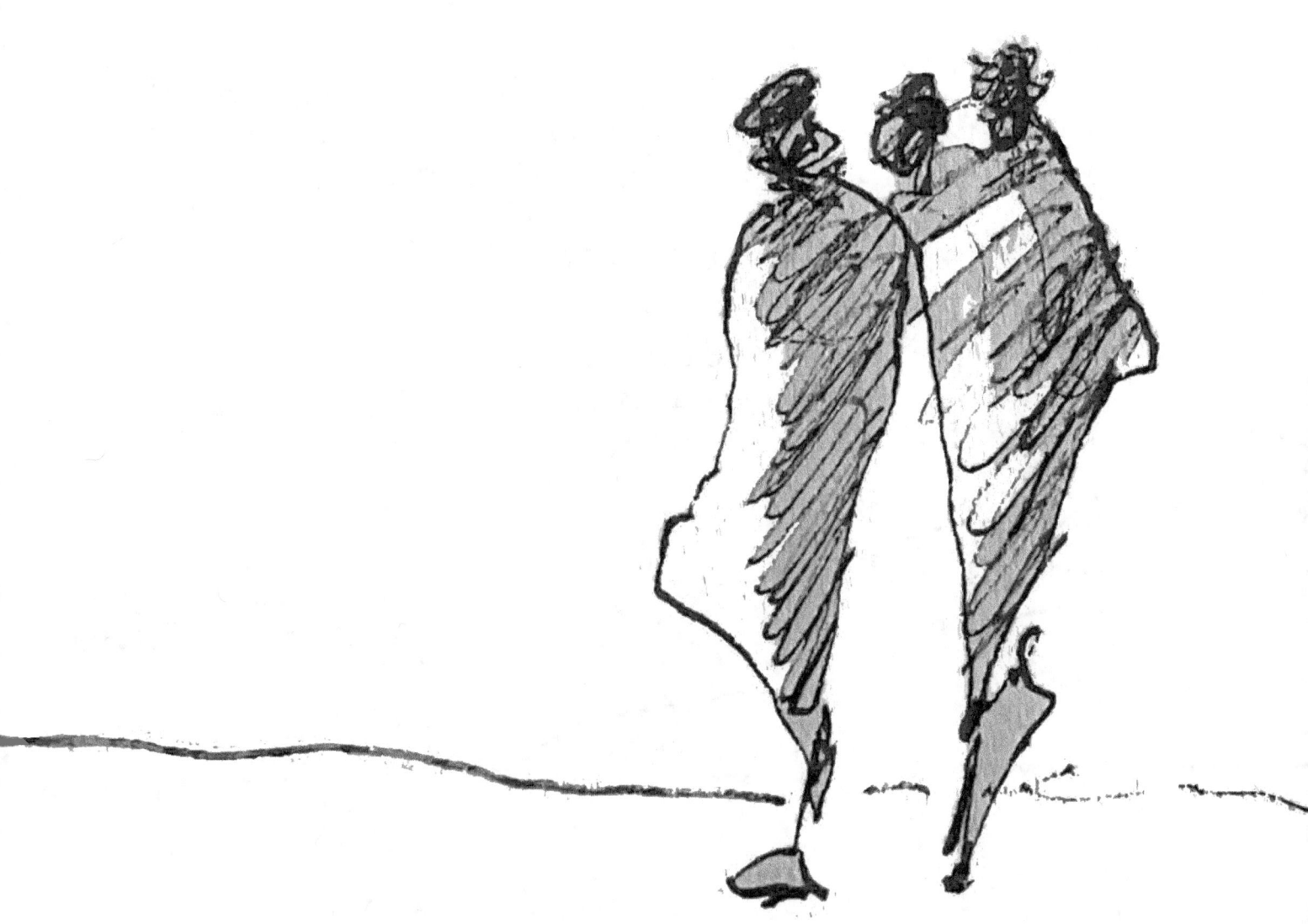

BLUE SEA

Endless blue
"Any benediction here?"
A whisper.

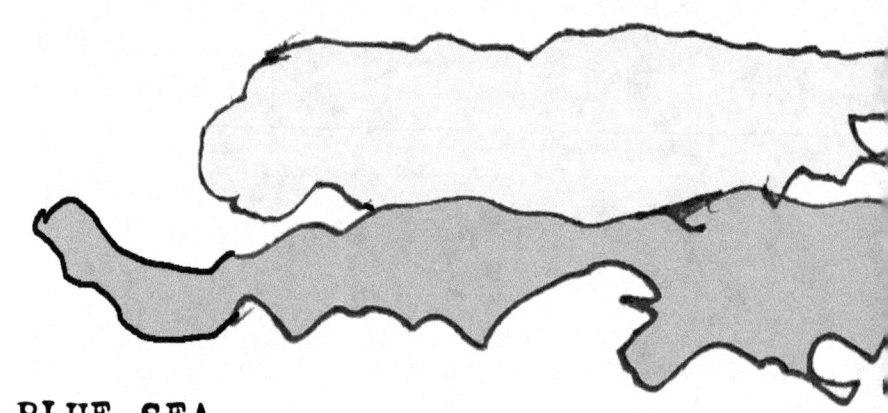

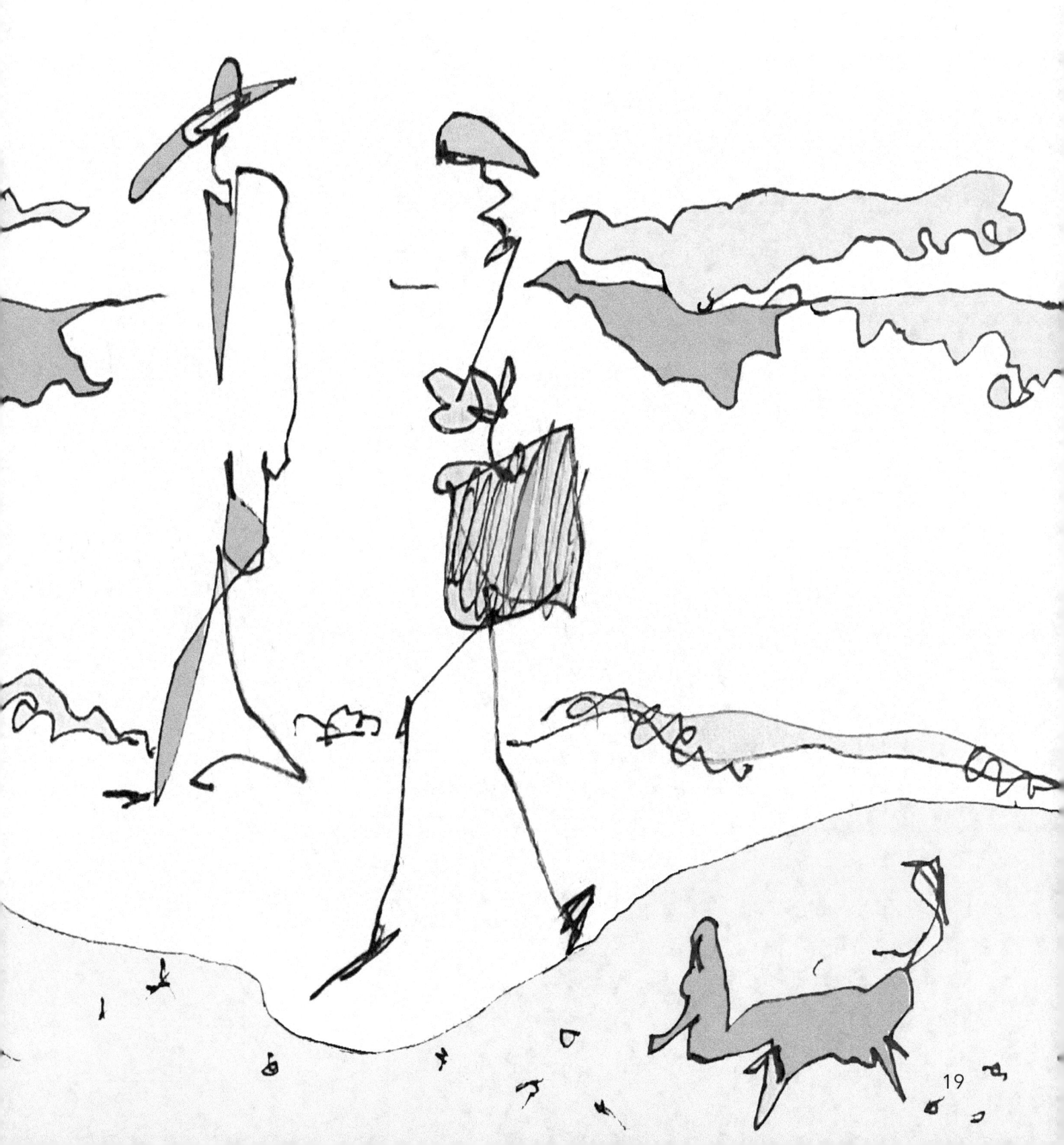

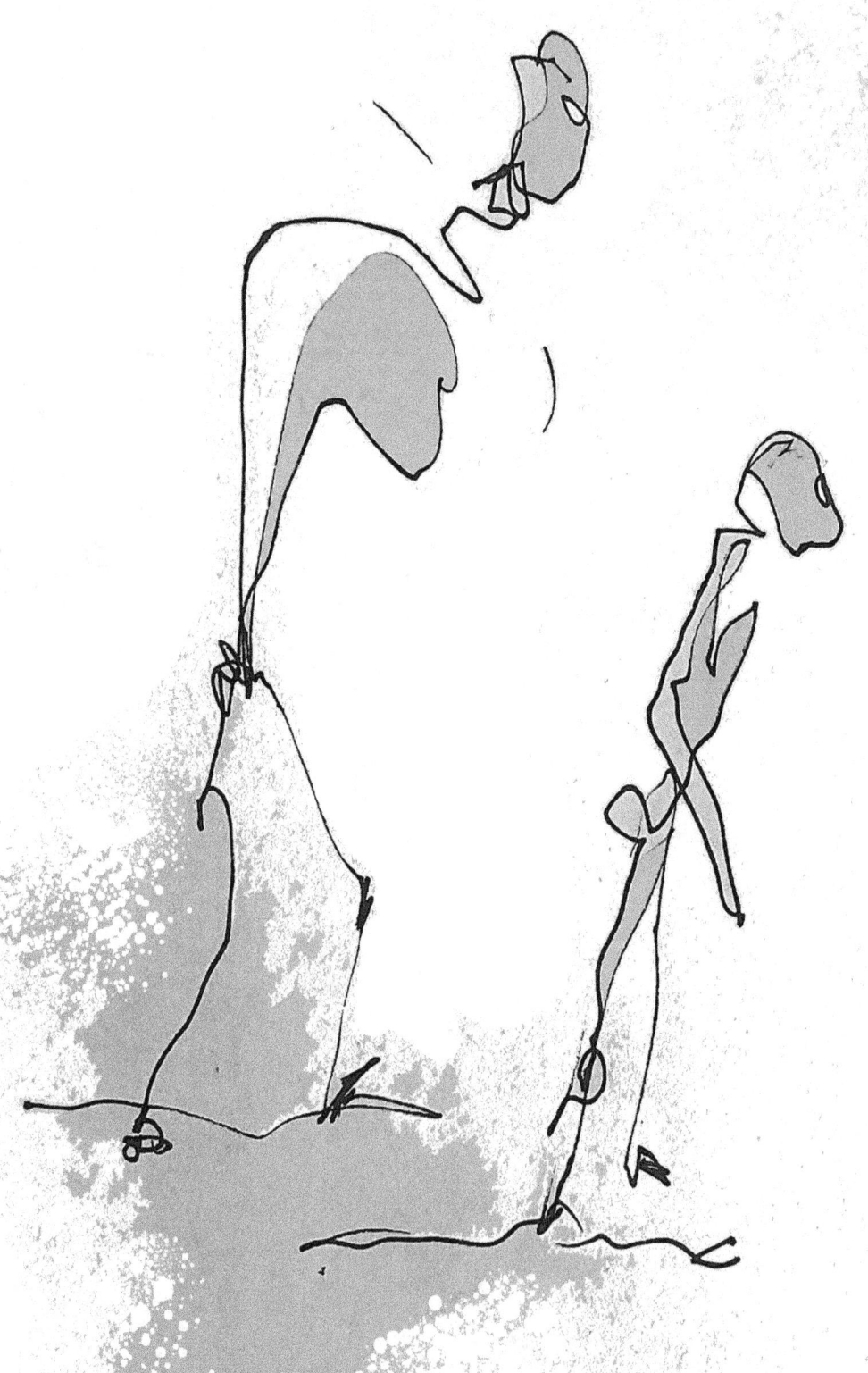

MAGNETIC BEACH

Waves pound
Water codes flash in retreat
Too fast to figure.

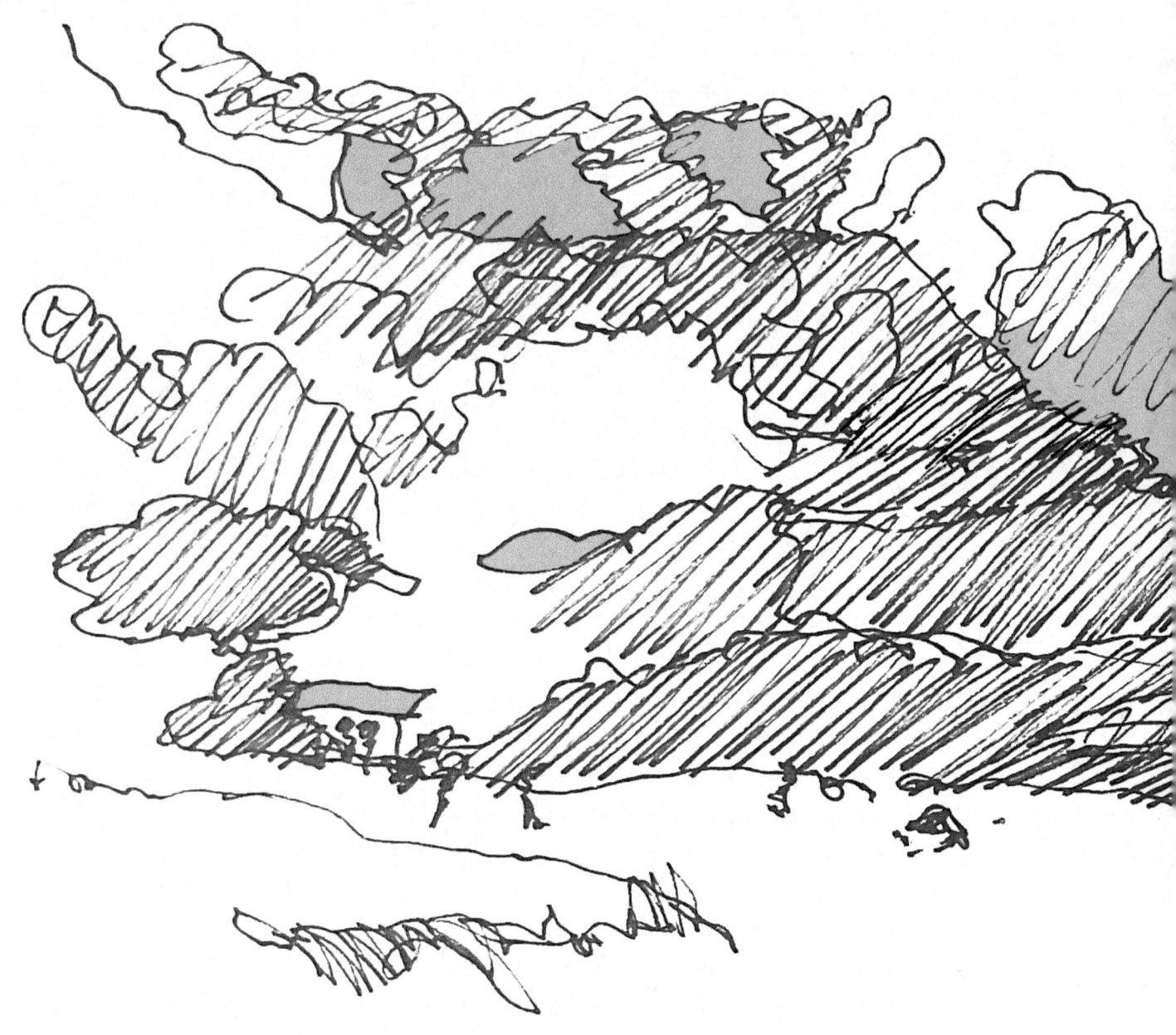

CLOUDY

Bloom of early flowers
Sunny smiles and sweet mango
Golden grains of sand.

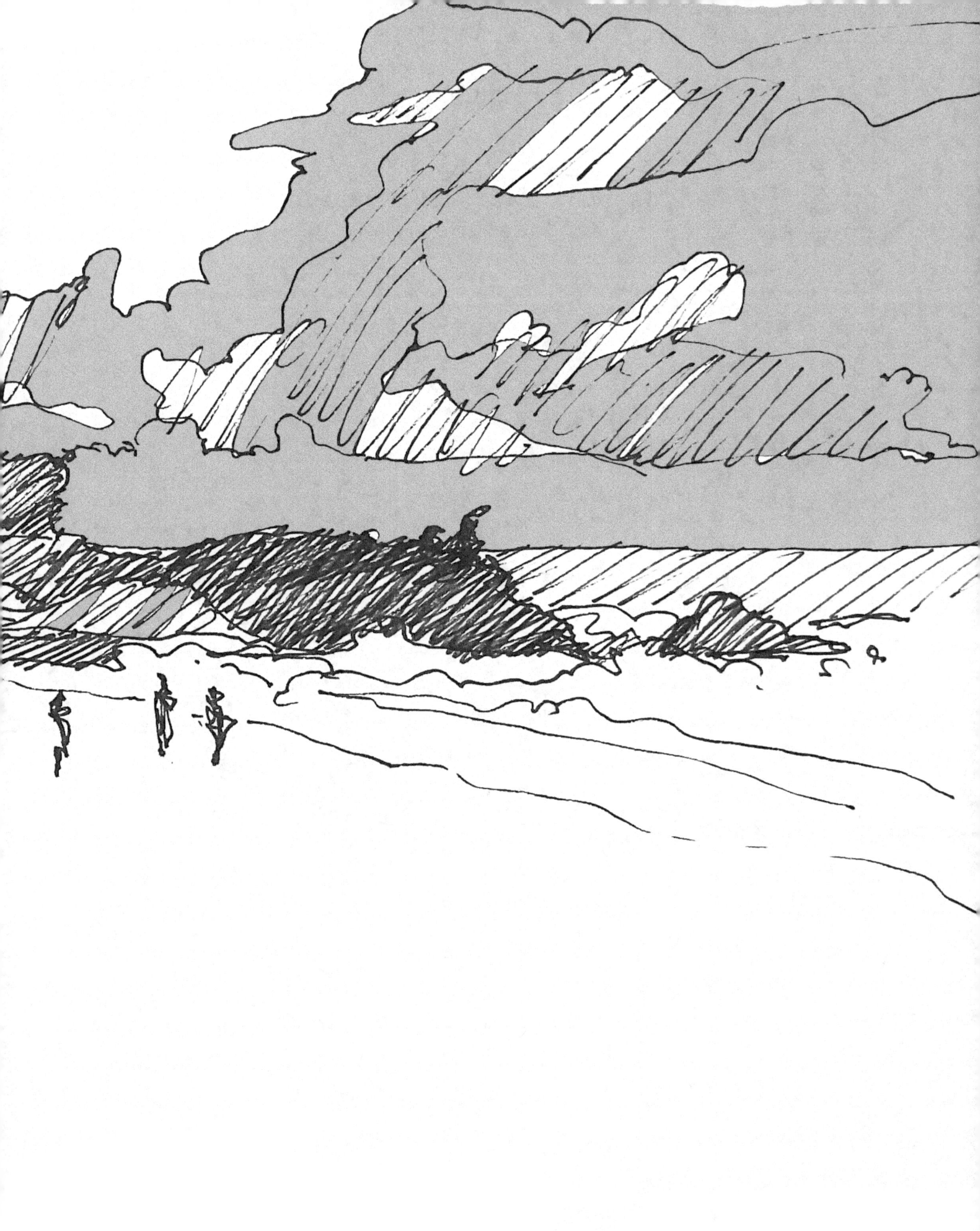

GULL

Curve of cyan sea
Seagull faces the breeze
Sandcastles melt.

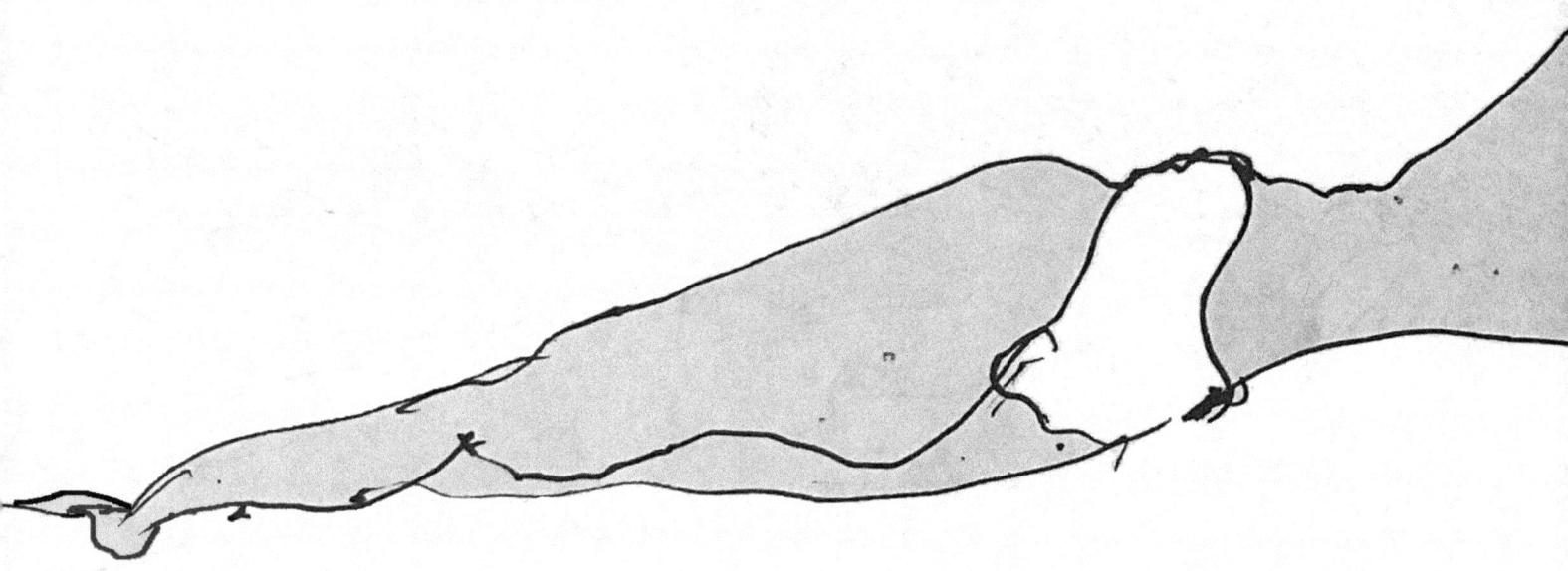

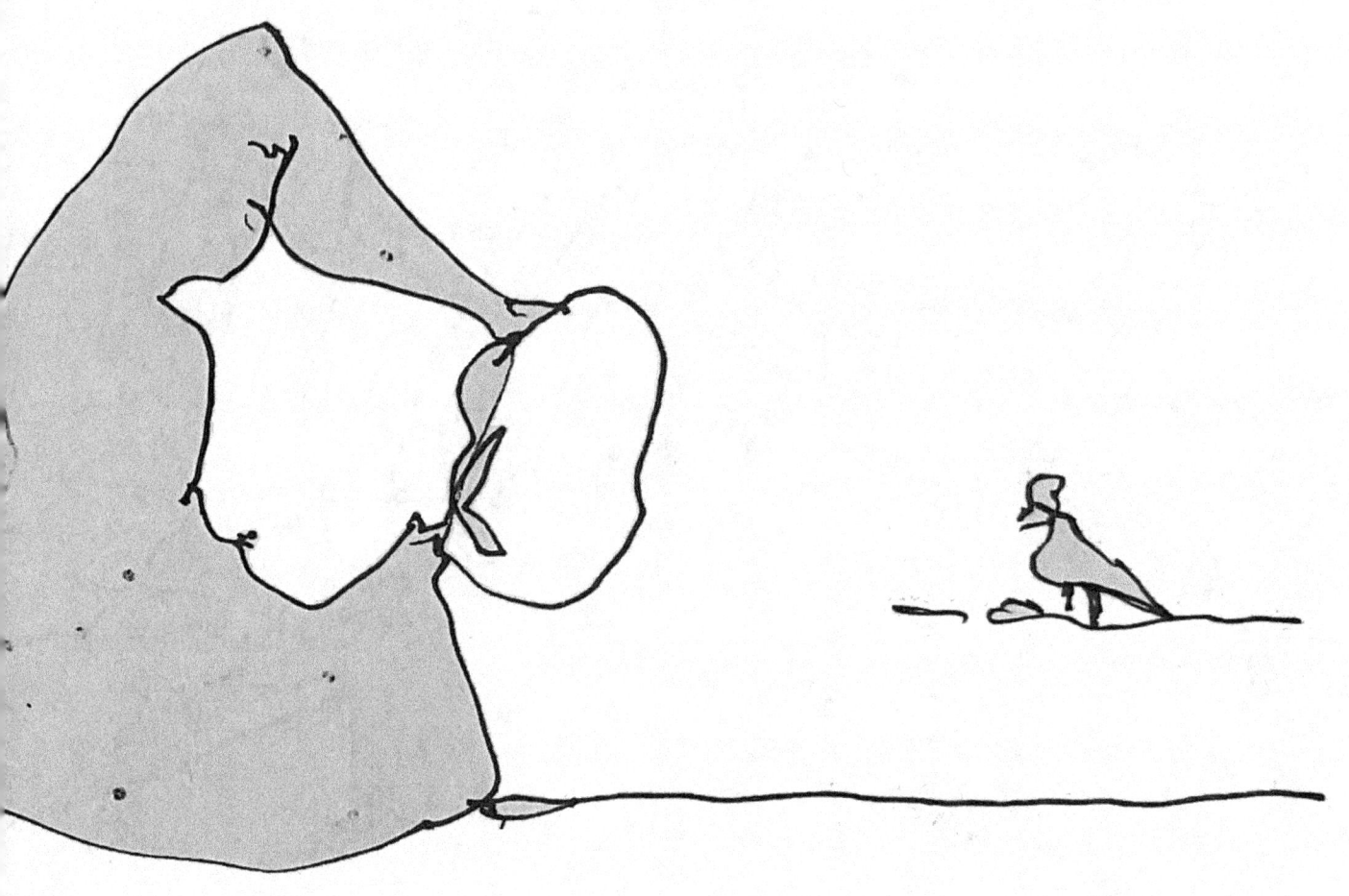

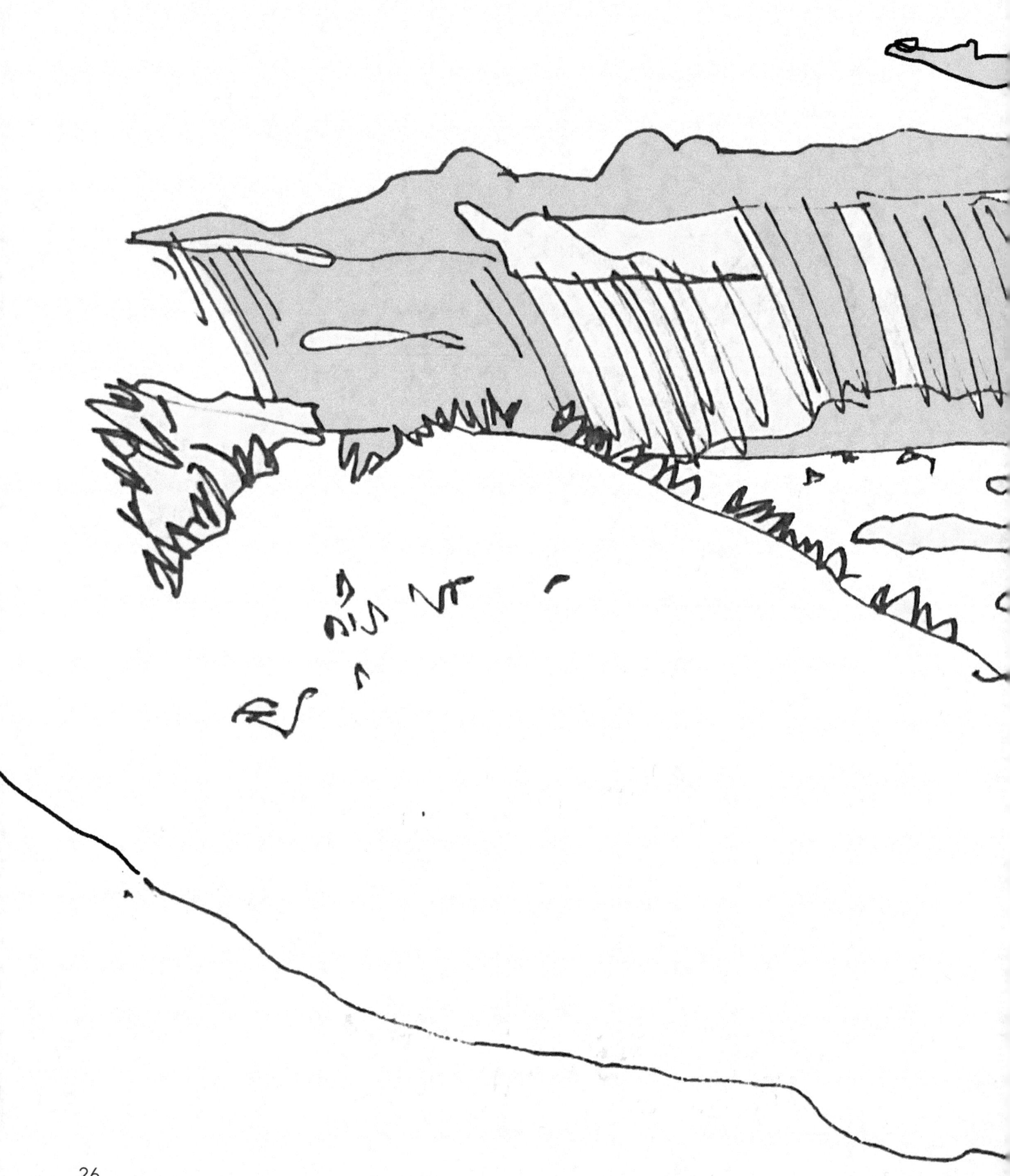

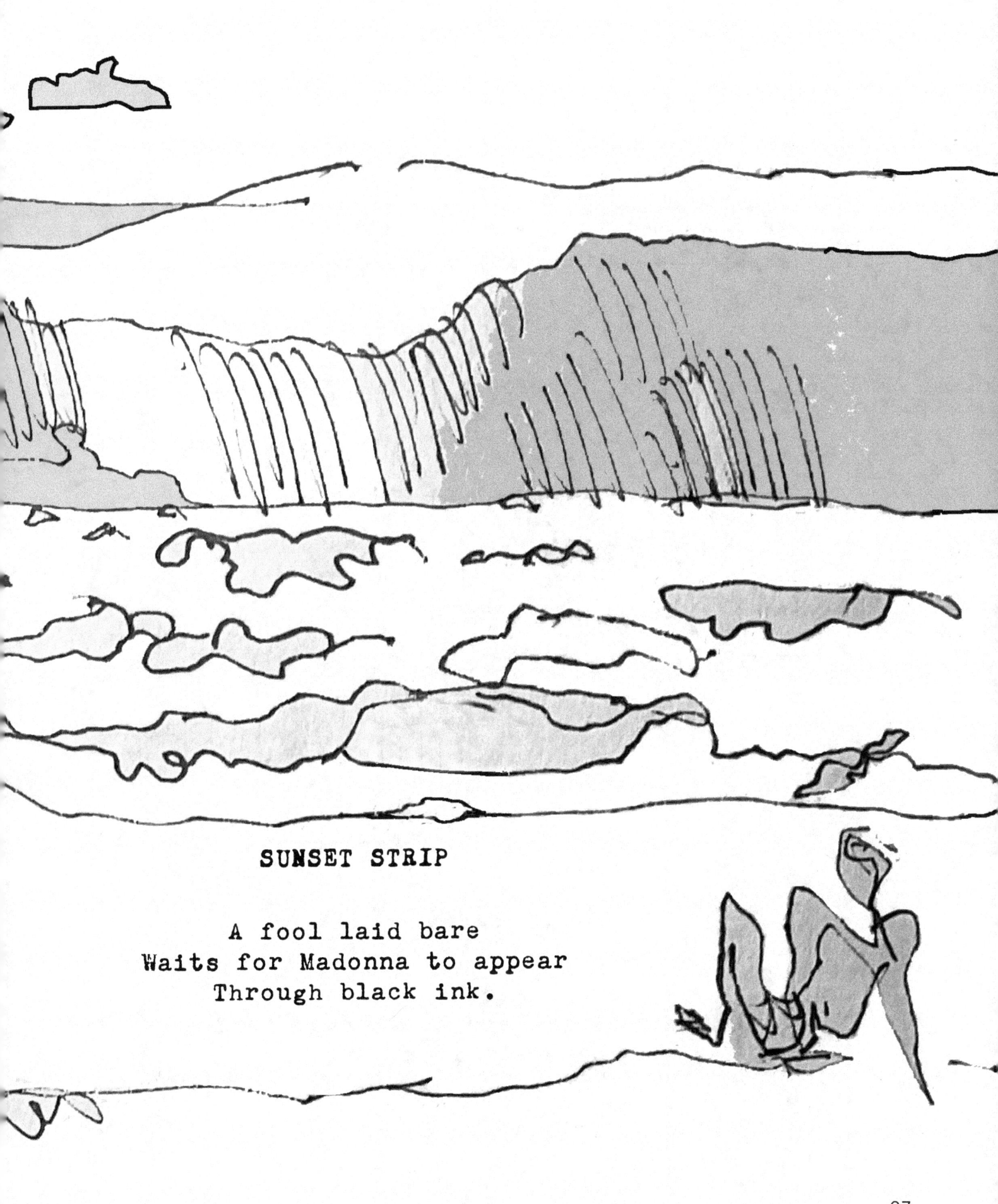

SUNSET STRIP

A fool laid bare
Waits for Madonna to appear
Through black ink.

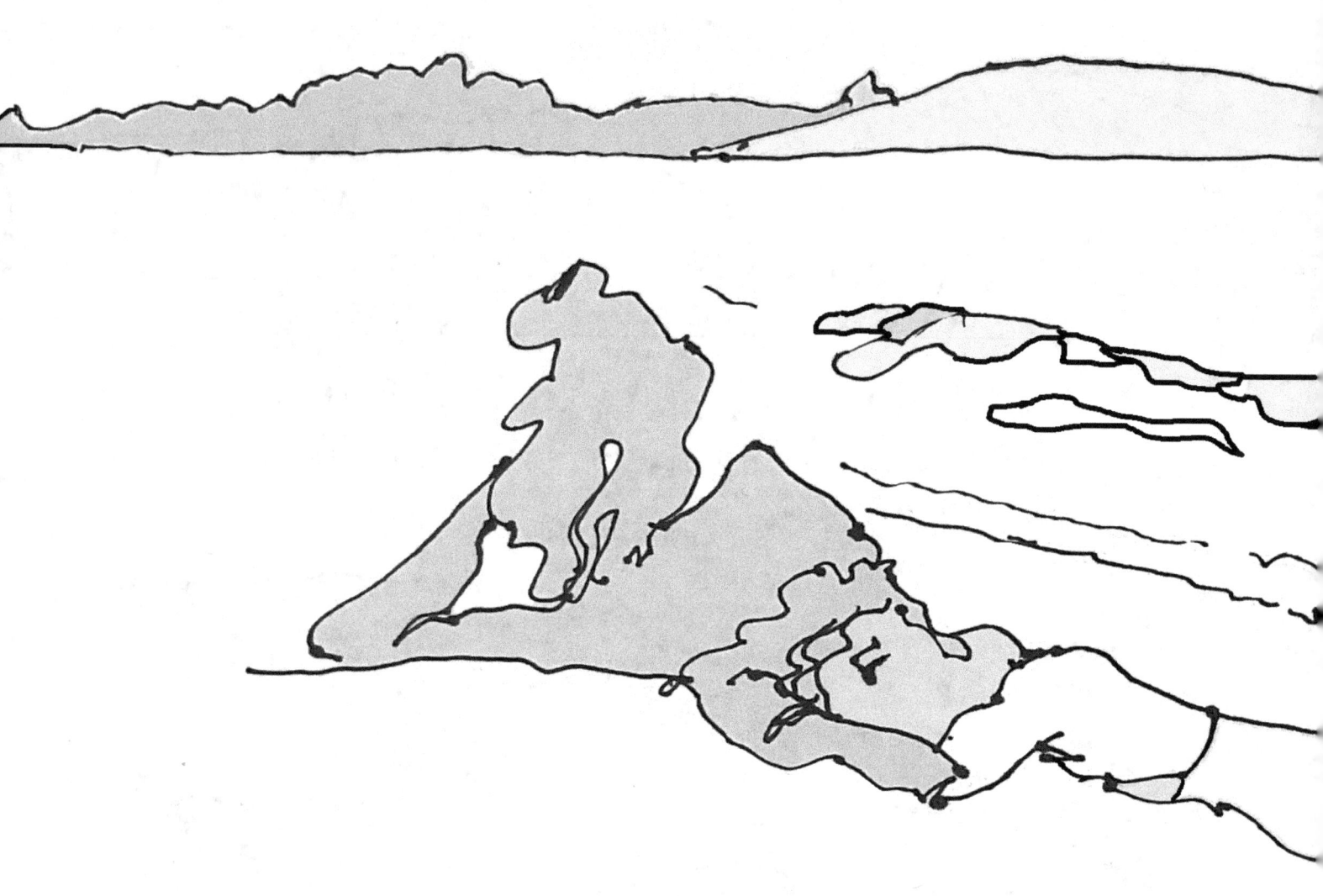

SAFE PASSAGE

Where dragons descend
Opal waves slap against wooden keel
Shrines wait in prayer.

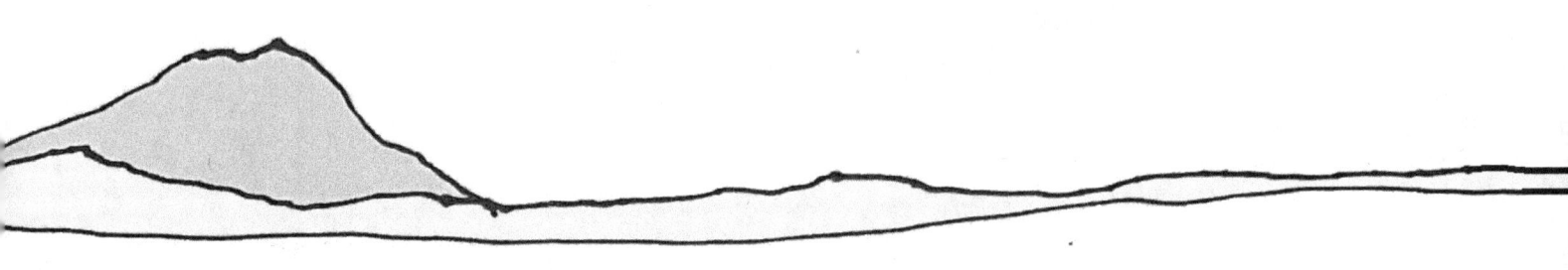

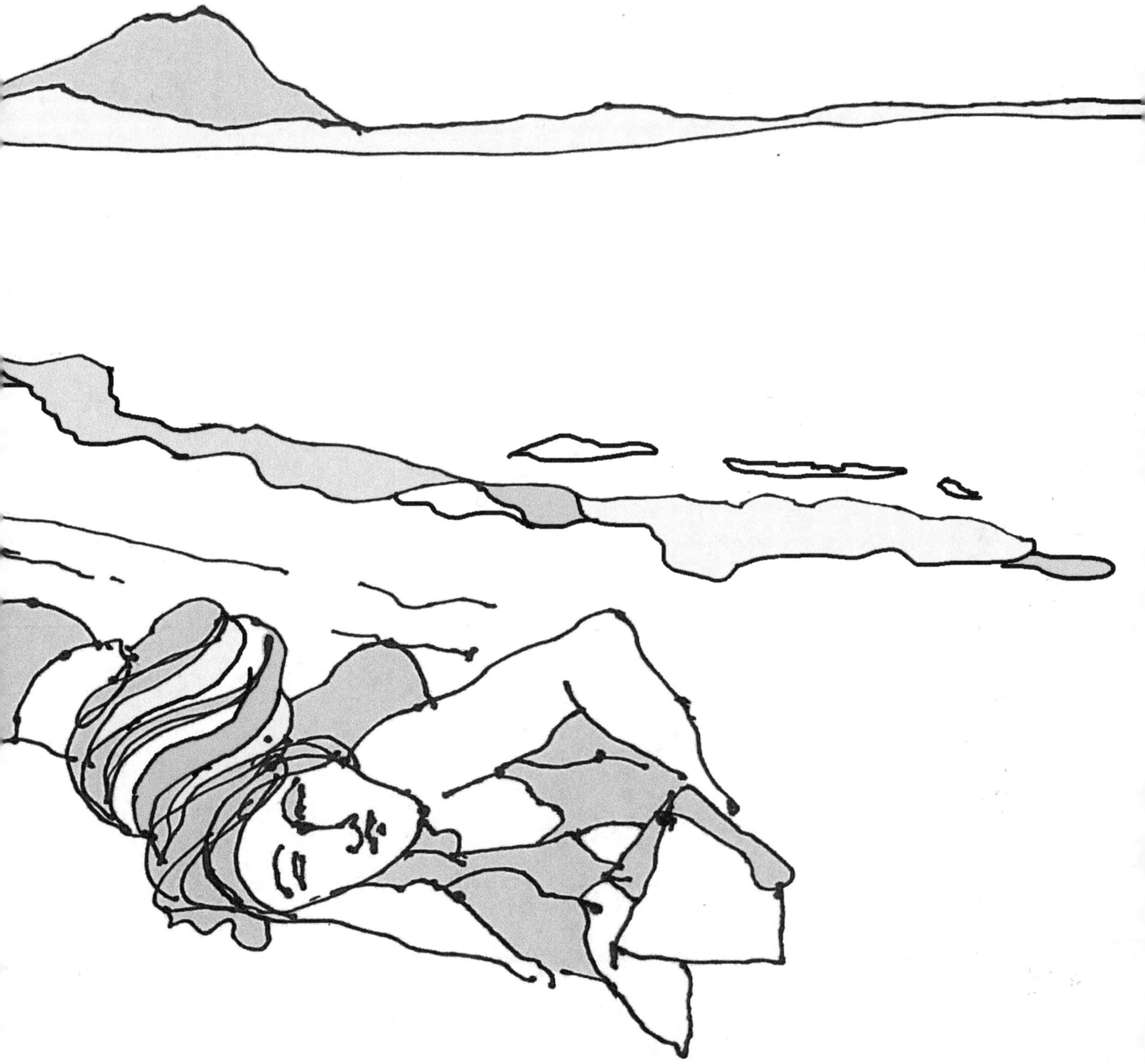

LIVE MARKET

Death on marble
Mucilaginous slab of egress
Butchered life.

———————————————————

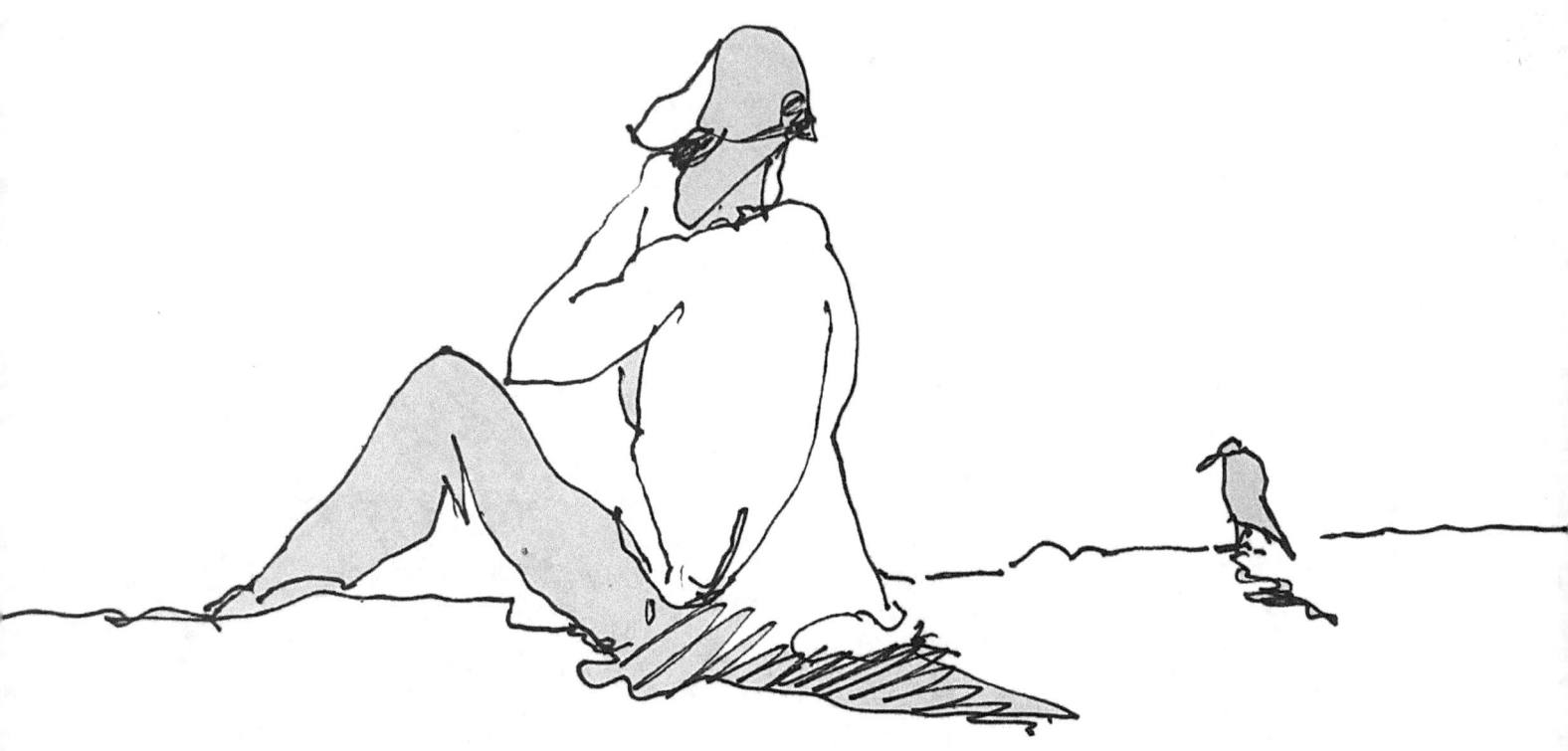

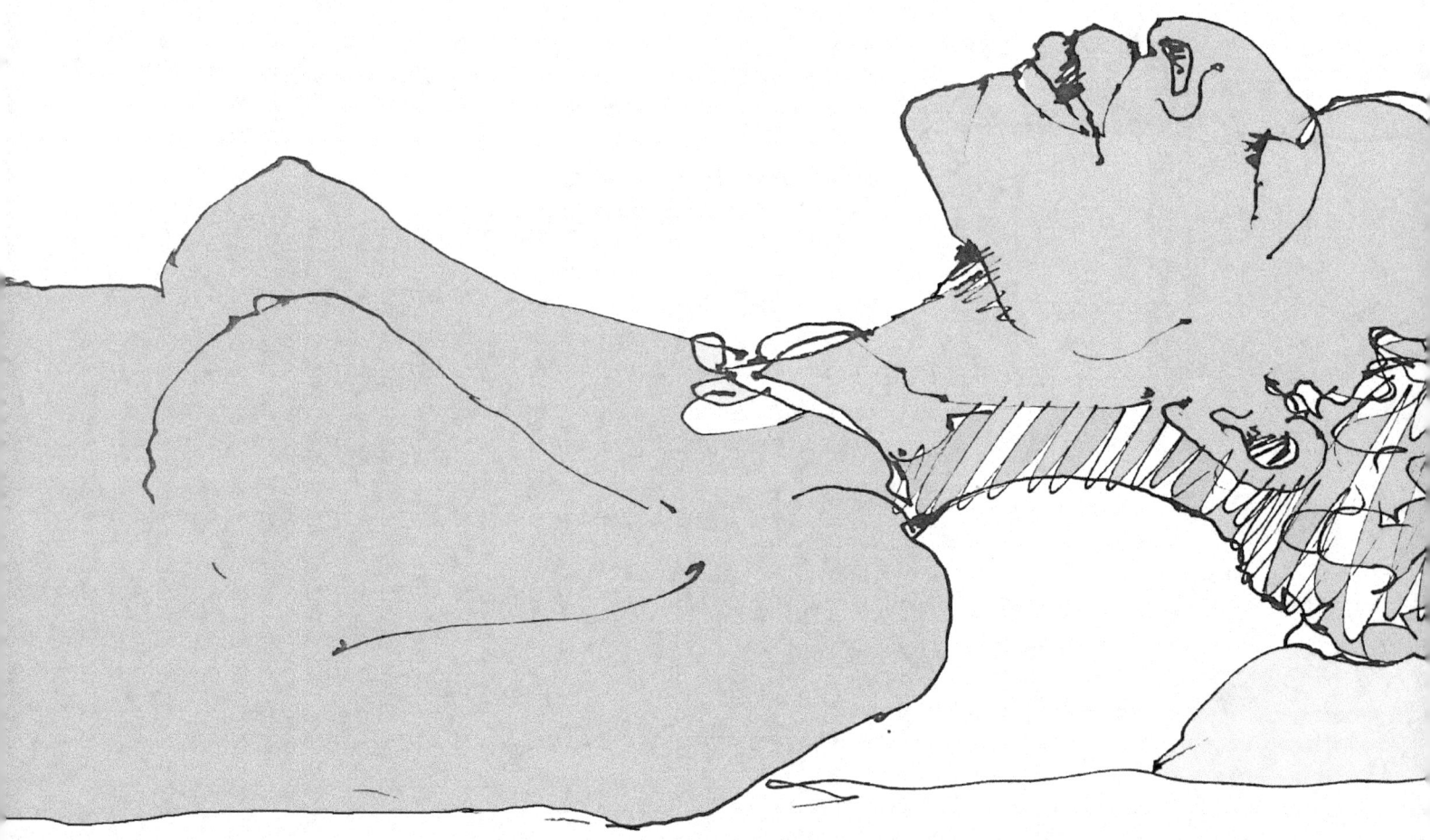

BACKDOOR

Small feet run the ghost path
Tell of dark attack
Tears in pain
Again, Again
Young feet flee
Hand of fire
Stars burn in heaven
Tears unnamed.

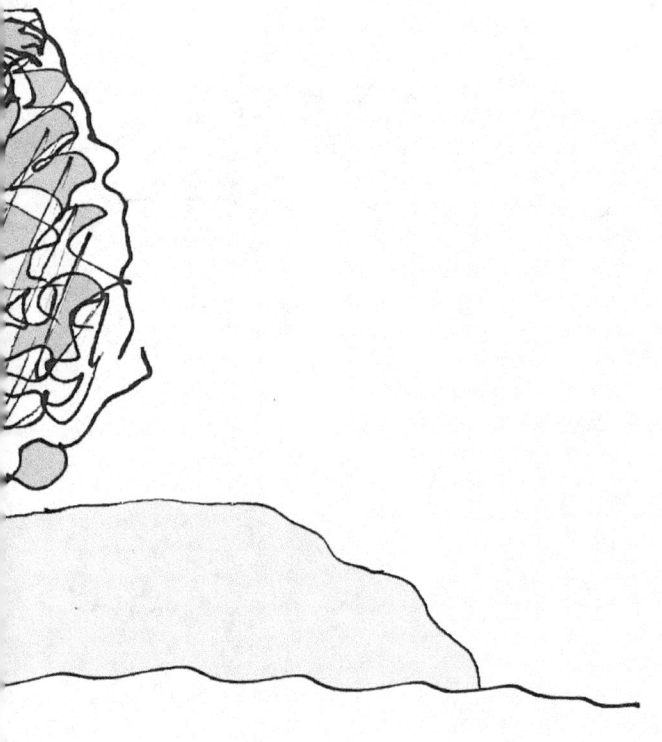

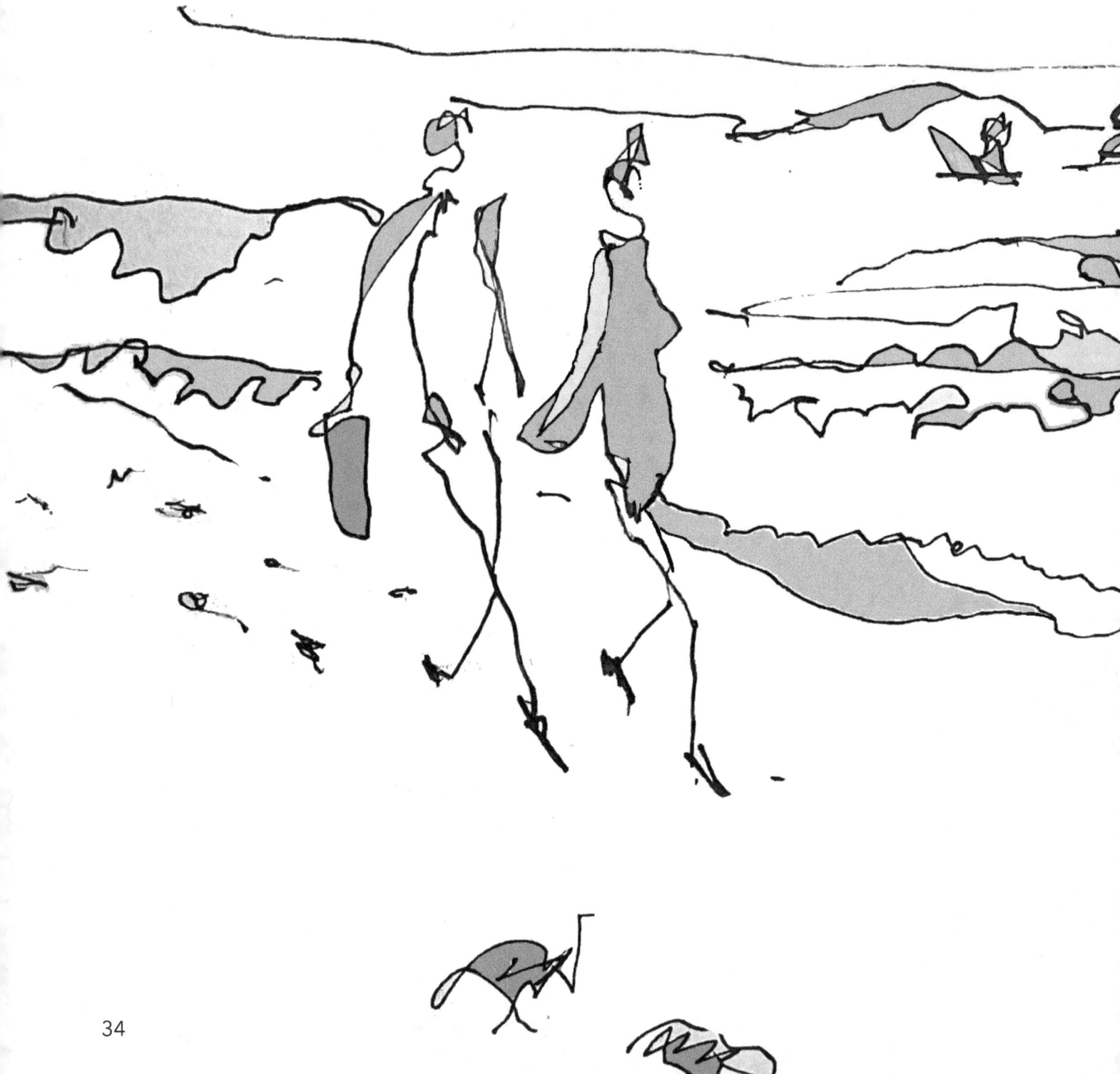

SEASHORE

The line is drawn
"Is this the infinite blessing?"
You hum faintly.

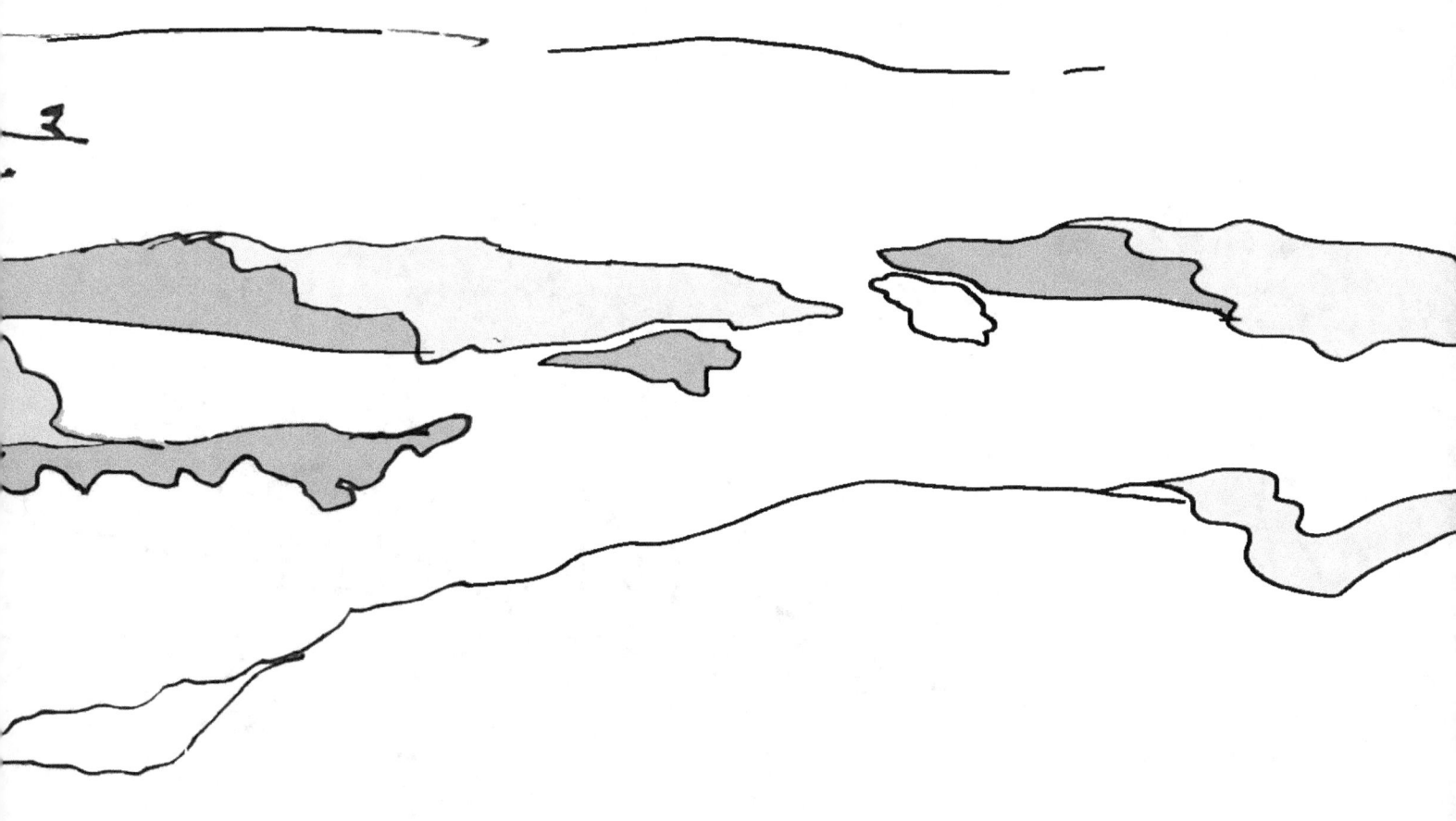

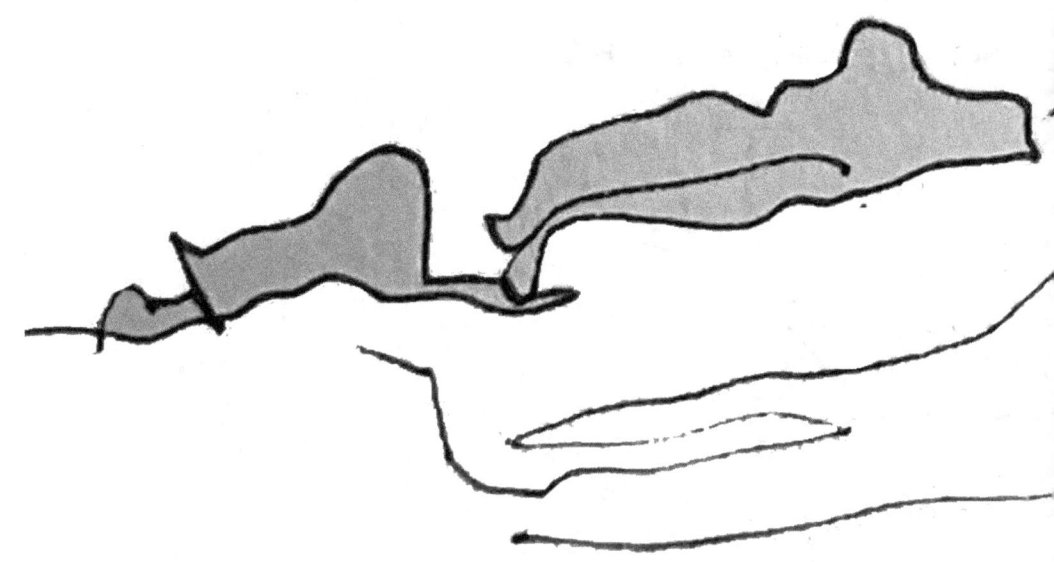

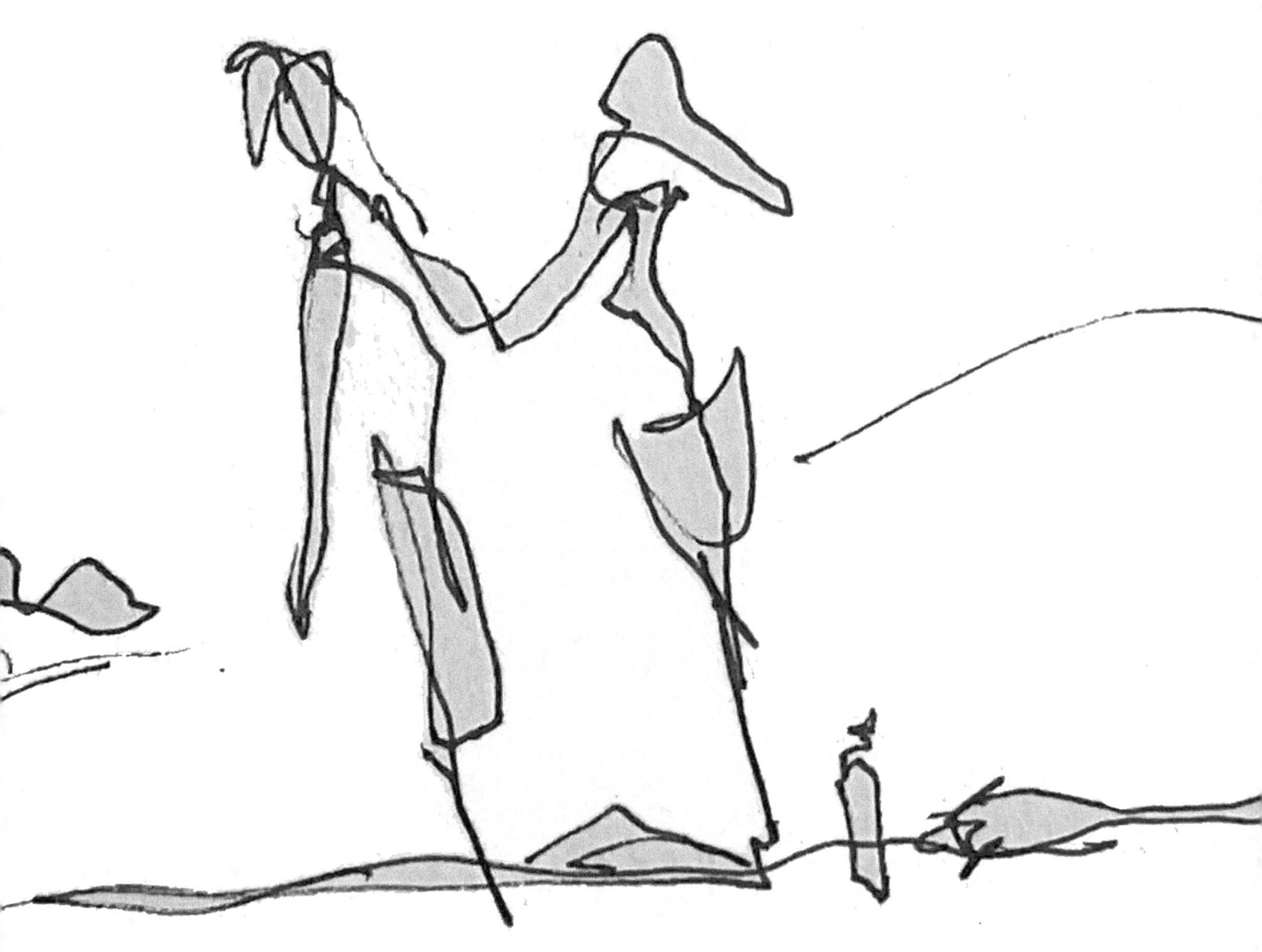

FIFTY SHADE

On hot sand
Short virgules of erotic code
Shadows delay.

DUNE GRASS

Sun burns red
Over verdant palette of sea
At the wilting time.

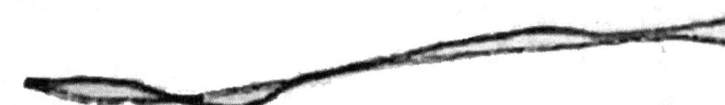

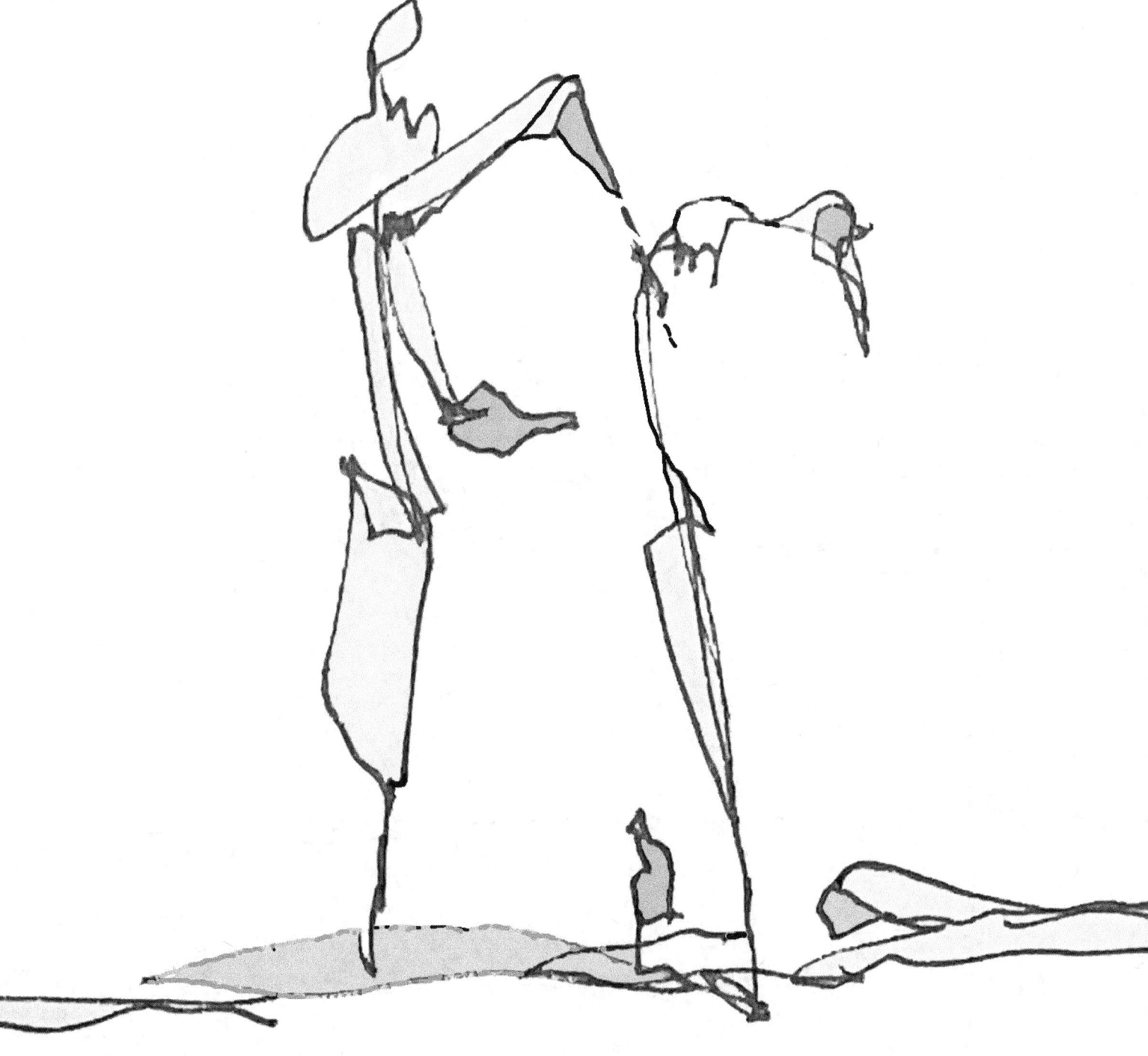

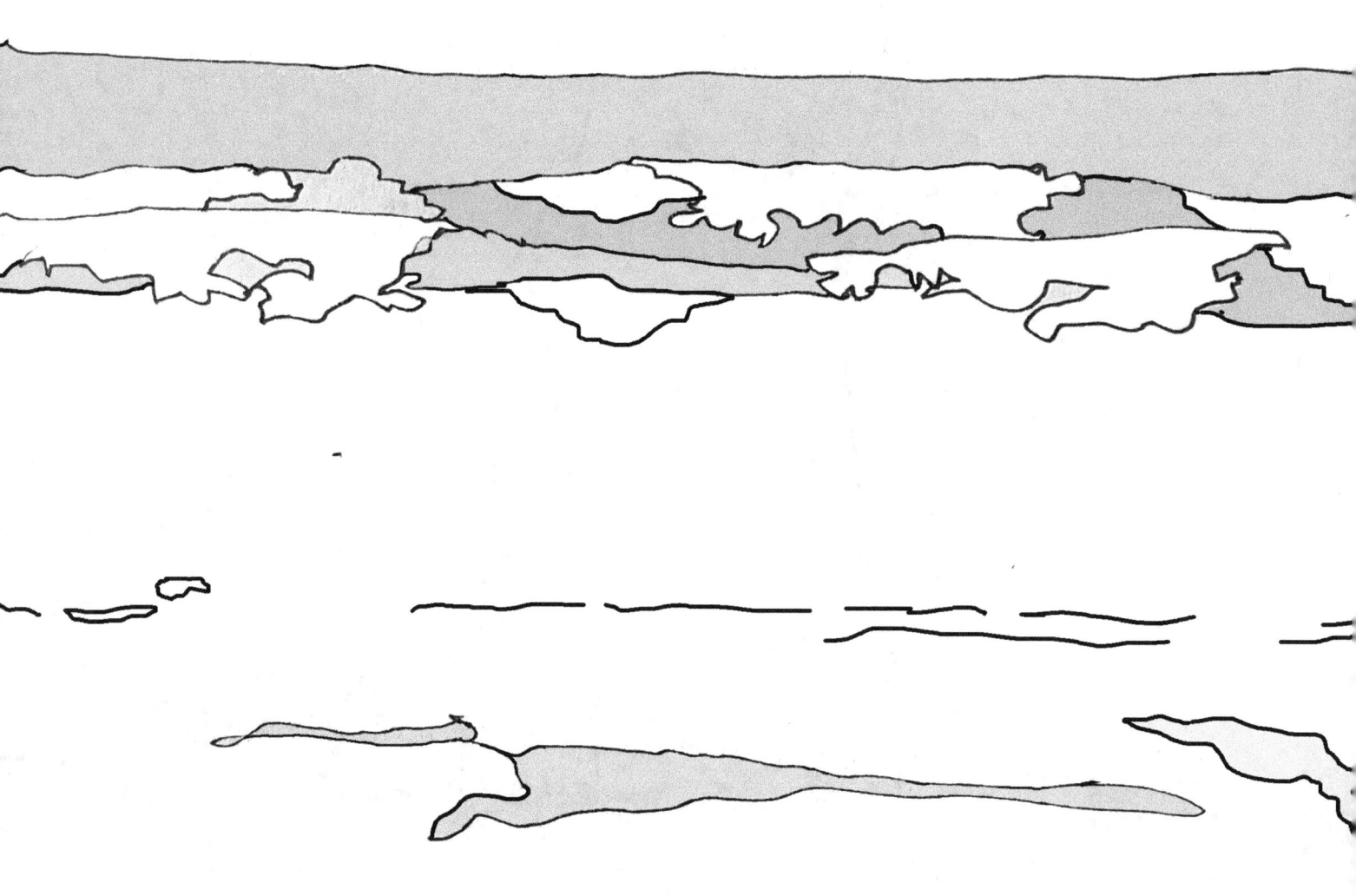

AUTUMN LIGHT

Sand dog
Waves caress crooked limbs
One last time.

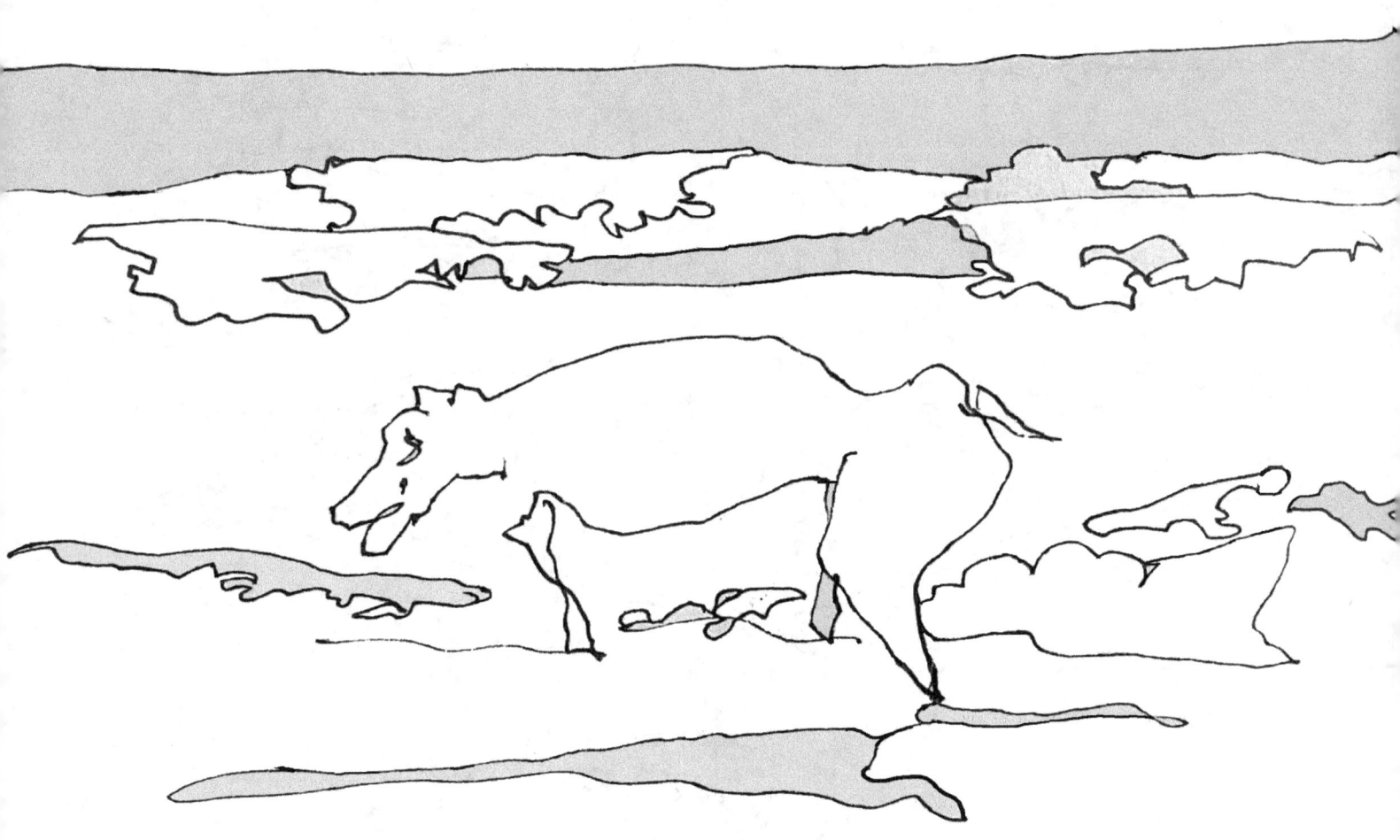

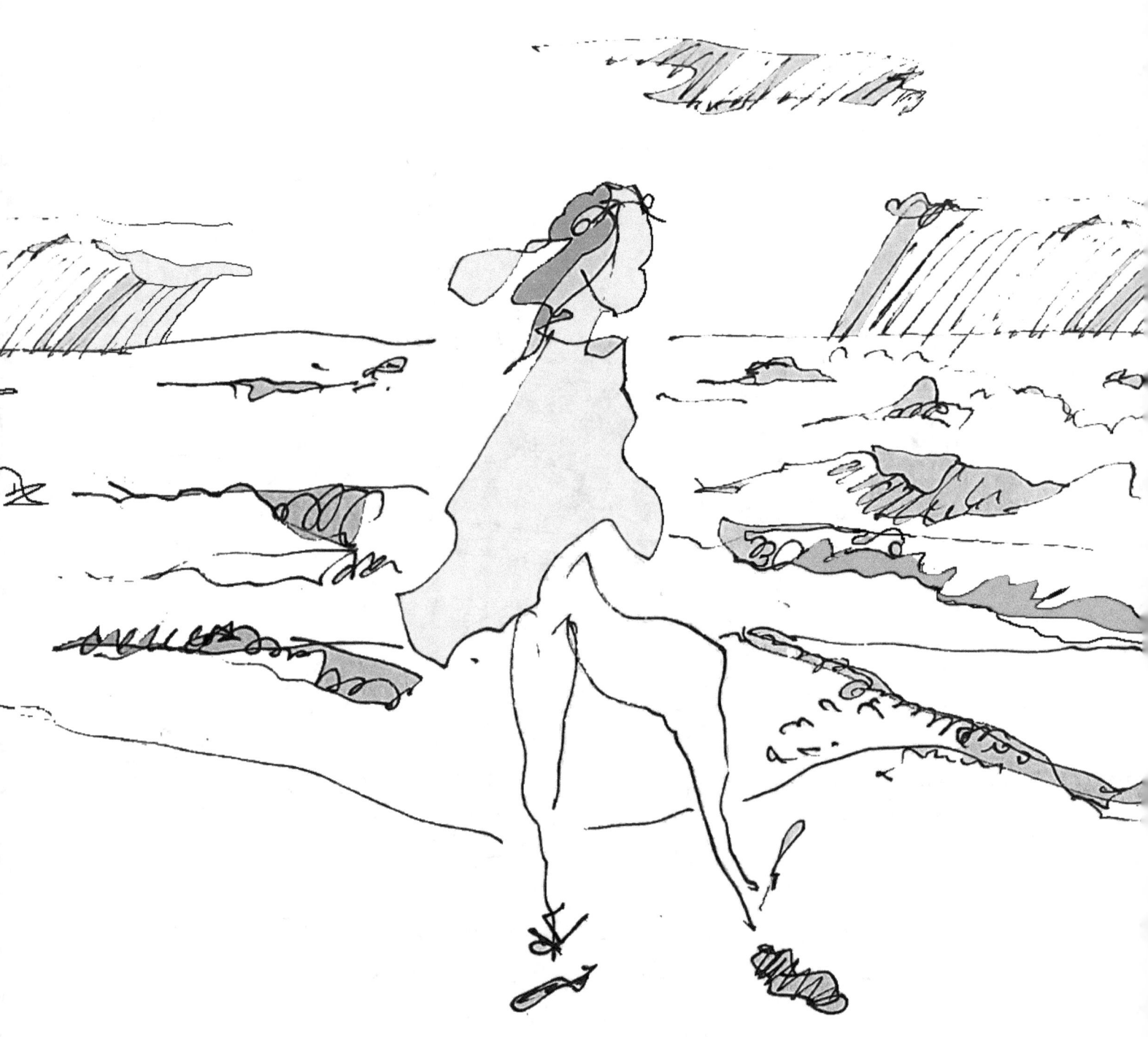

SHADOW PRINTS

Clouds drop rain
Yellow cotton dress flickers
Tempest wind.

BROKEN LADDER

Orphaned kittens
Mother leaves an empty space
A dark place.

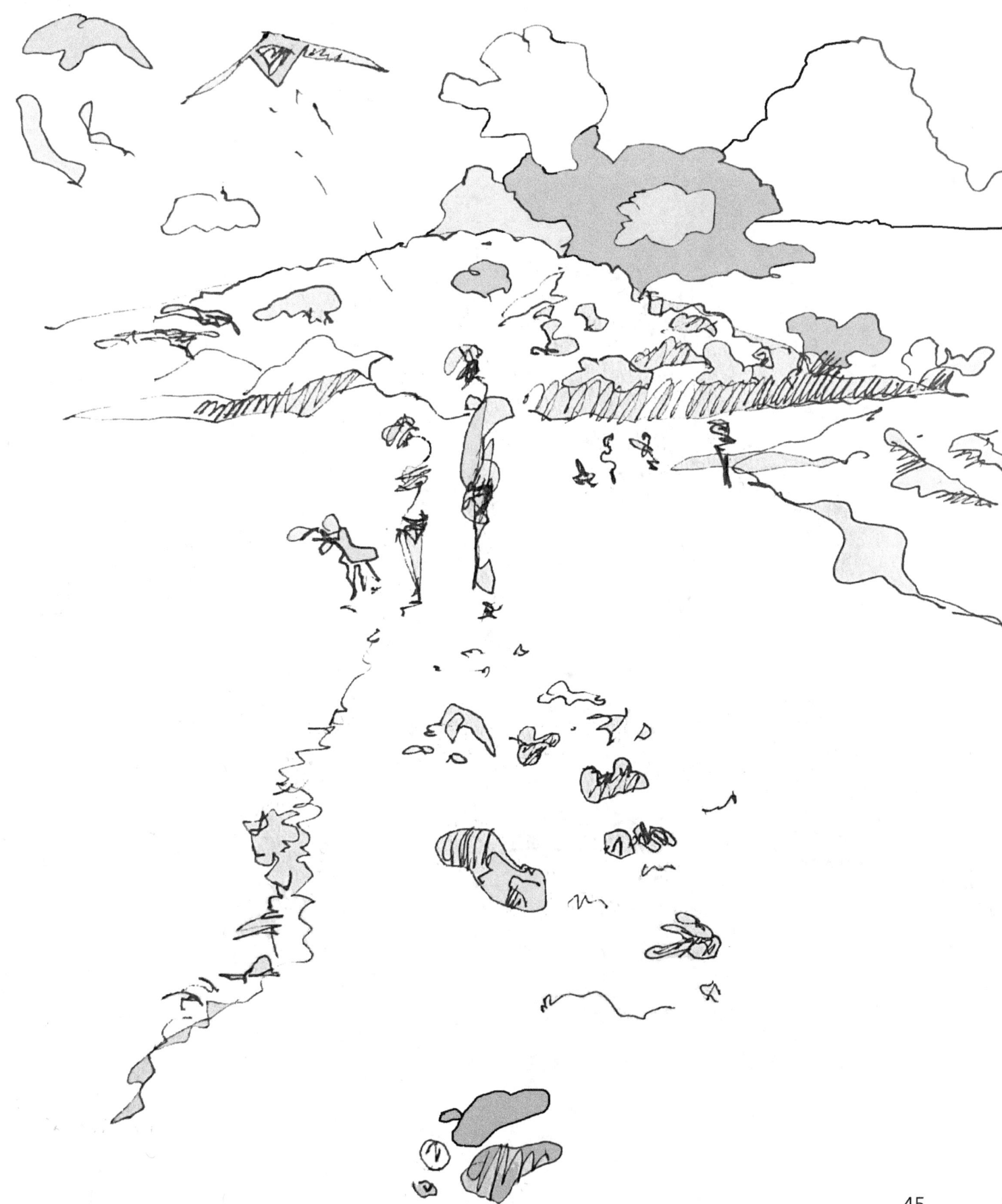

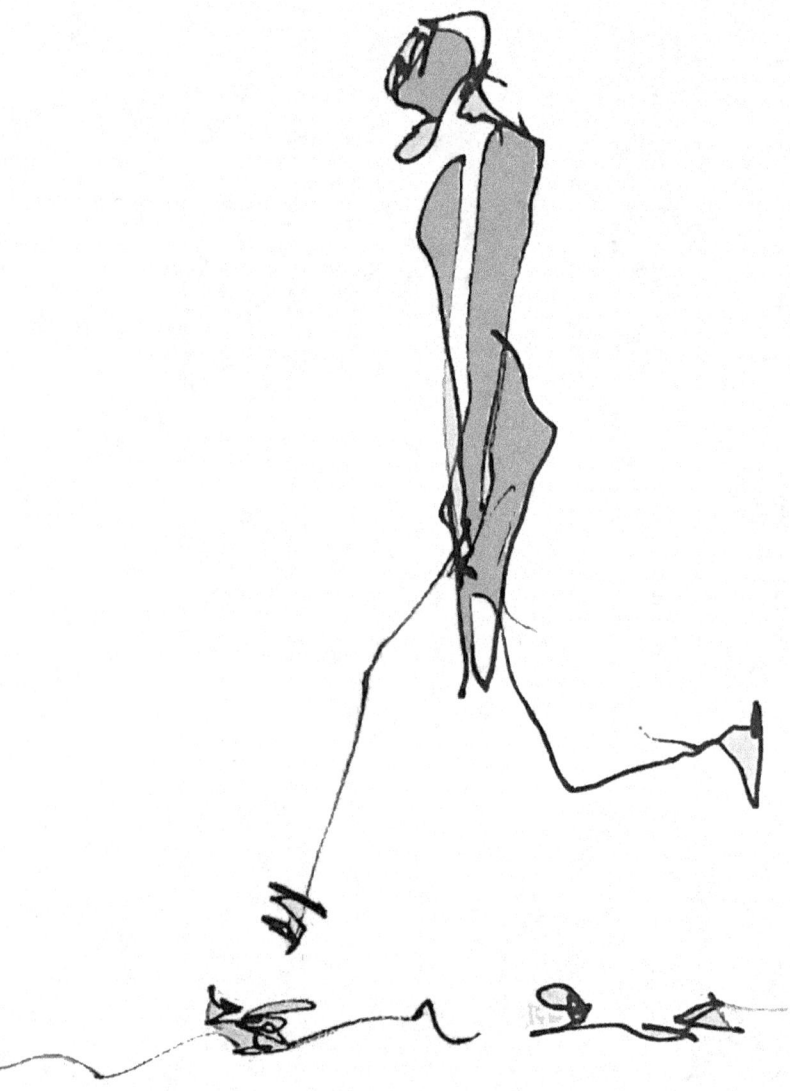

SILVER RING

Fickle sand
Diamond grains, lost at edge of sea
Sadness held down.

ANHEDONIA

Love beyond fear
Hold fast the ruthless animal in chains
I tumble out the door.

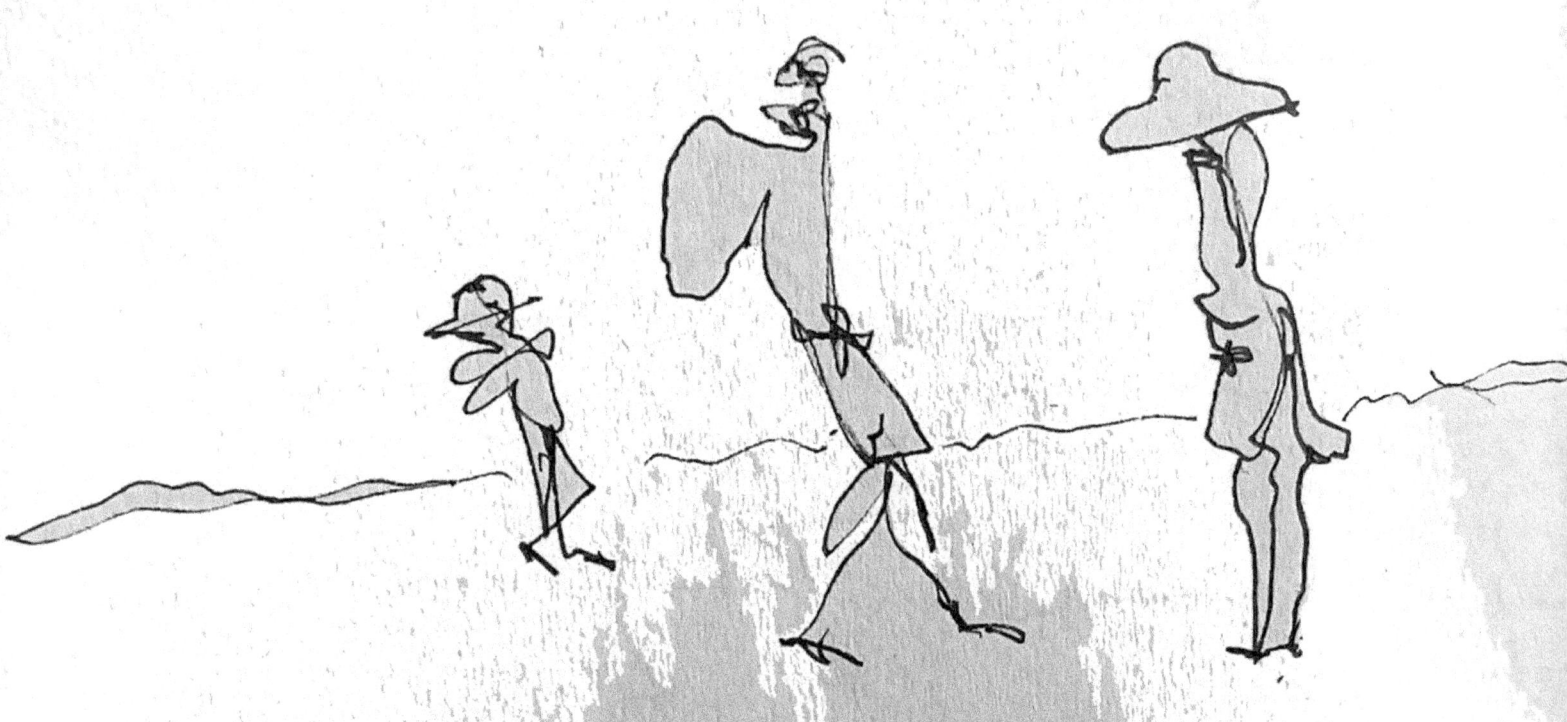

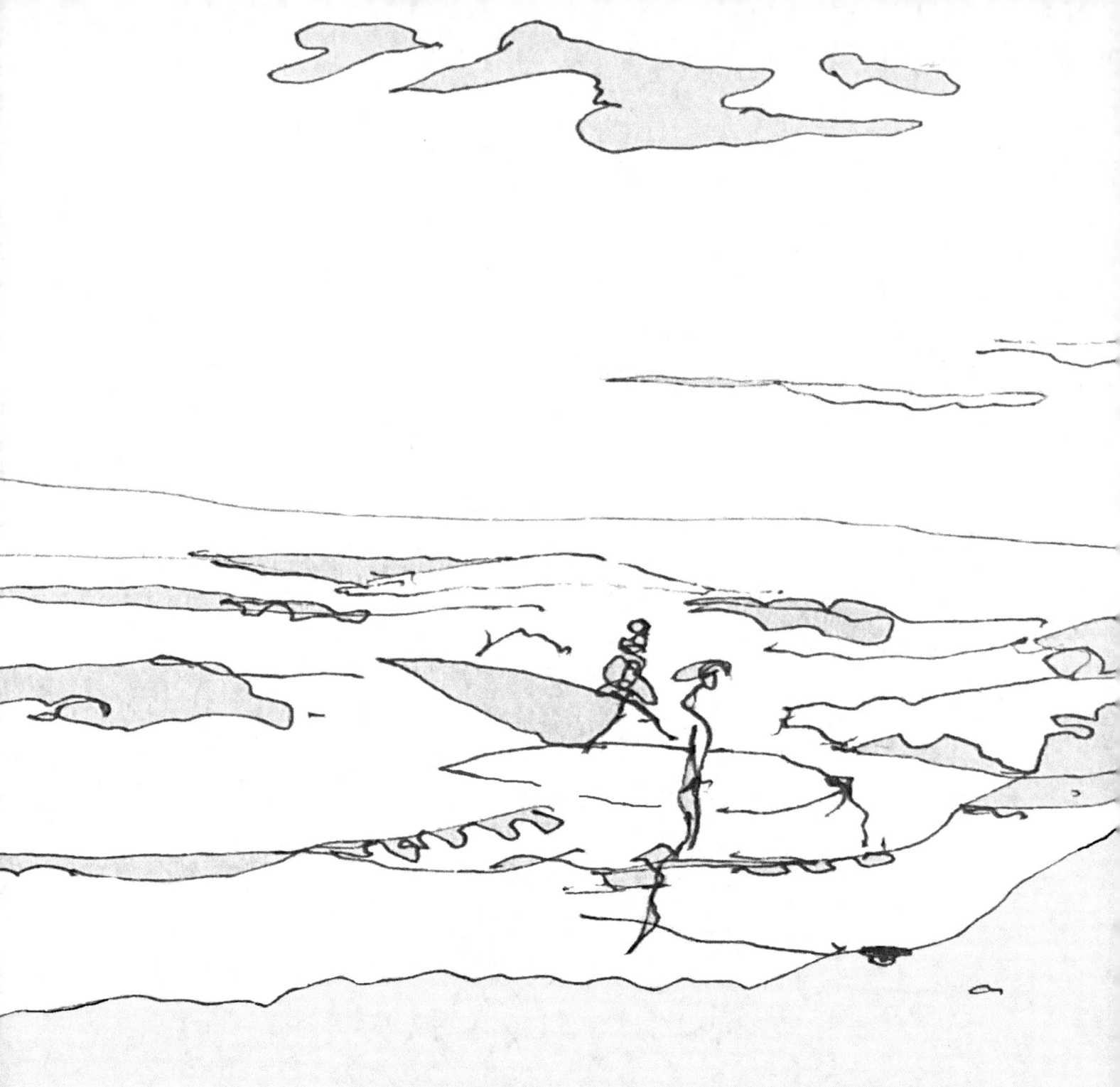

BRICK WORK

Dust of rubble chokes
Steel hammers pound away the night
Lungs suffused.

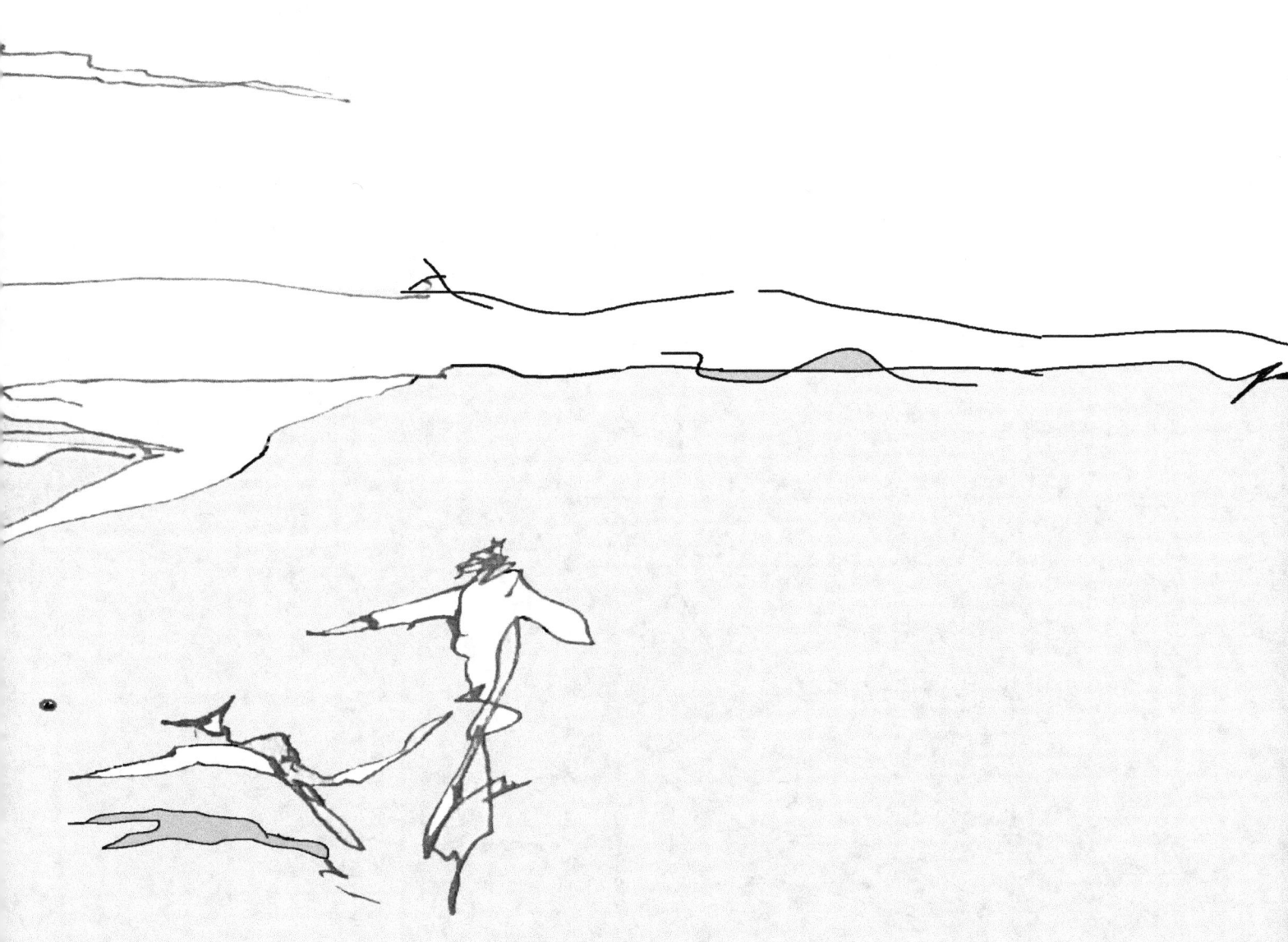

STRANDS

Pearls in spasm
Loose ends of necklace fray
Shells unravel.

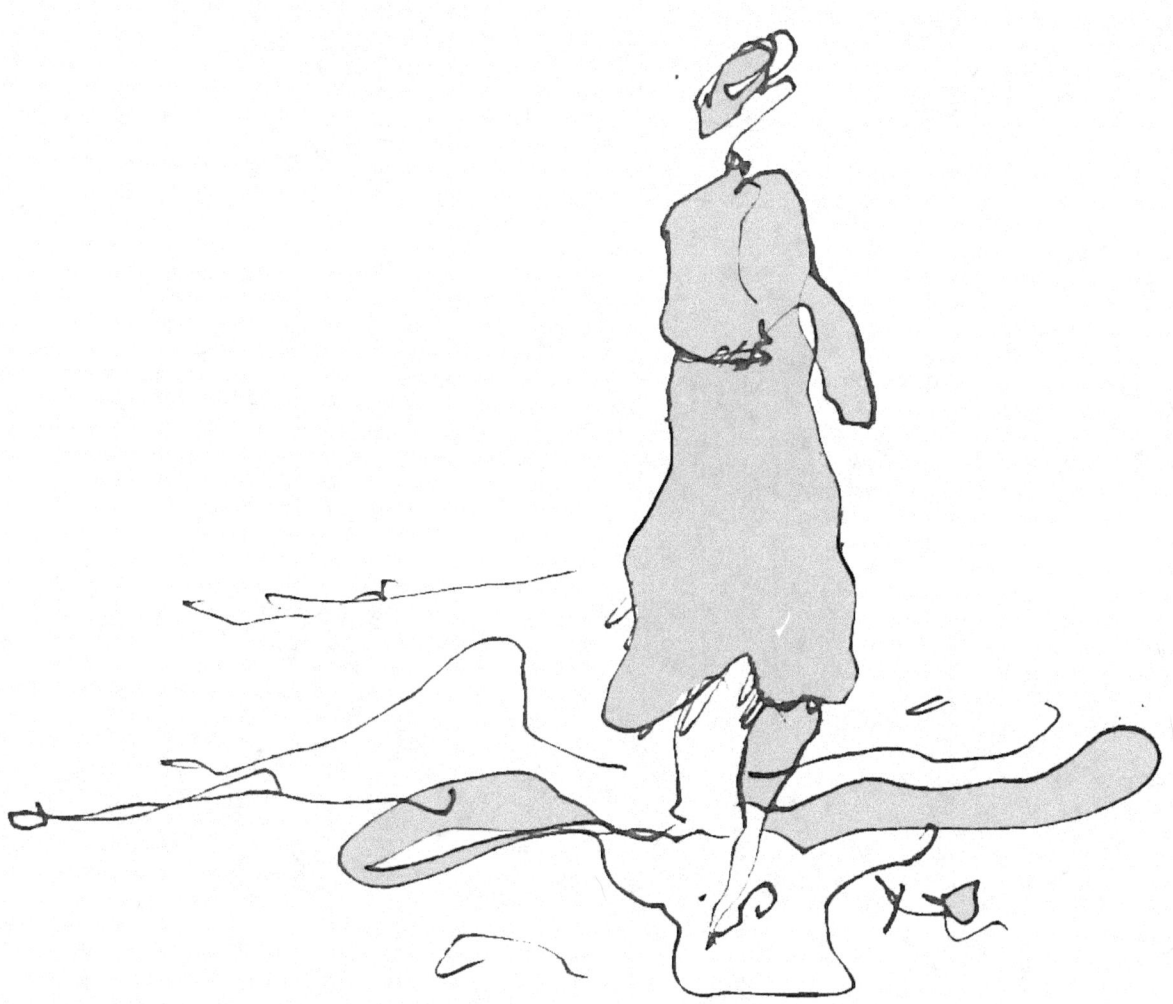

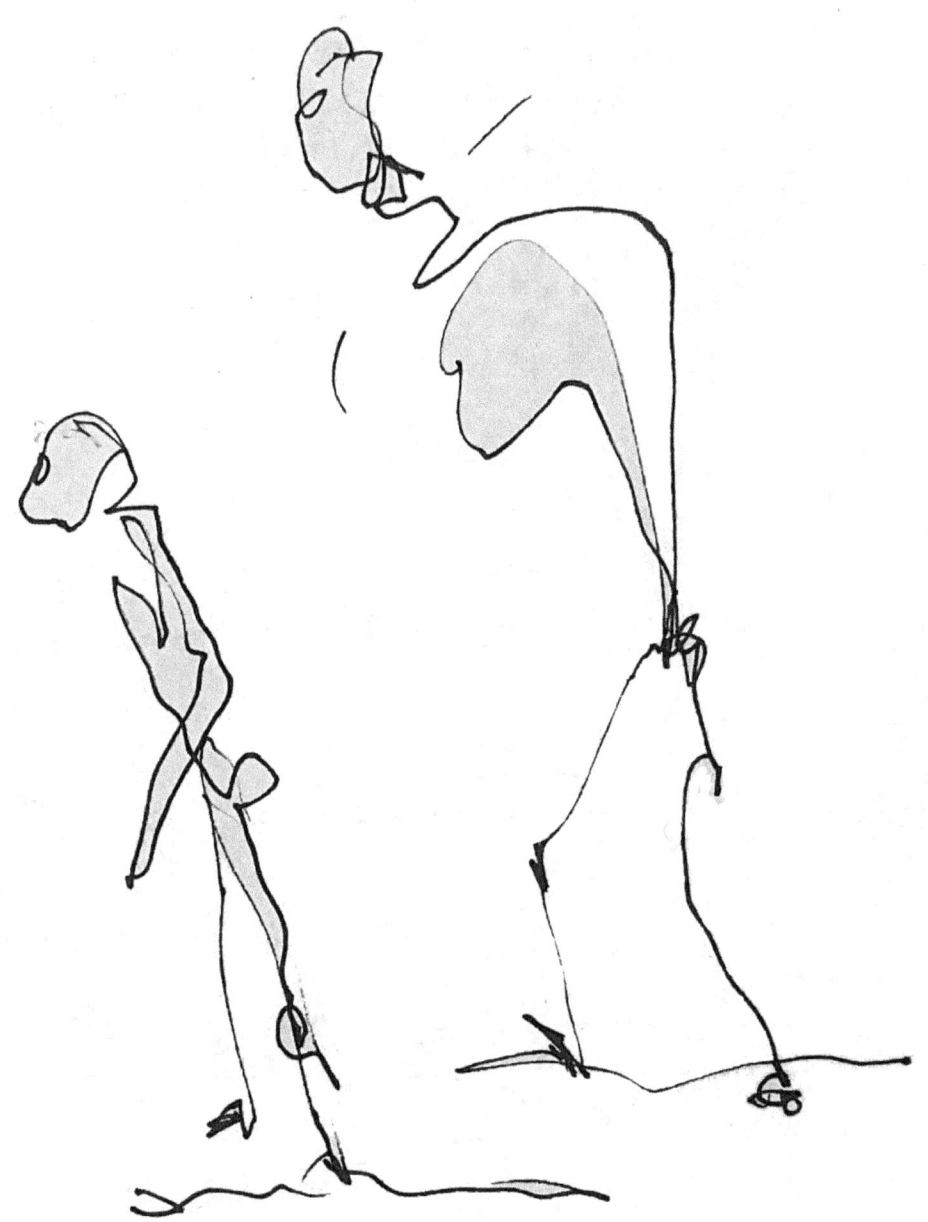

TIN PAN BLUES

Tin door in yellow wall
Hammers out buckled rhythms
Wind unhinged.

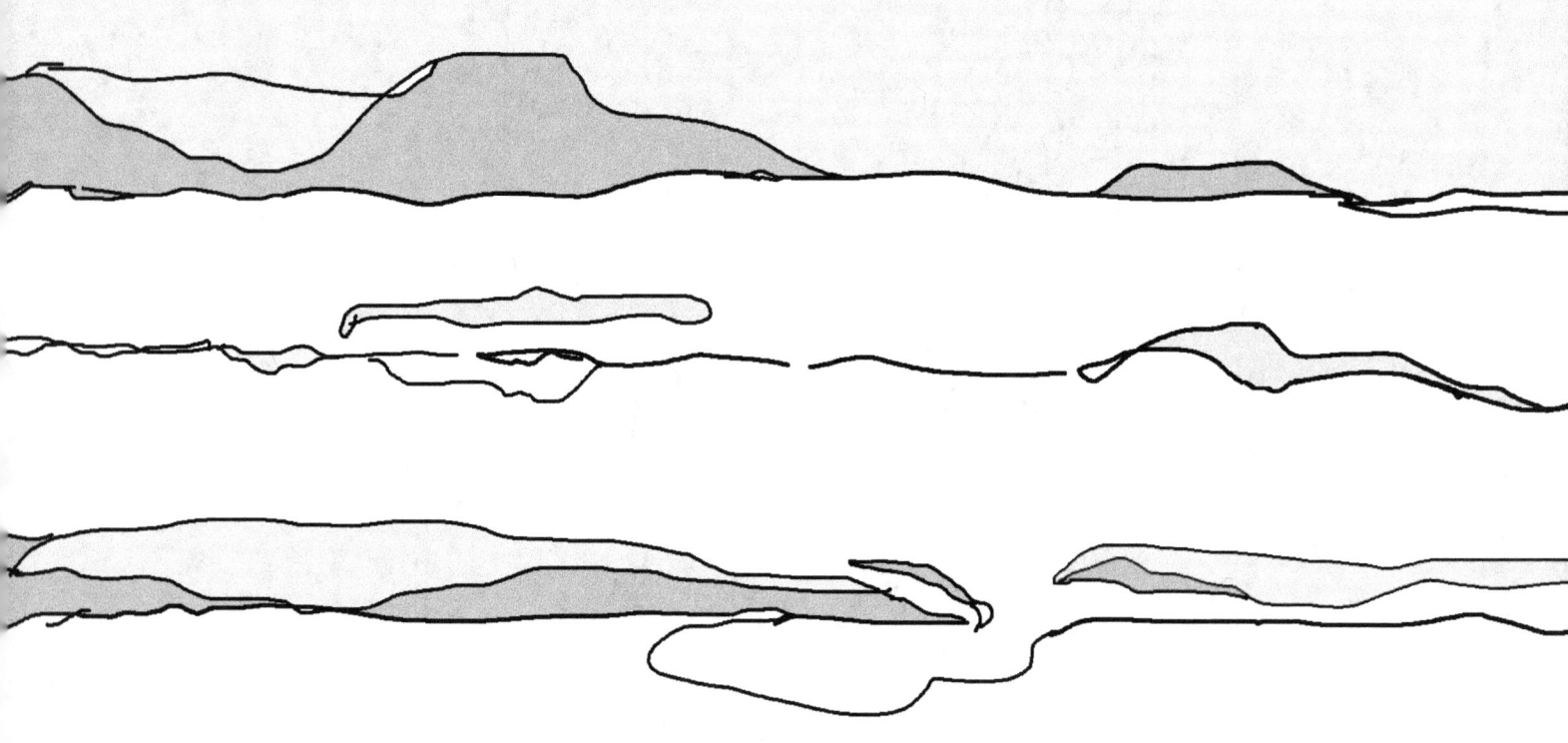

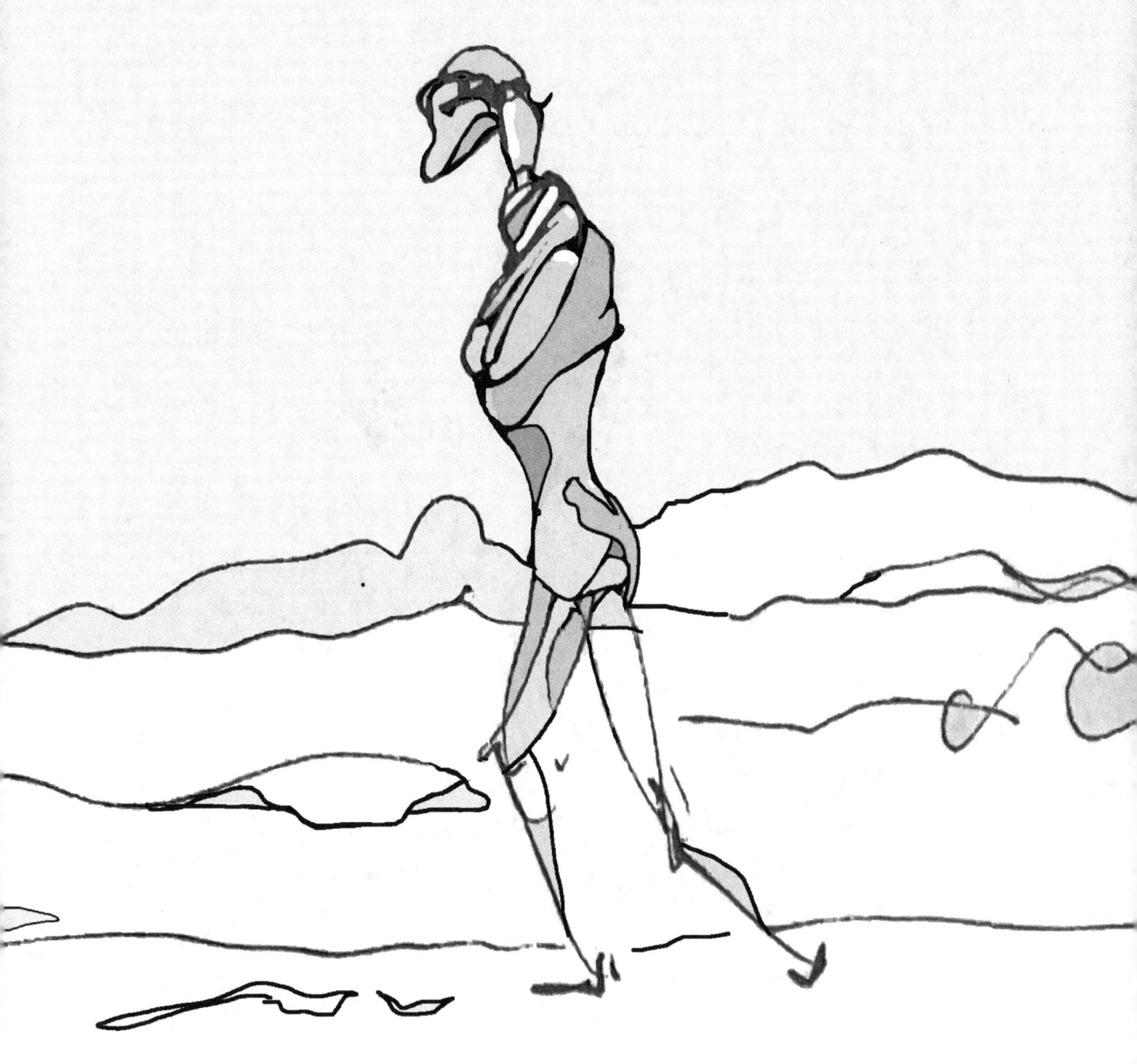

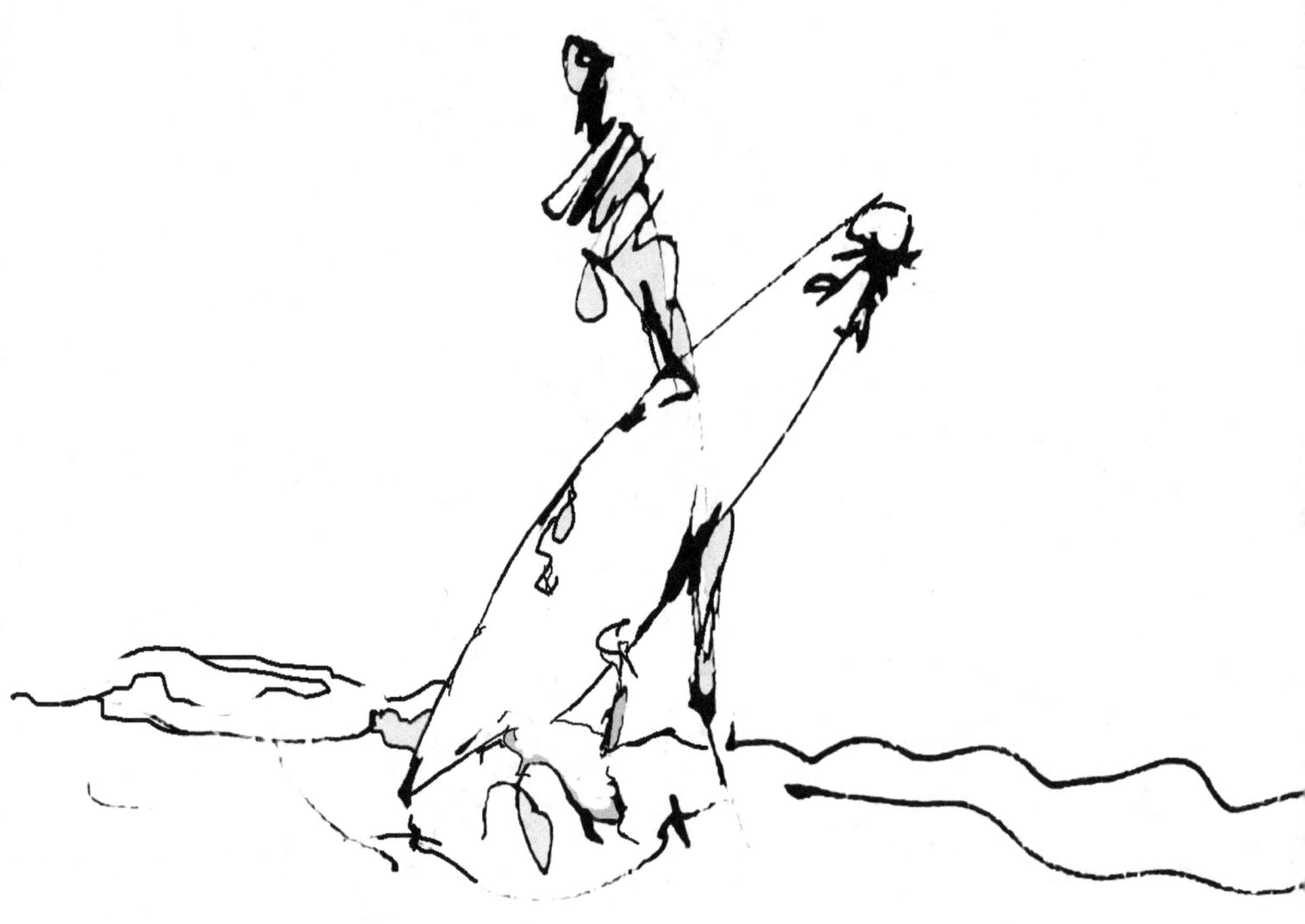

WAIST DEEP

The boy waits
Wheat pods rattle in afternoon breeze
Winged pheasant rises.

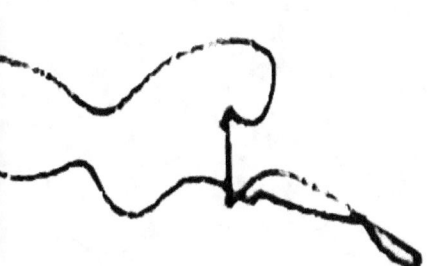

HEADLAND

End of beach
Ocean waves pop along the shore
Flutter of a butterfly.

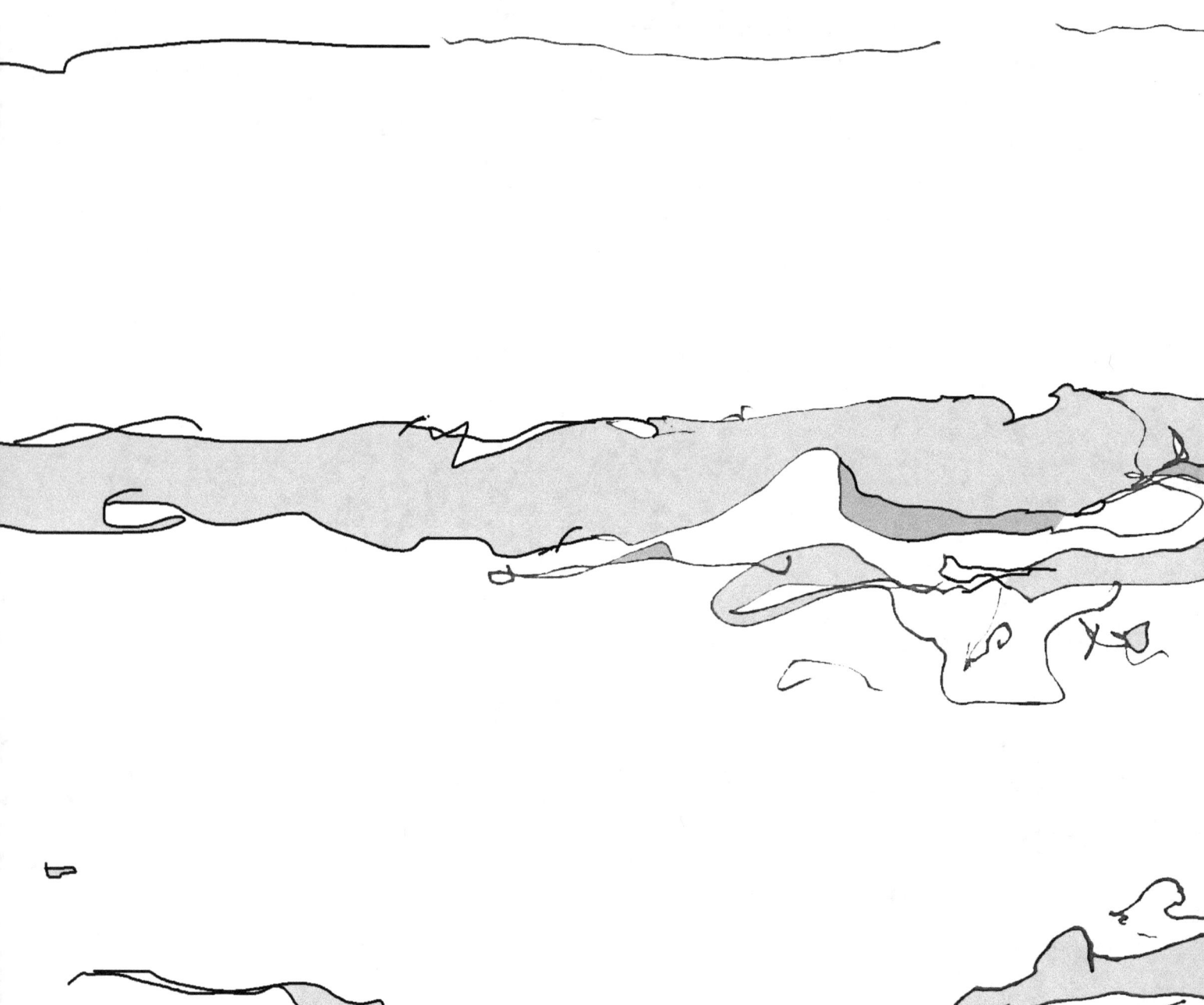

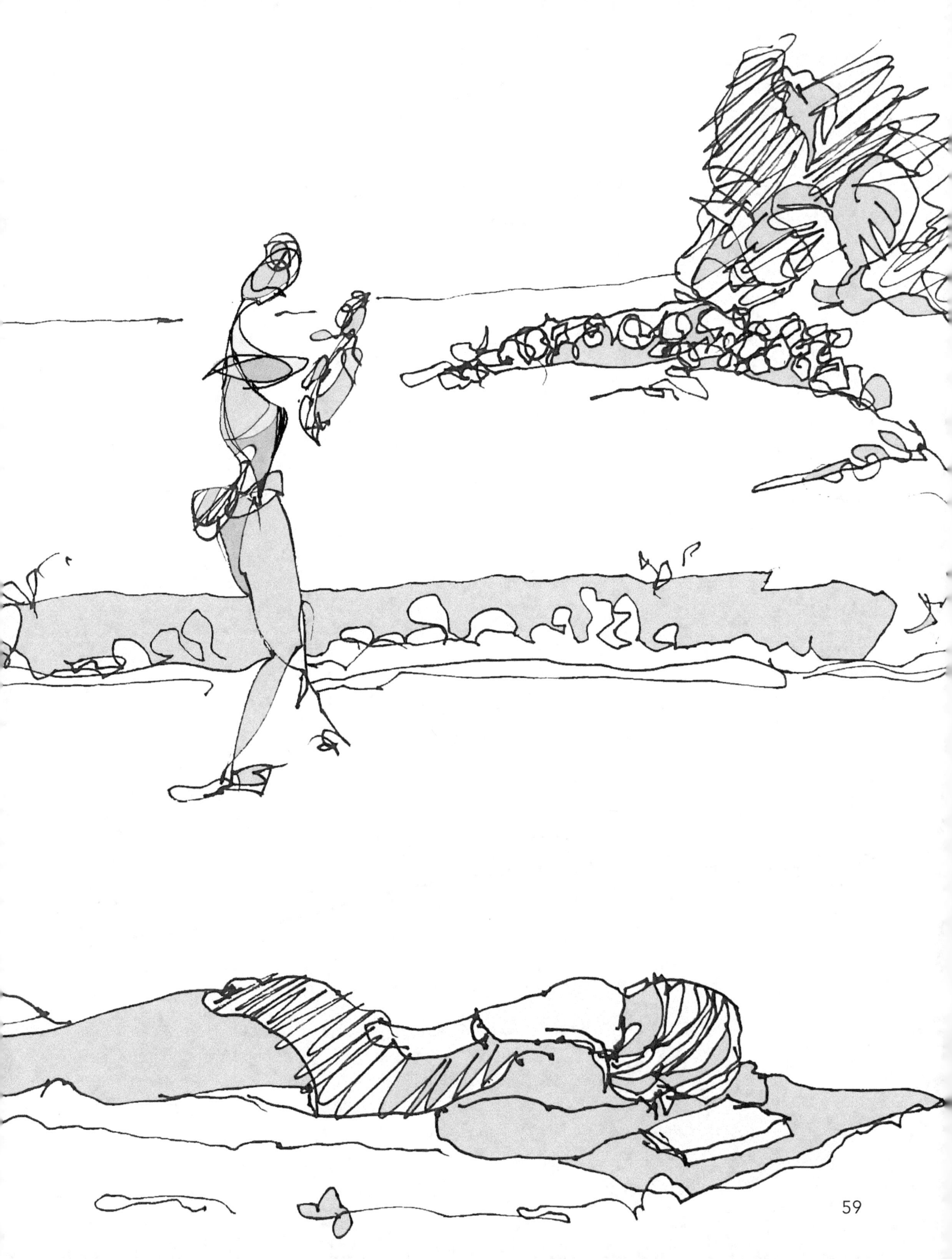

SIRIUS

The dog star
Black ink and faded yellow sand
Shadows lengthen.

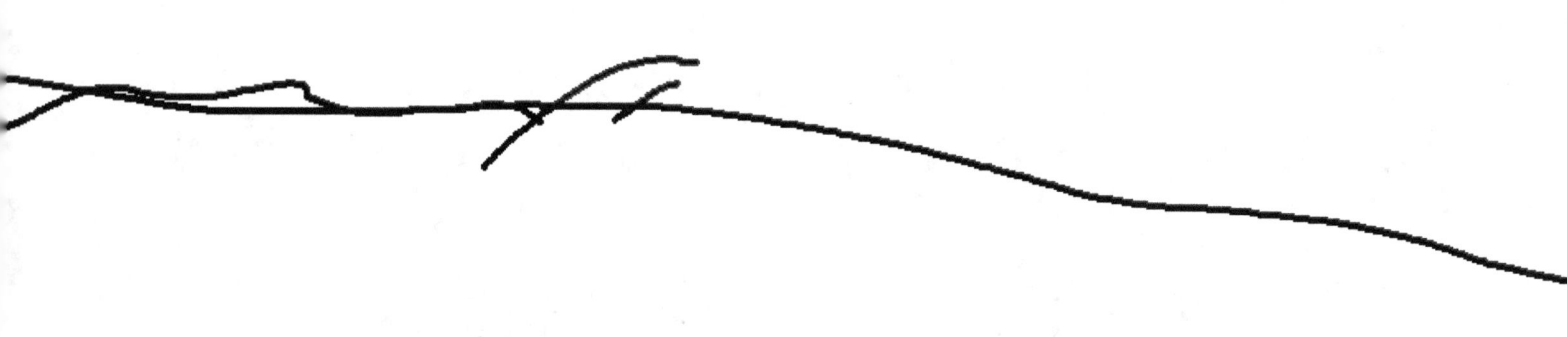

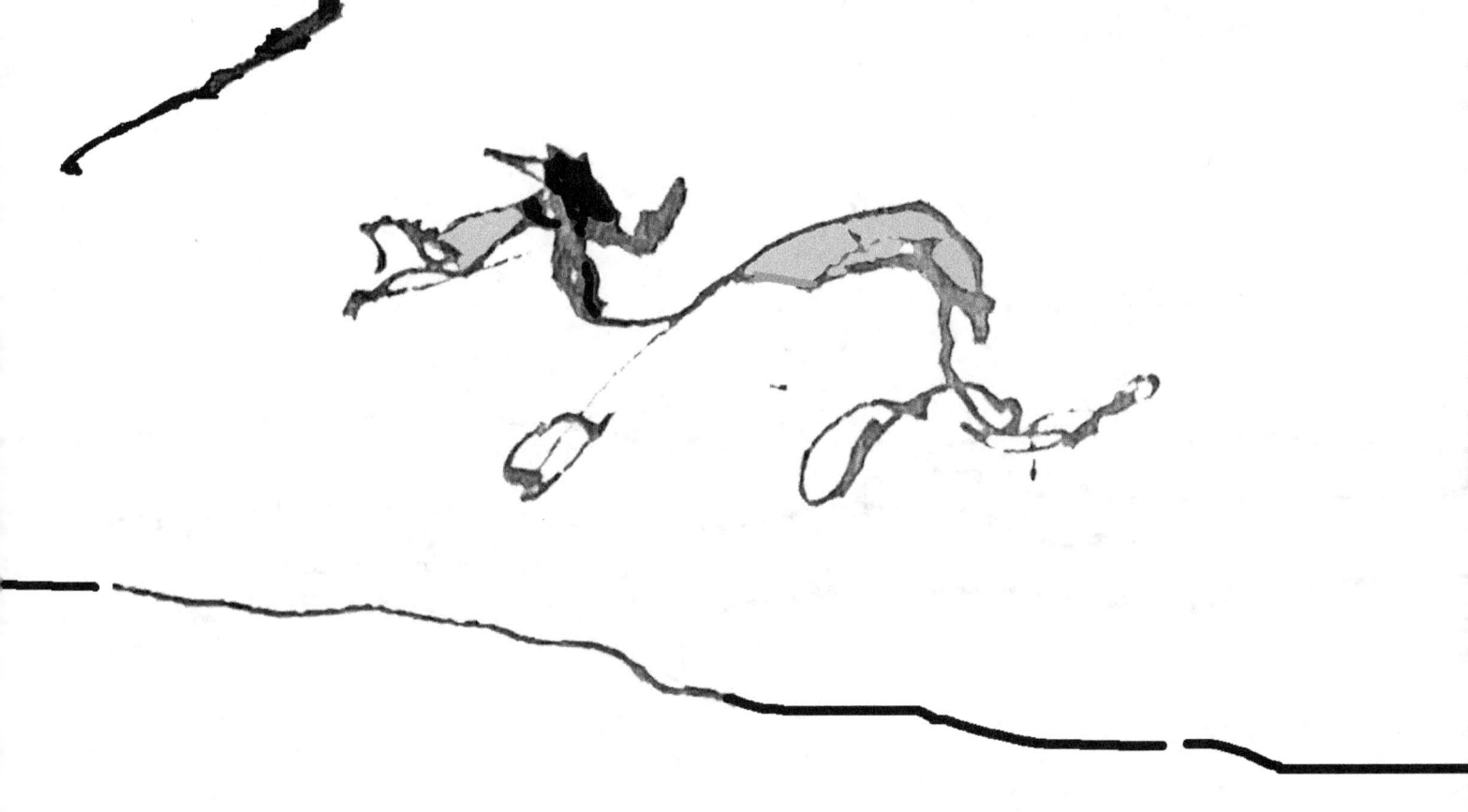

AT SEA

Thought waves
On turquoise oceans of nothingness
Whisperers of questions.

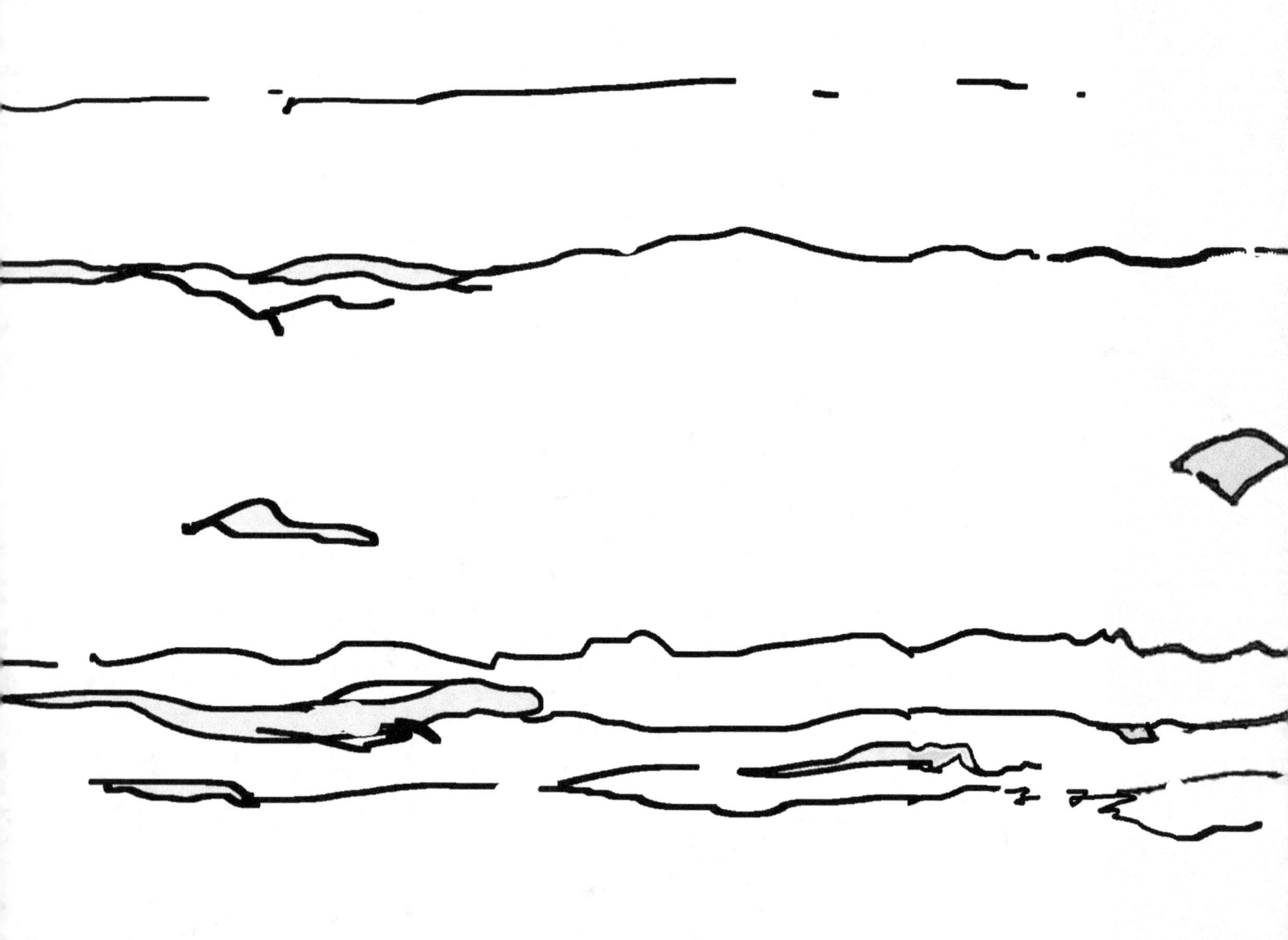

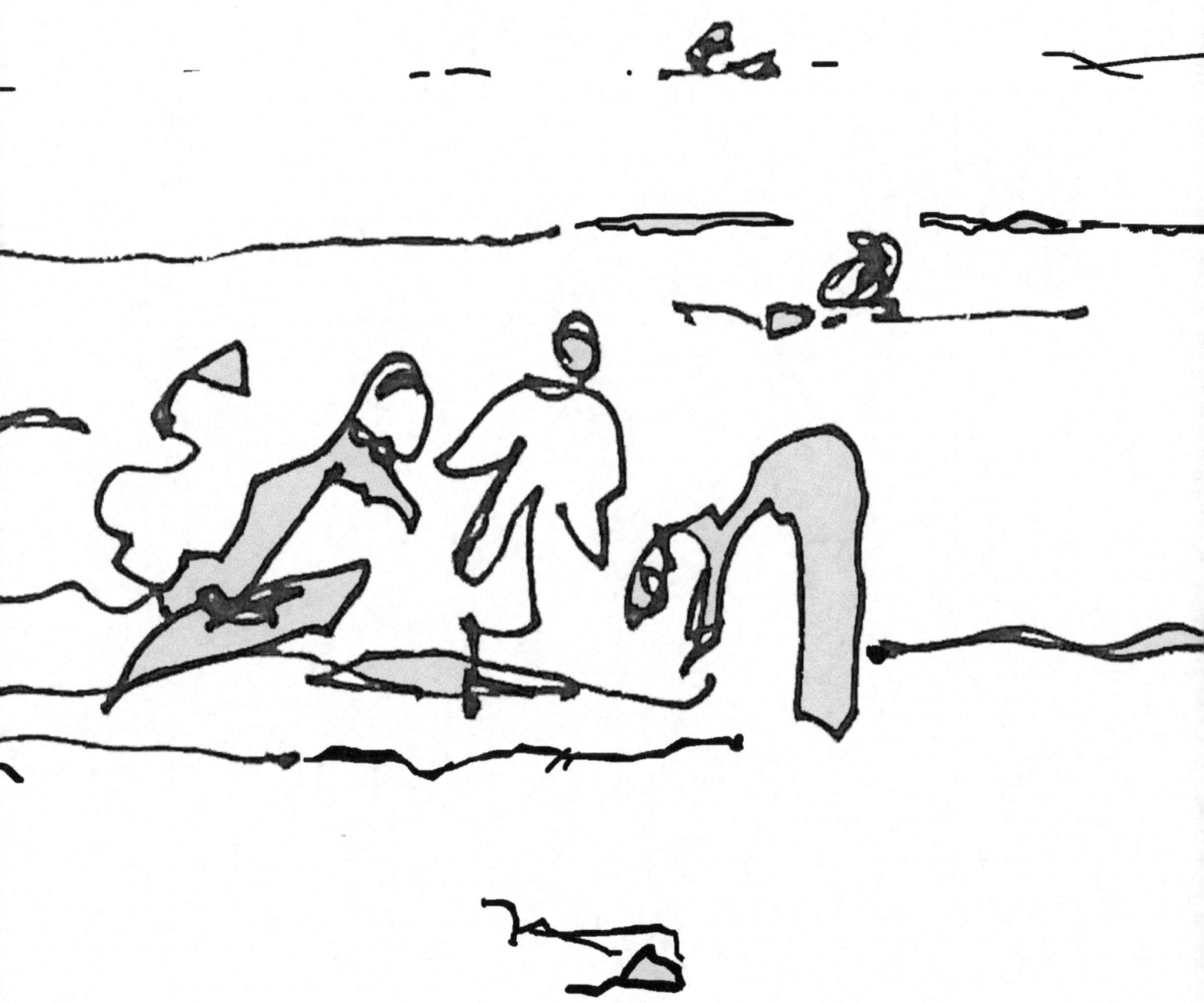

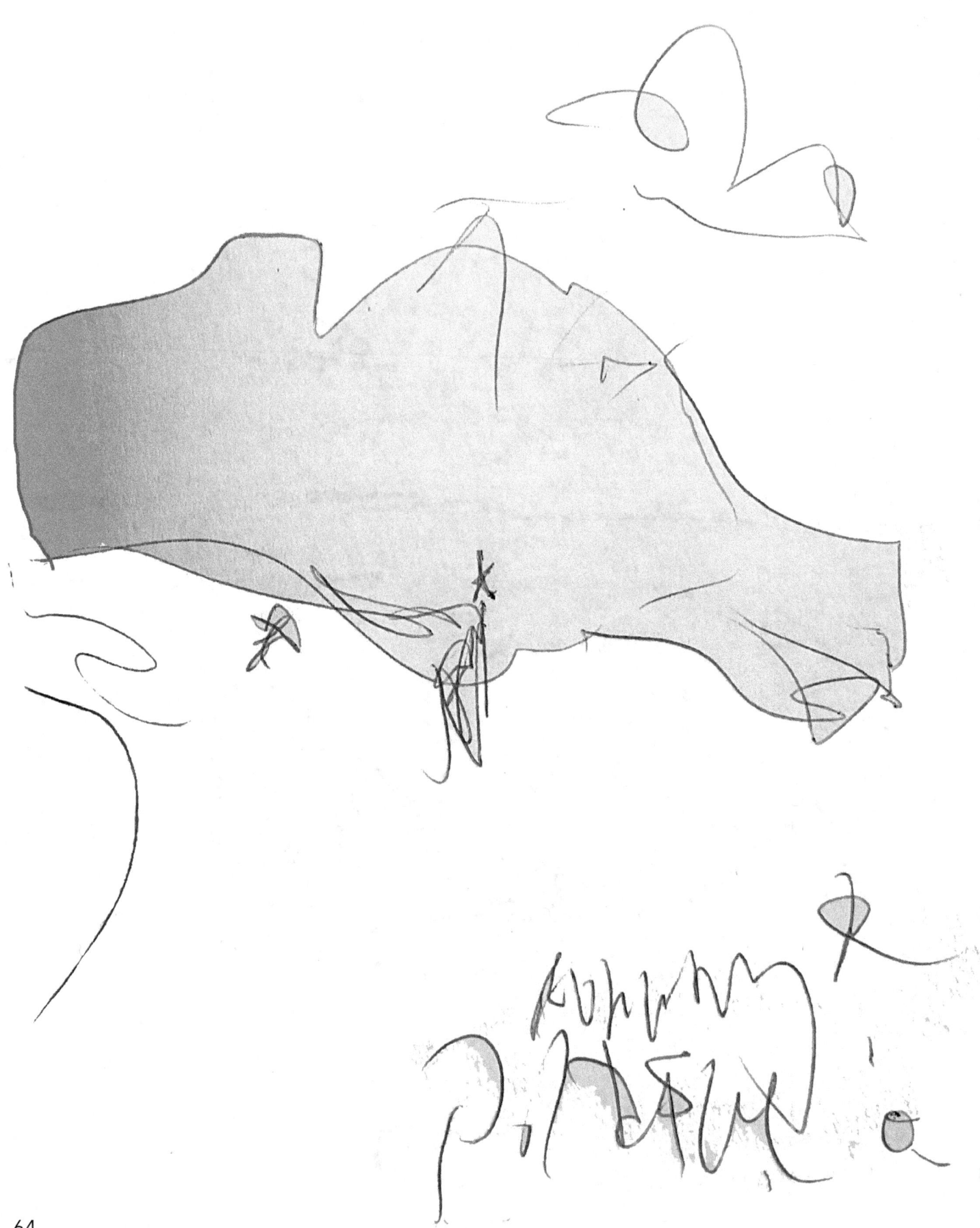

SHADOW LIFE

Seeds shudder
Iron buds swaddled in gossamer
Silent passing of night.

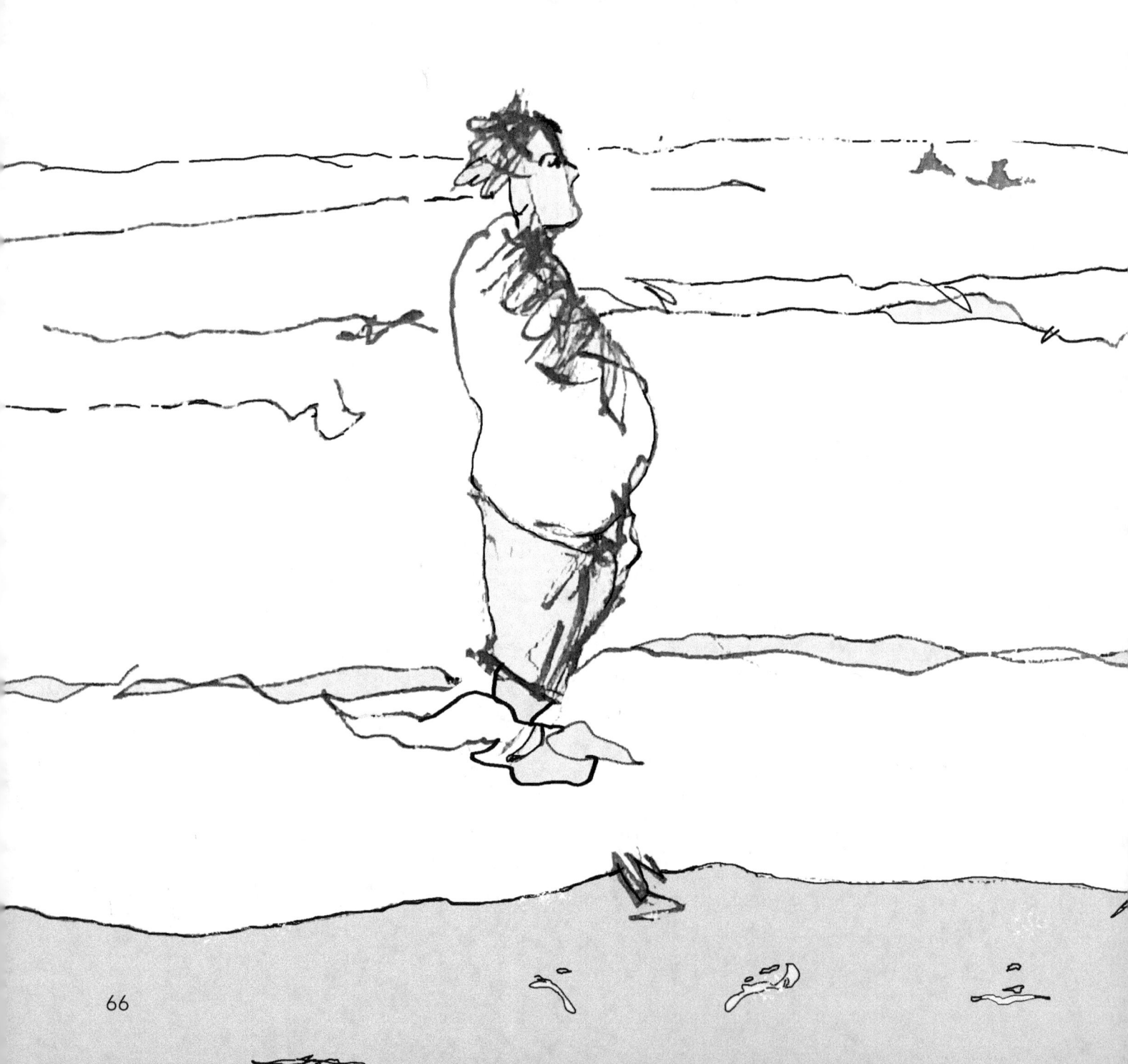

EVENING LIGHT

Black ink figurines
Trapped in ragged line
Nugatory in time.

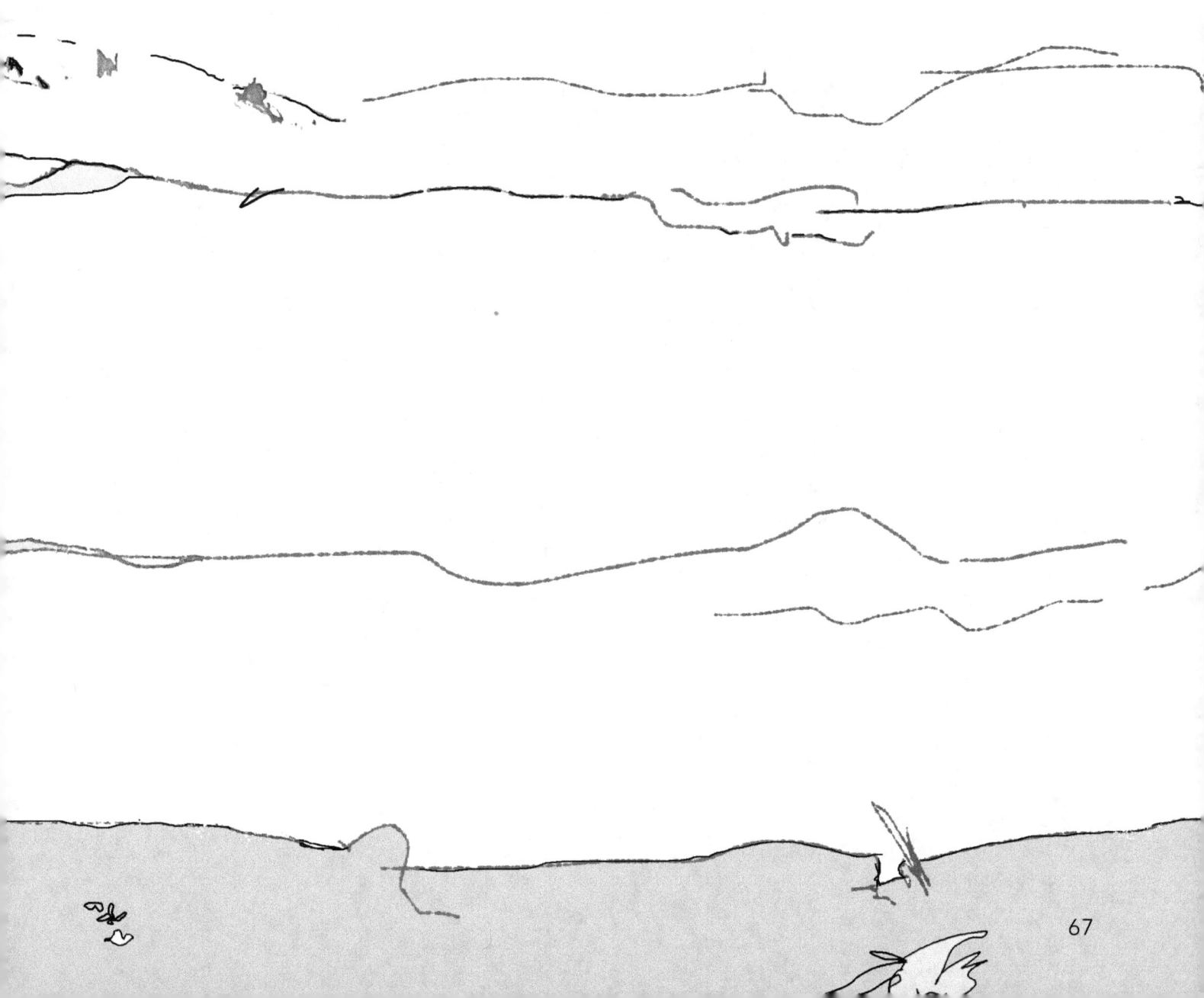

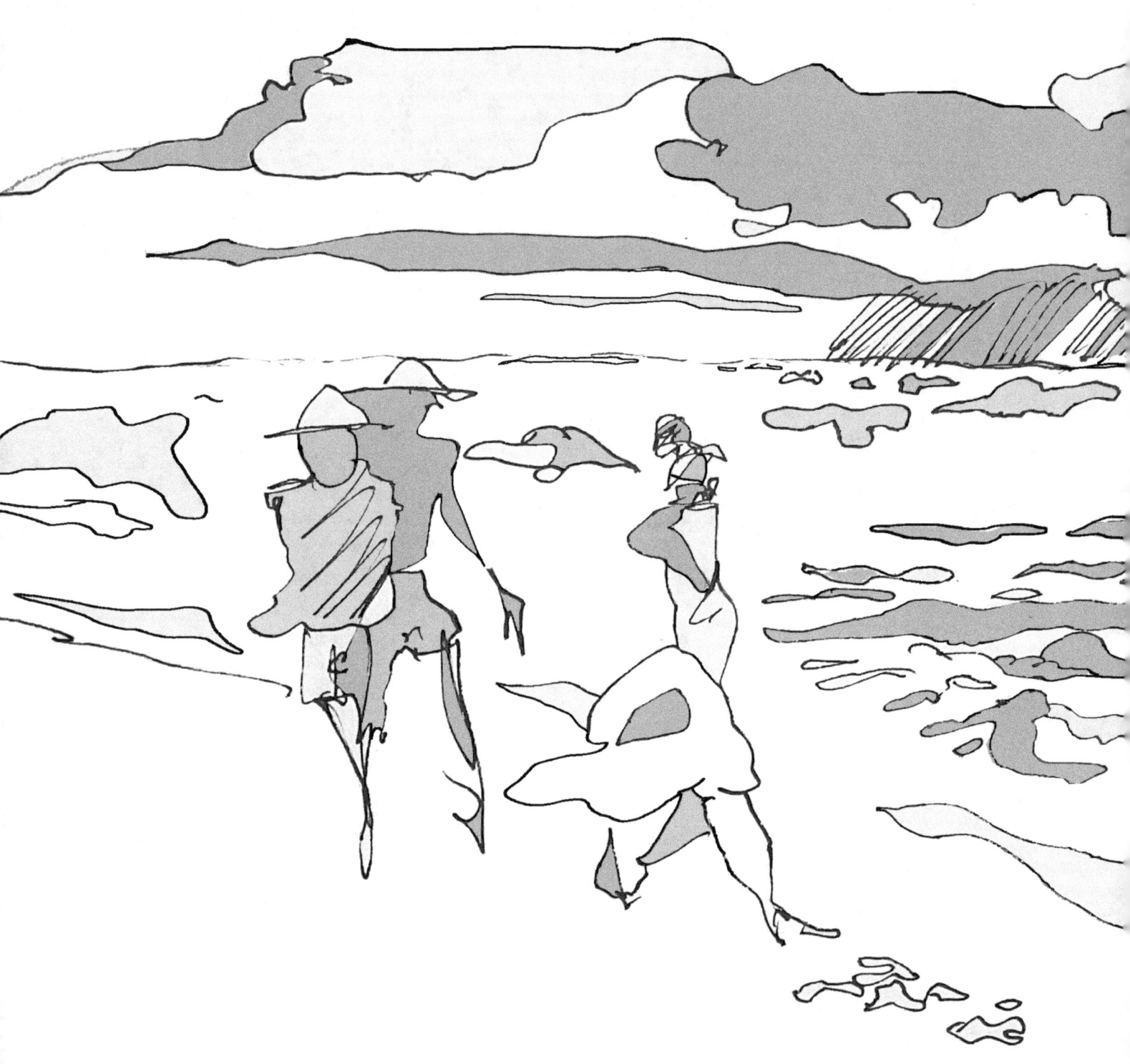

OYSTER BAY

Fishing pole nods
Fingers of rising tide flood the hour
Passing slivers of fish.

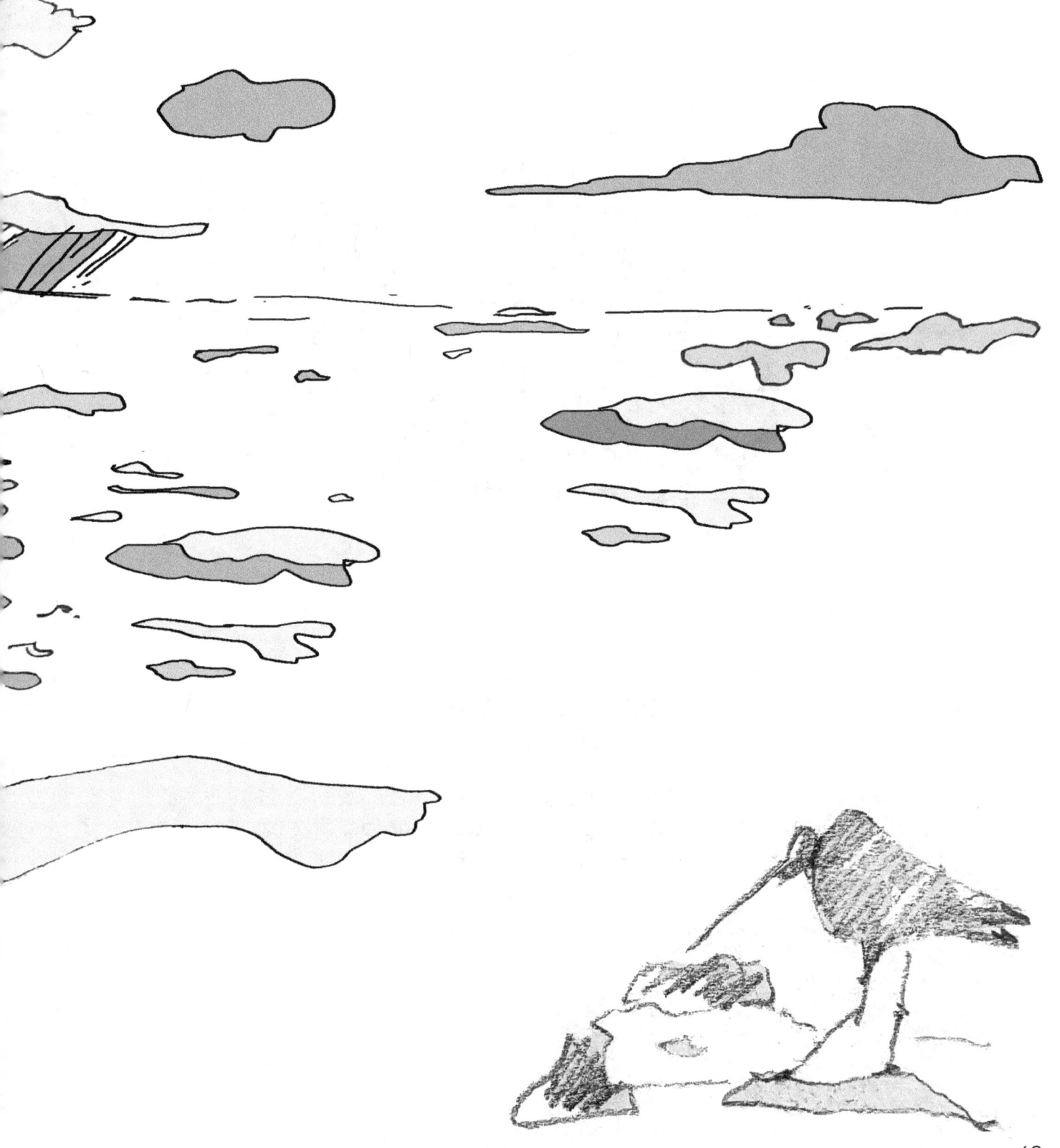

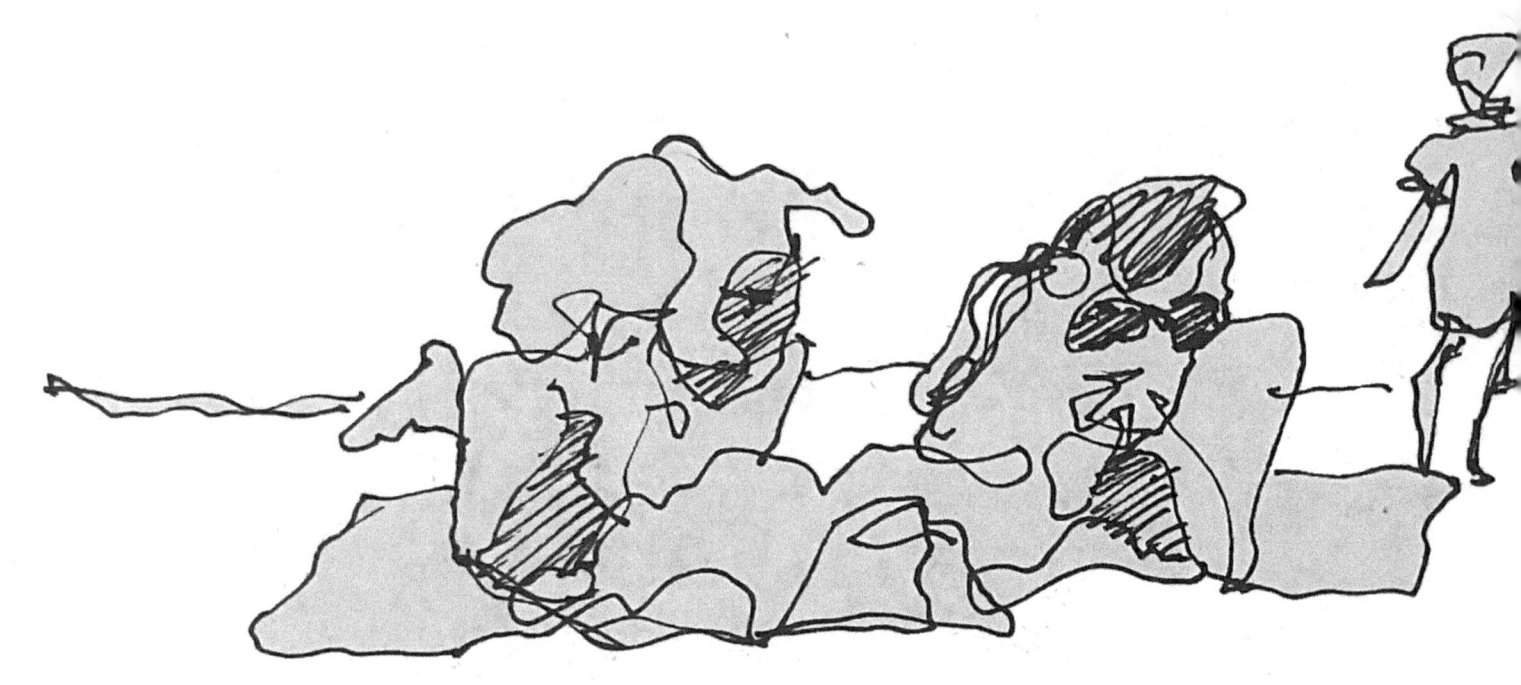

SPECKLED EGGS

Warm egg alone
Nest cradled high in bough of tree
The hawk awaits.

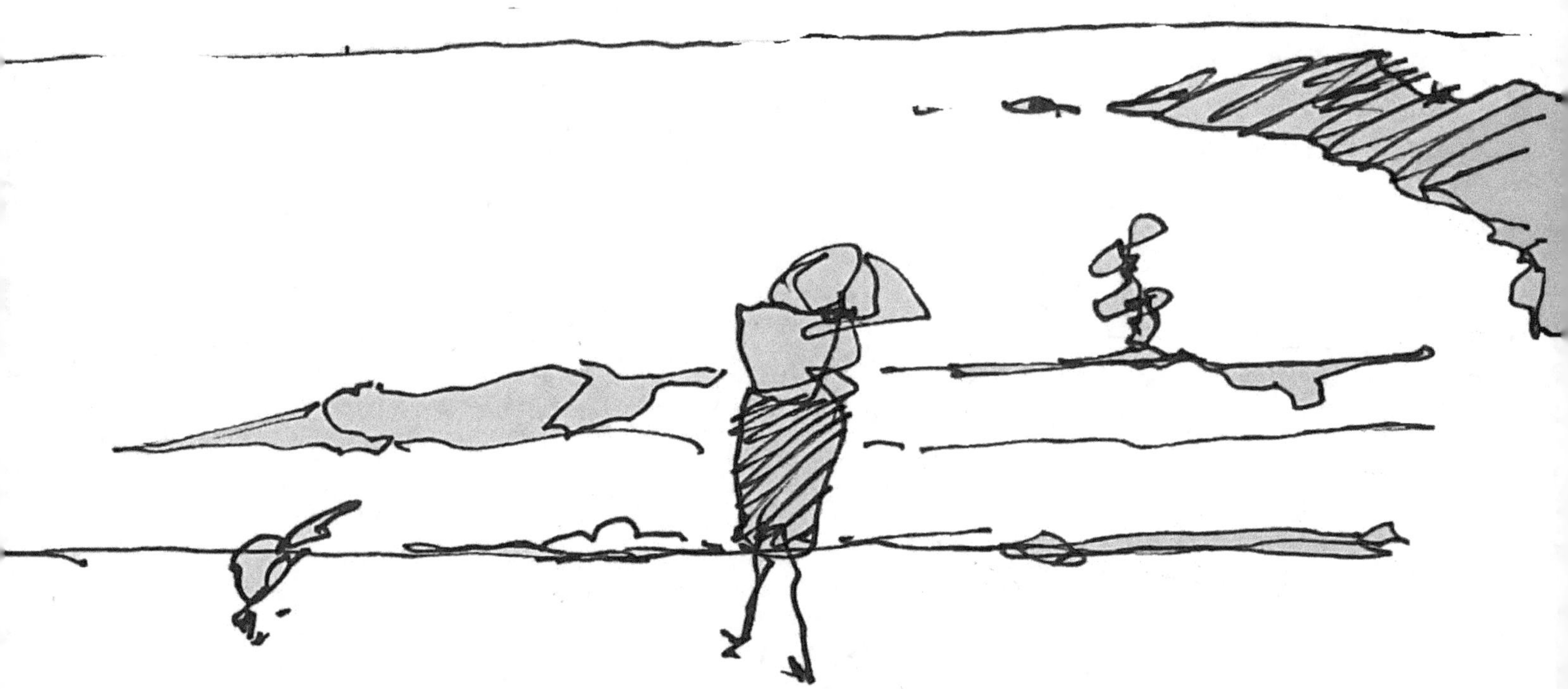

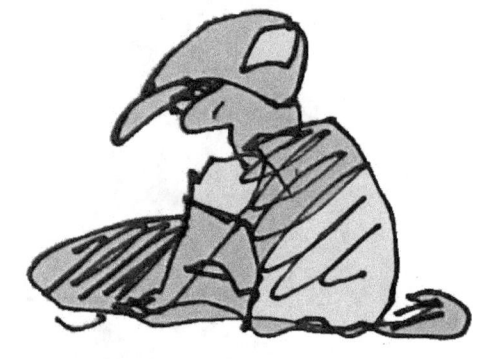

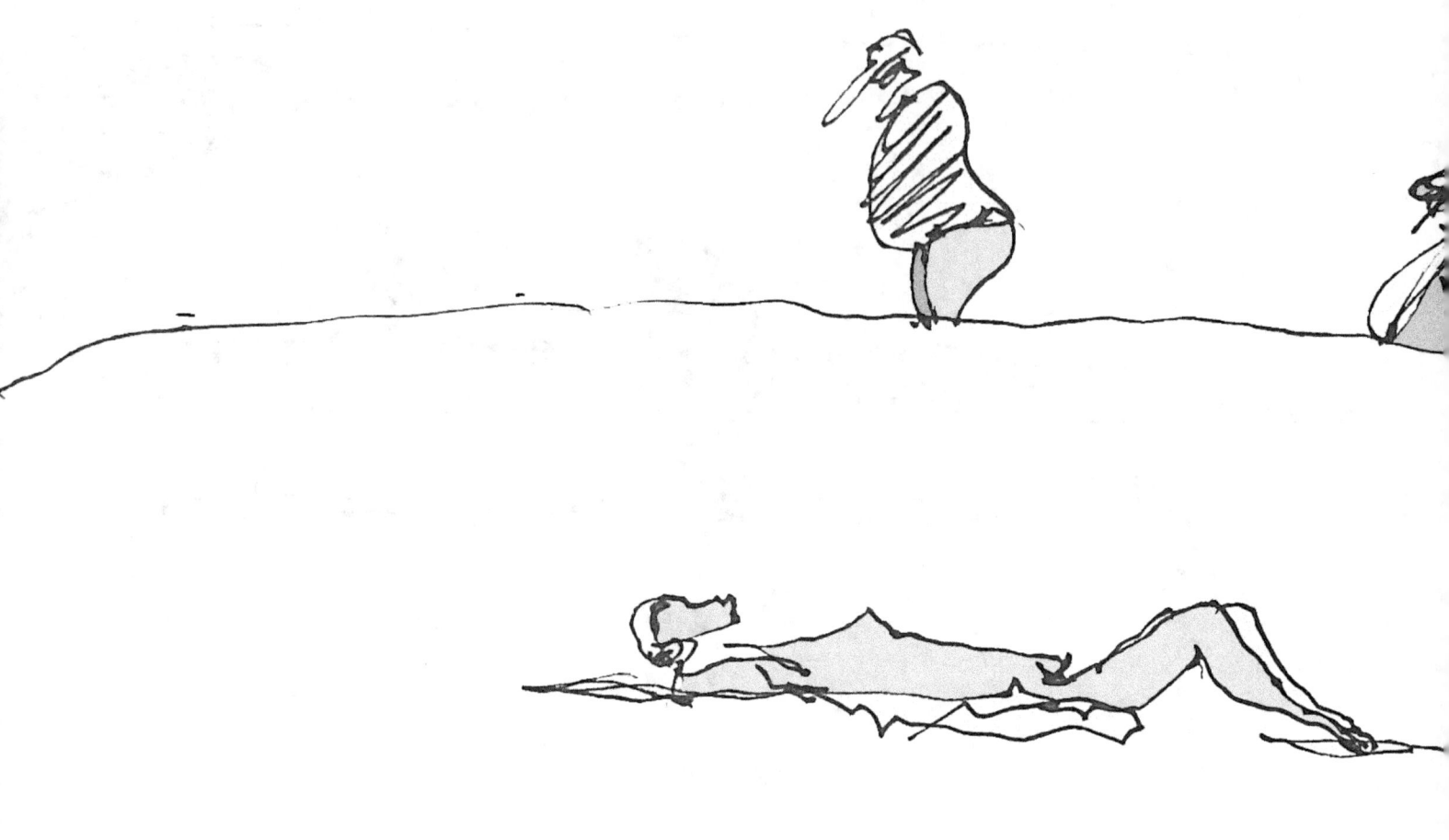

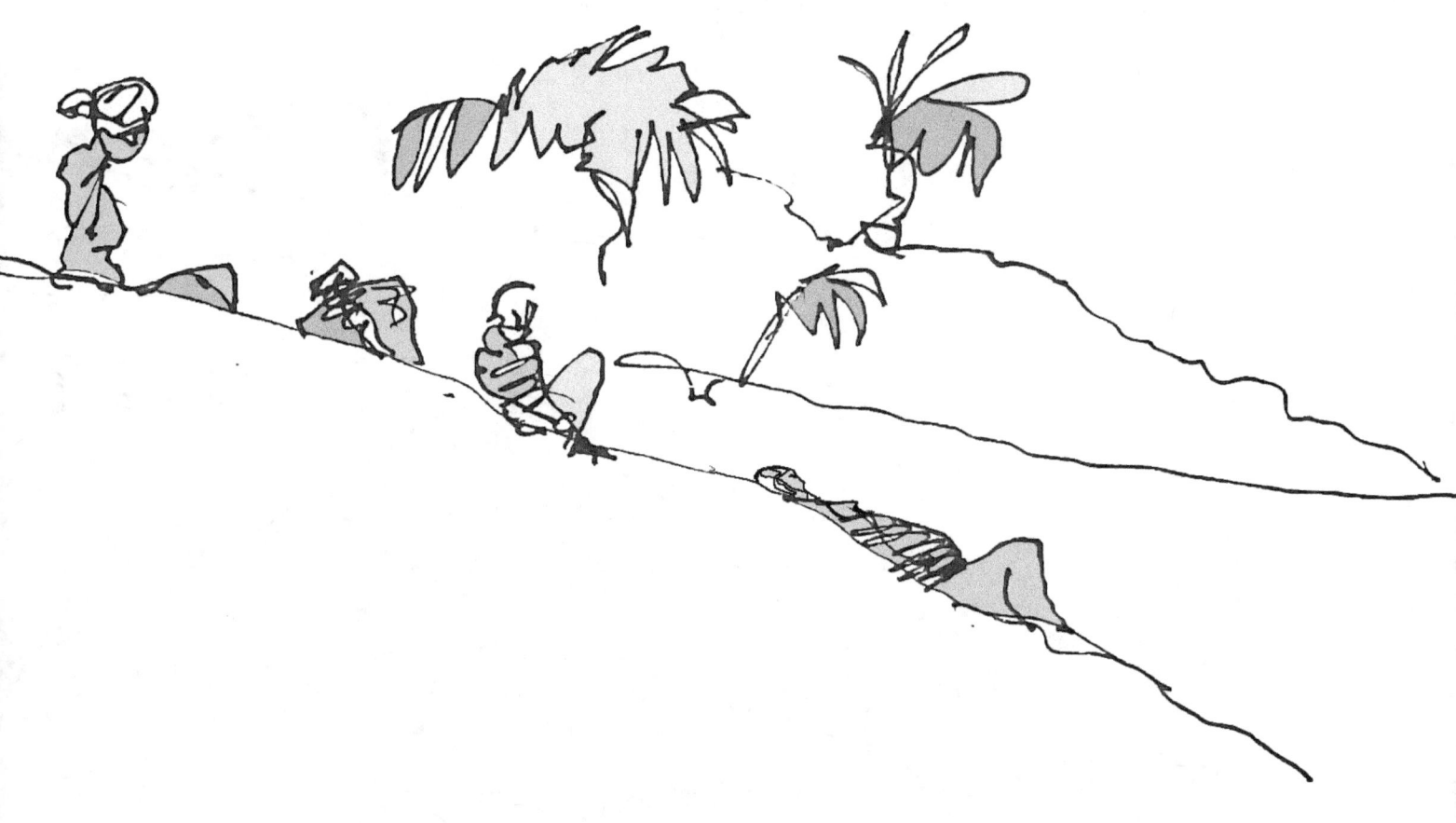

SAND HILL

A rippled horizon
The artist sees what the poet hears
Vacancy of place.

SHALLOWS

Bay of life
Fish flash, hominoids splash
Tenuous bliss.

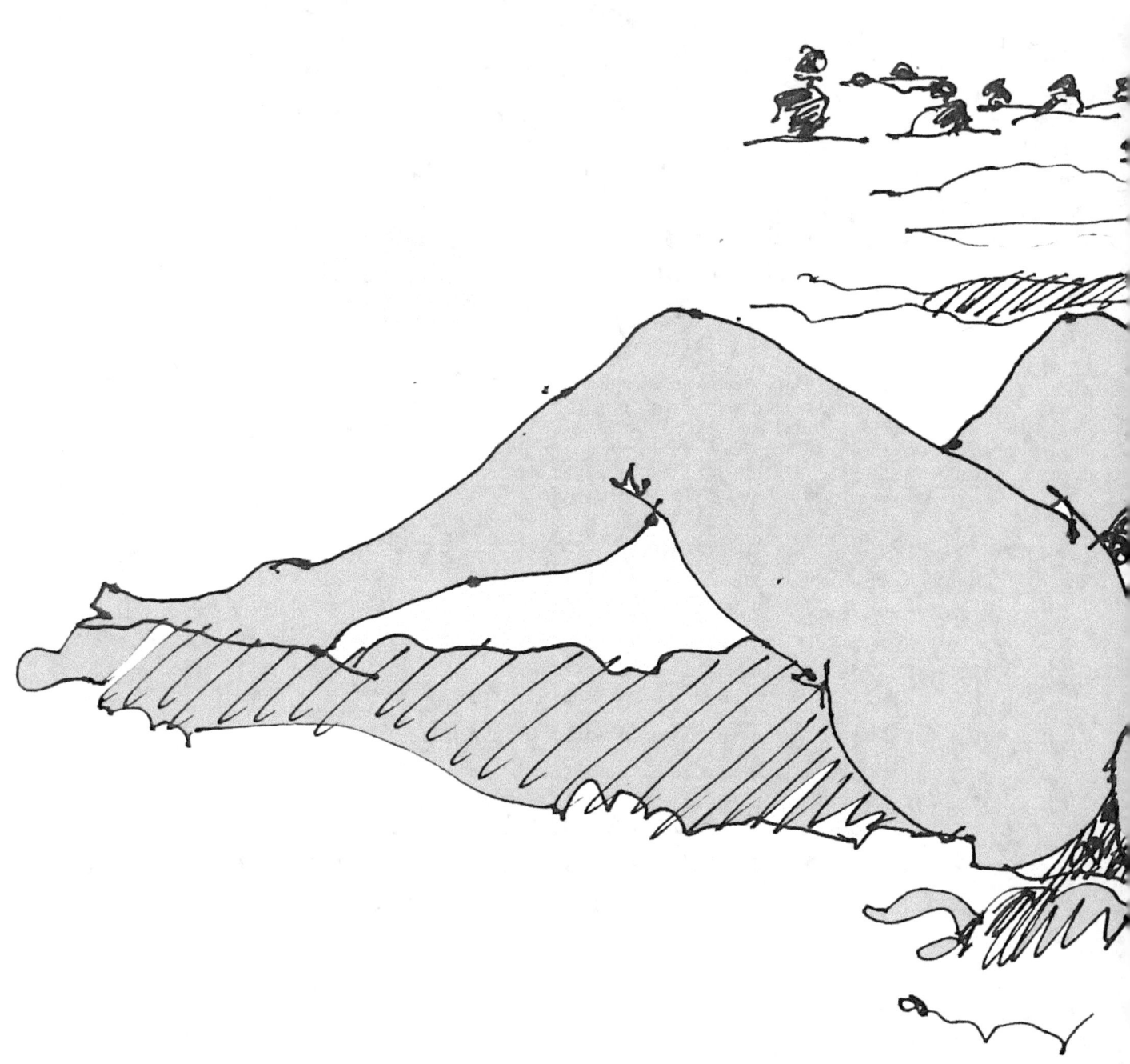

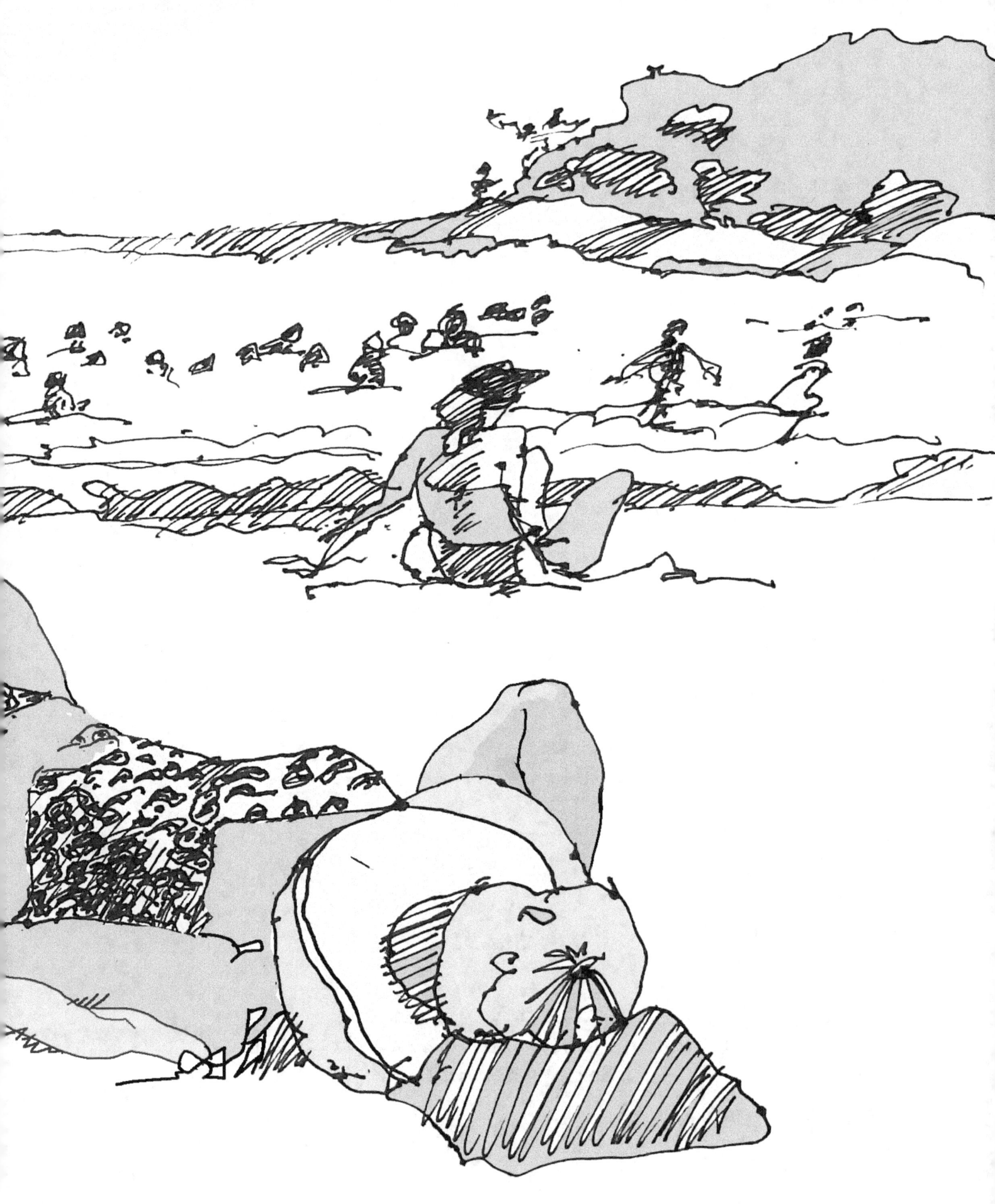

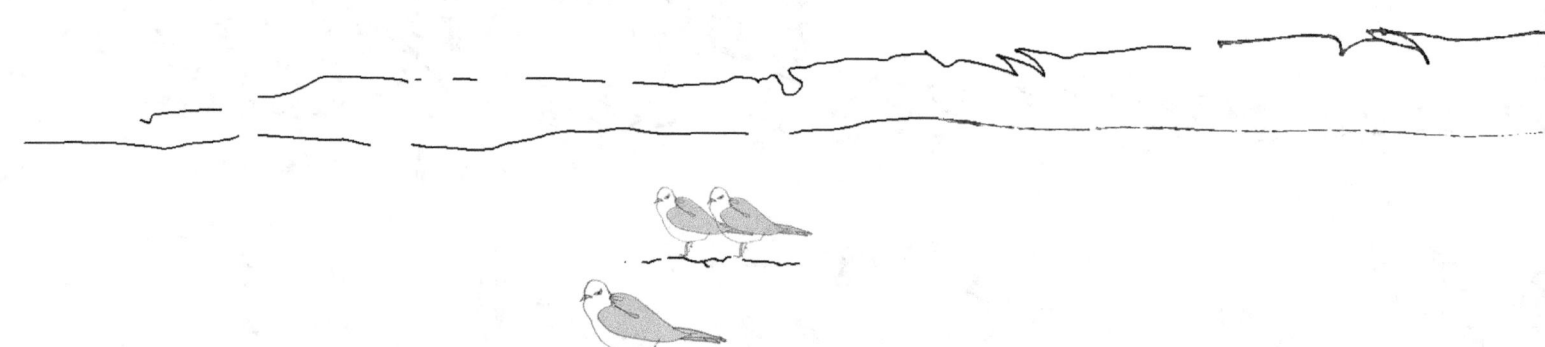
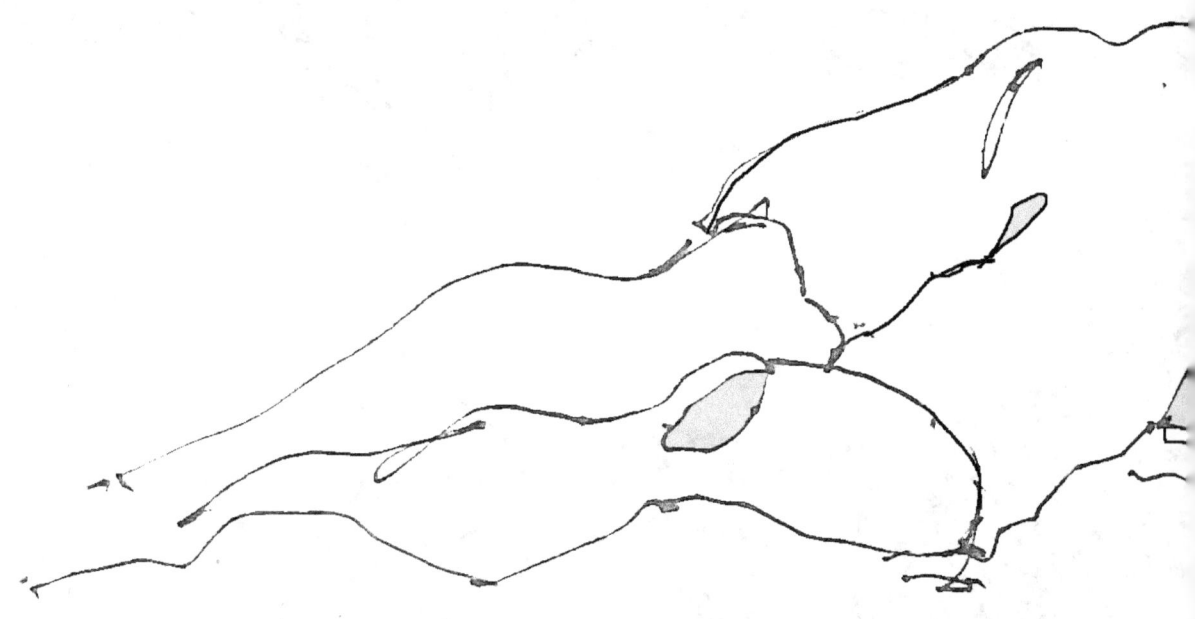

SHADE

Bodhi tree stands
Newborns left for monks to find
Hide the snakes.

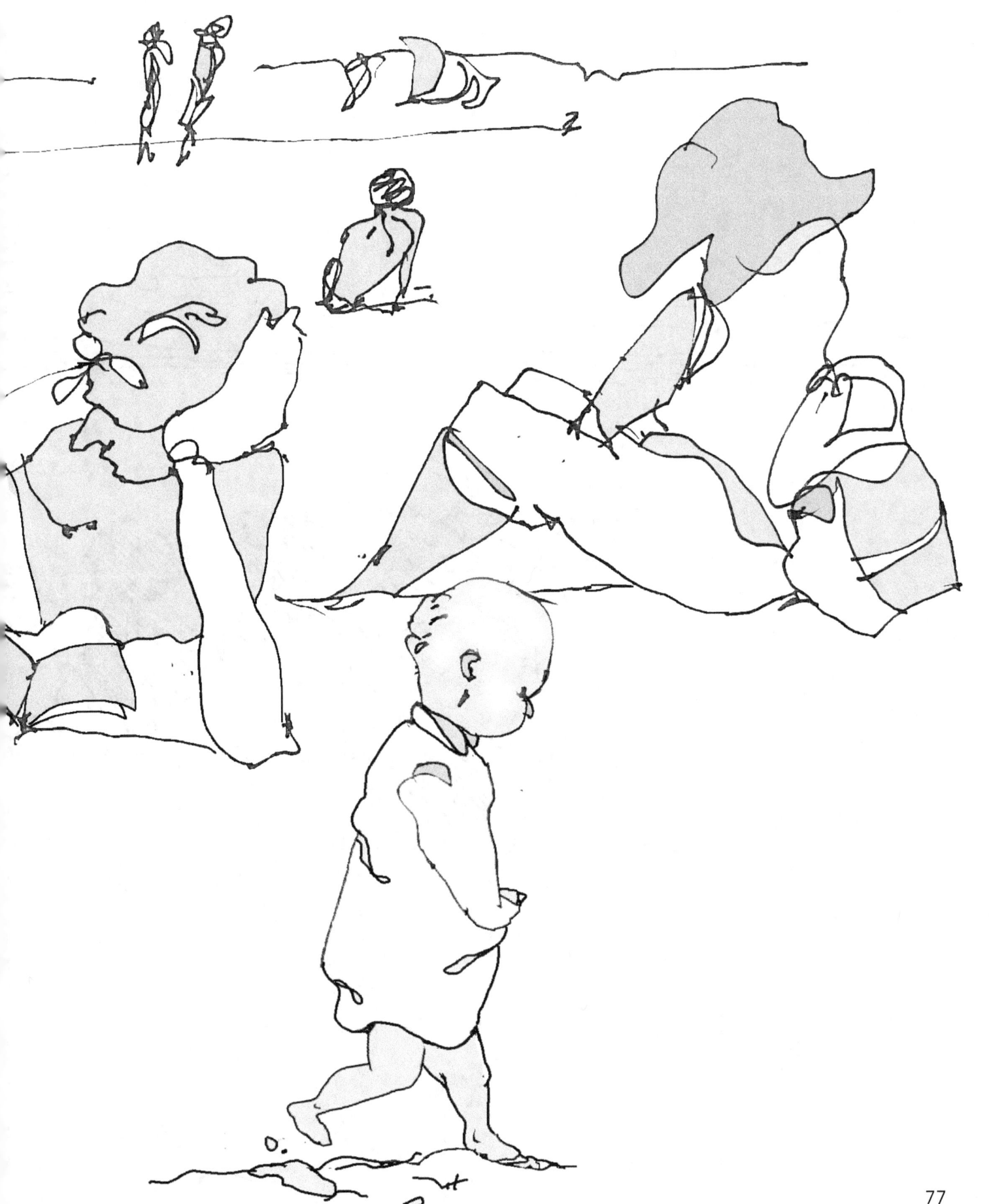

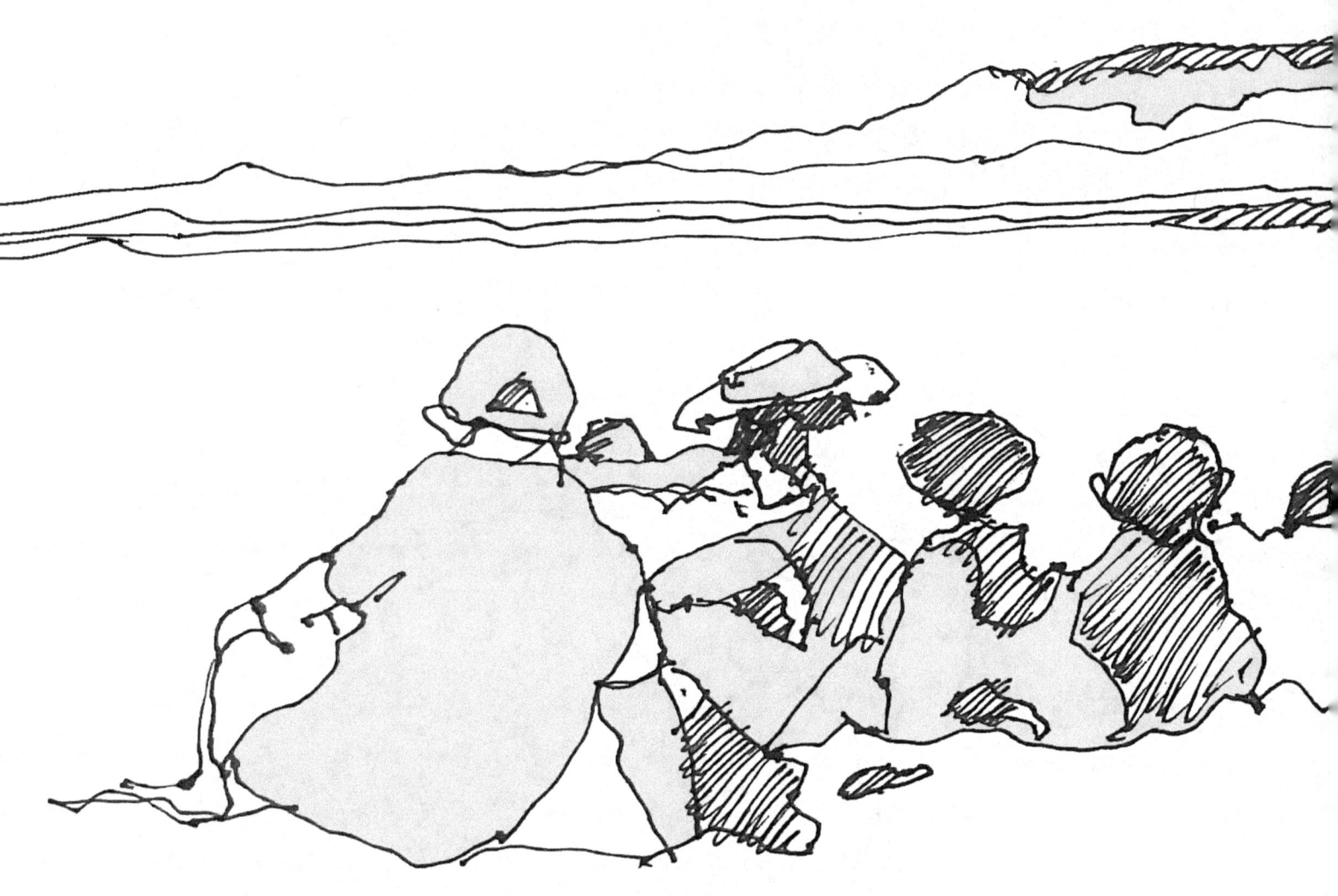

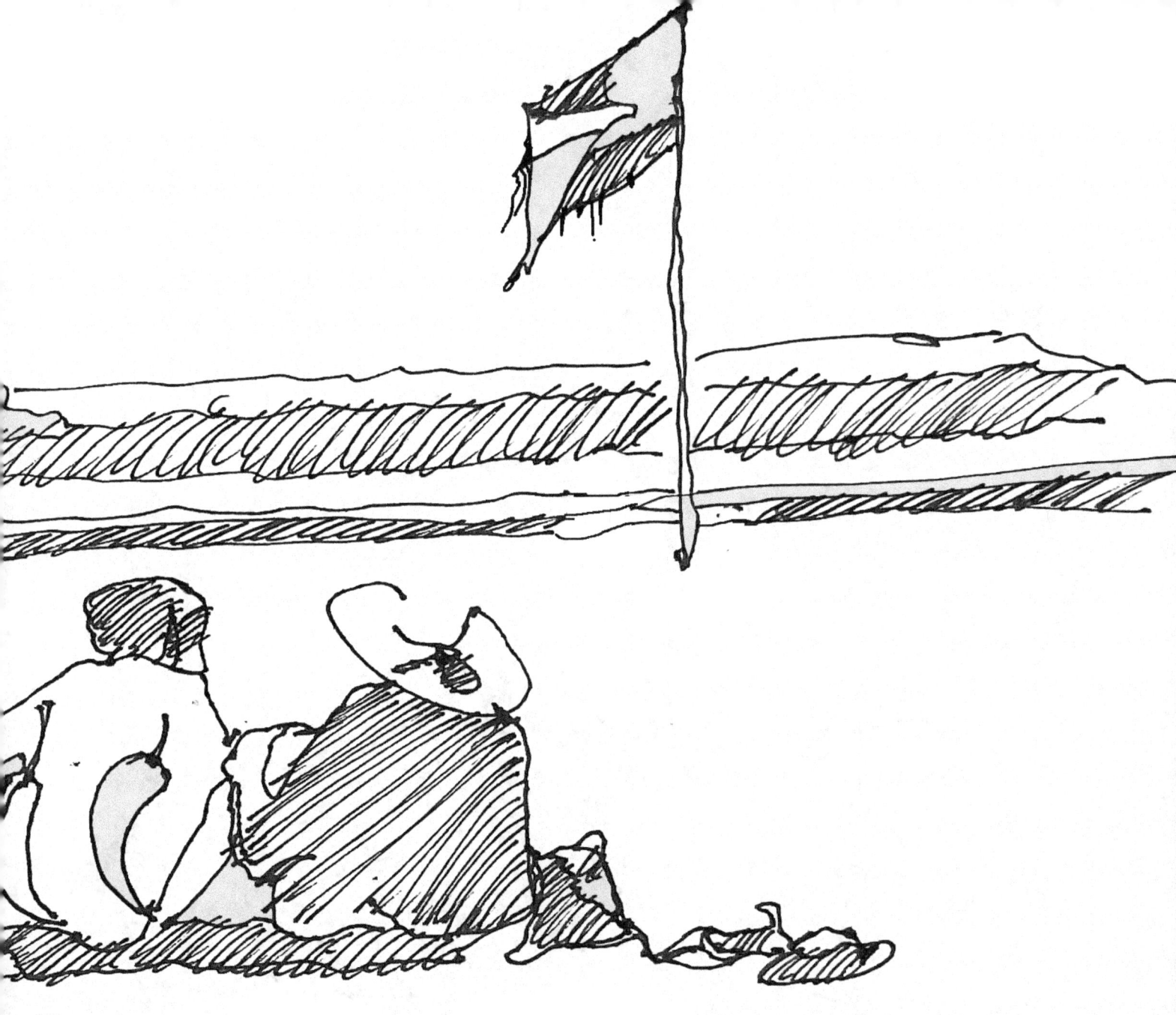

RAGGED

Flag torn weary
Warns daily of water graves
Look away.

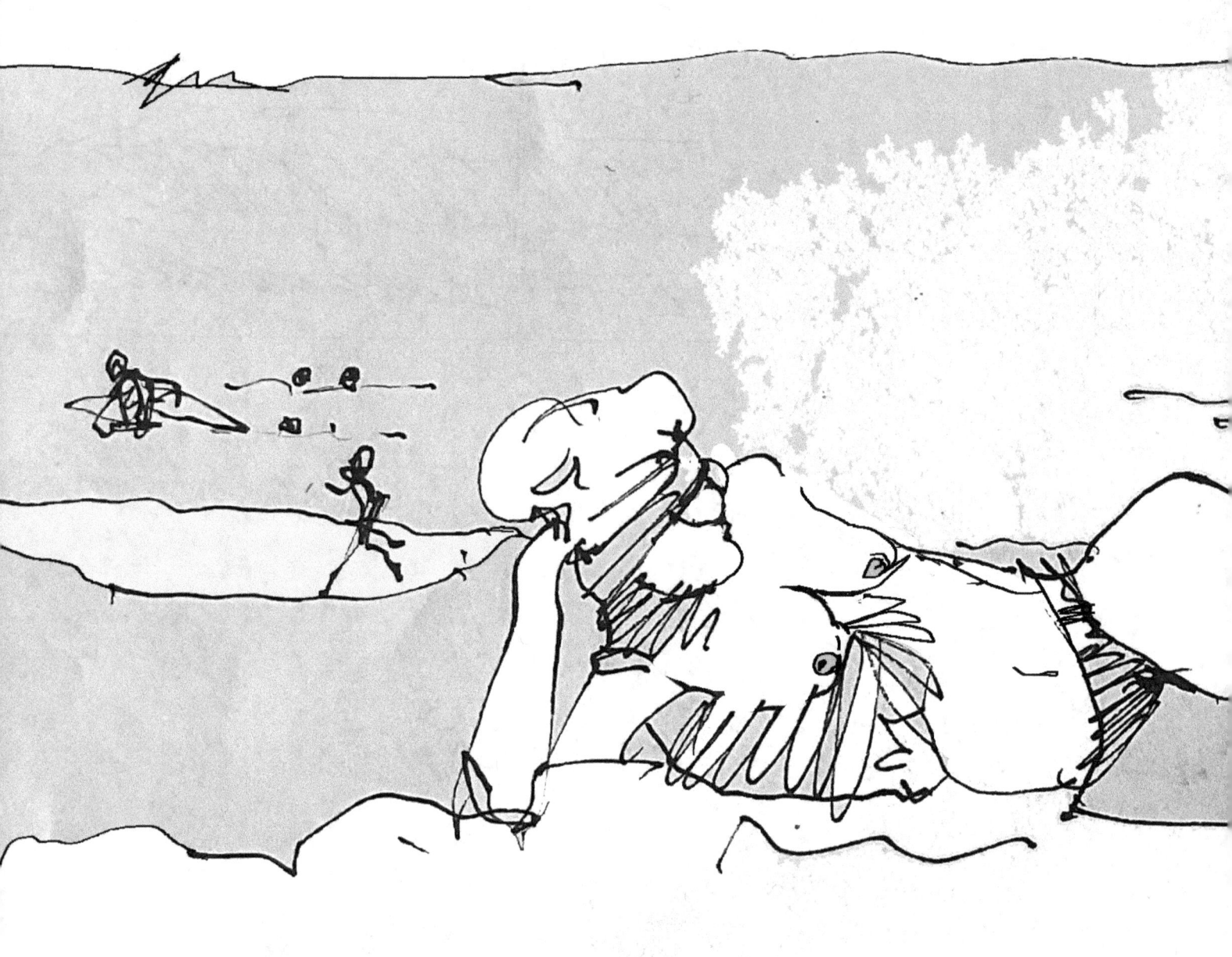

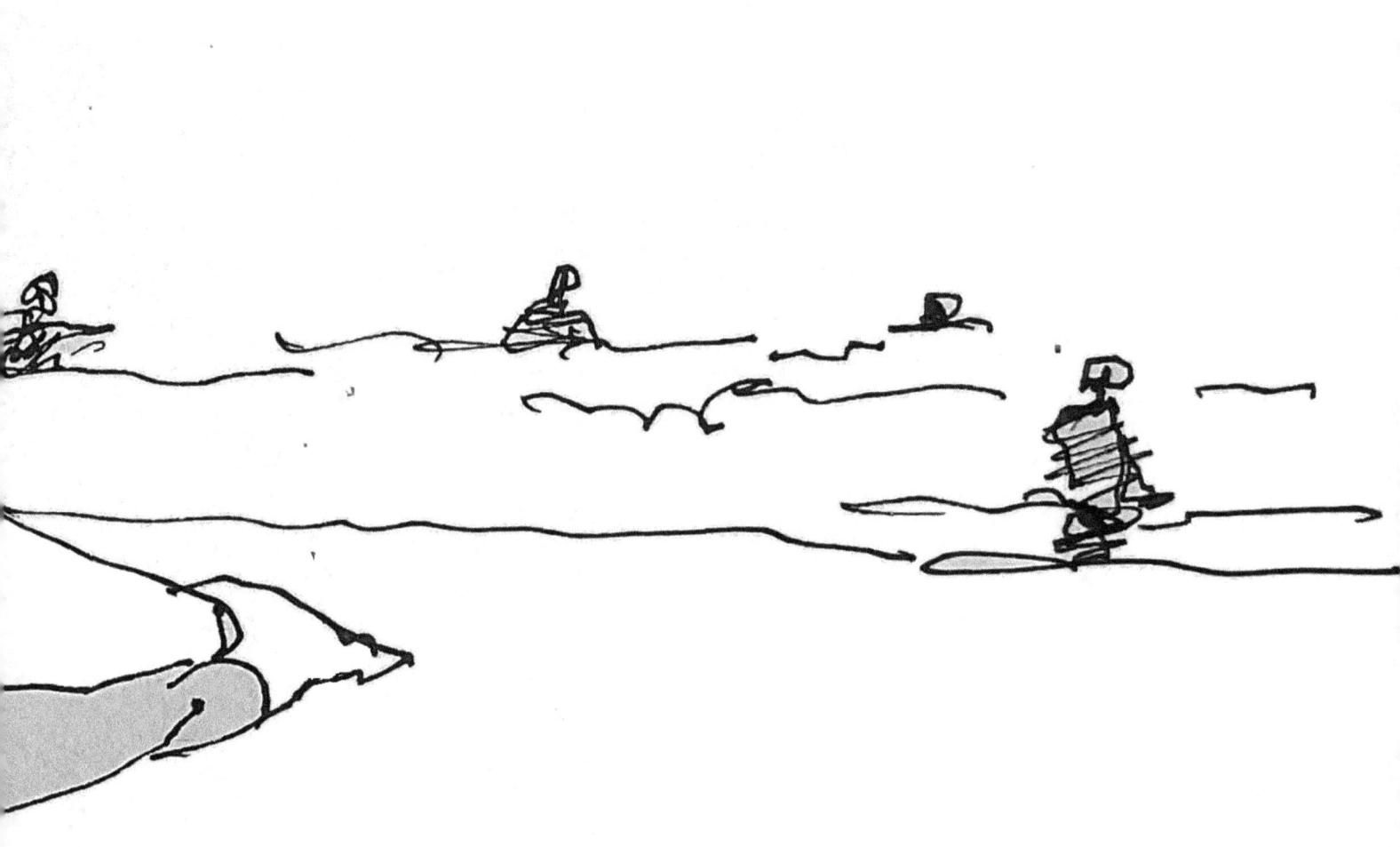

SWEET CAFFEINE

Ceiling fan clatters
Silver urn in curve of spoon
Silent in reflection.

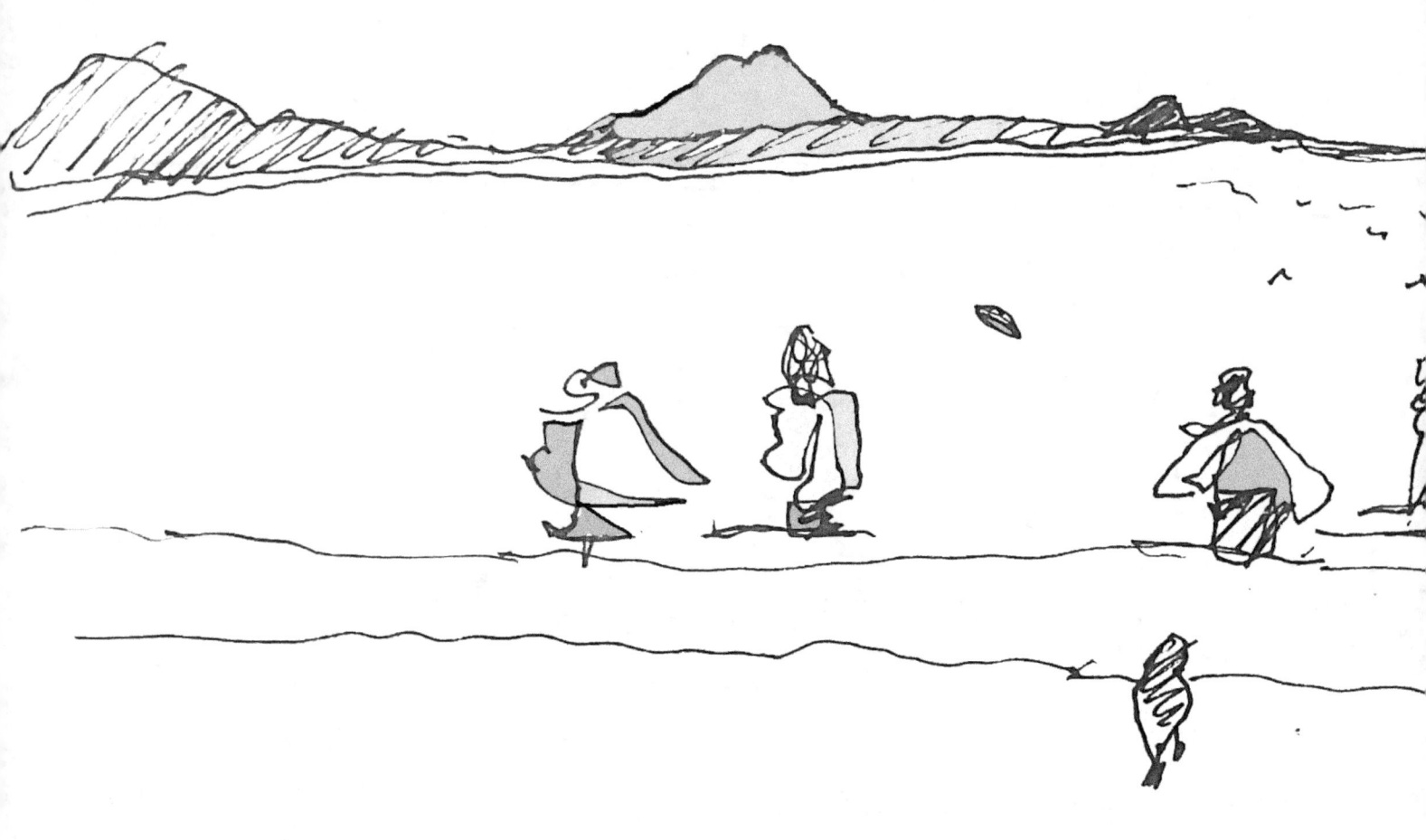

FORECAST

Sunday sandcastles
At the sacrificial verge of sea
Stand guard.

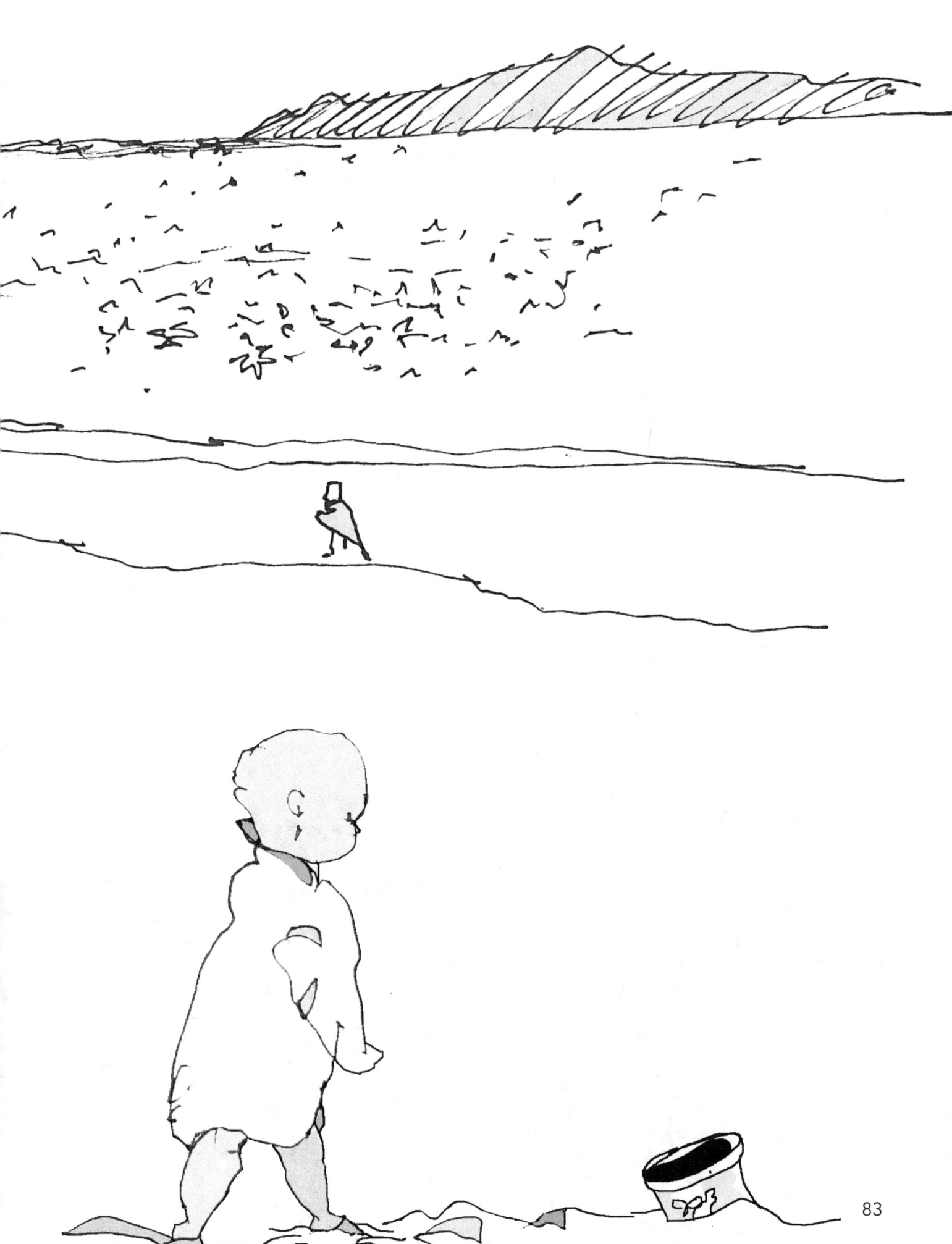

BIRDING

Watching bird
Watching bird watching bird
Bird watching.

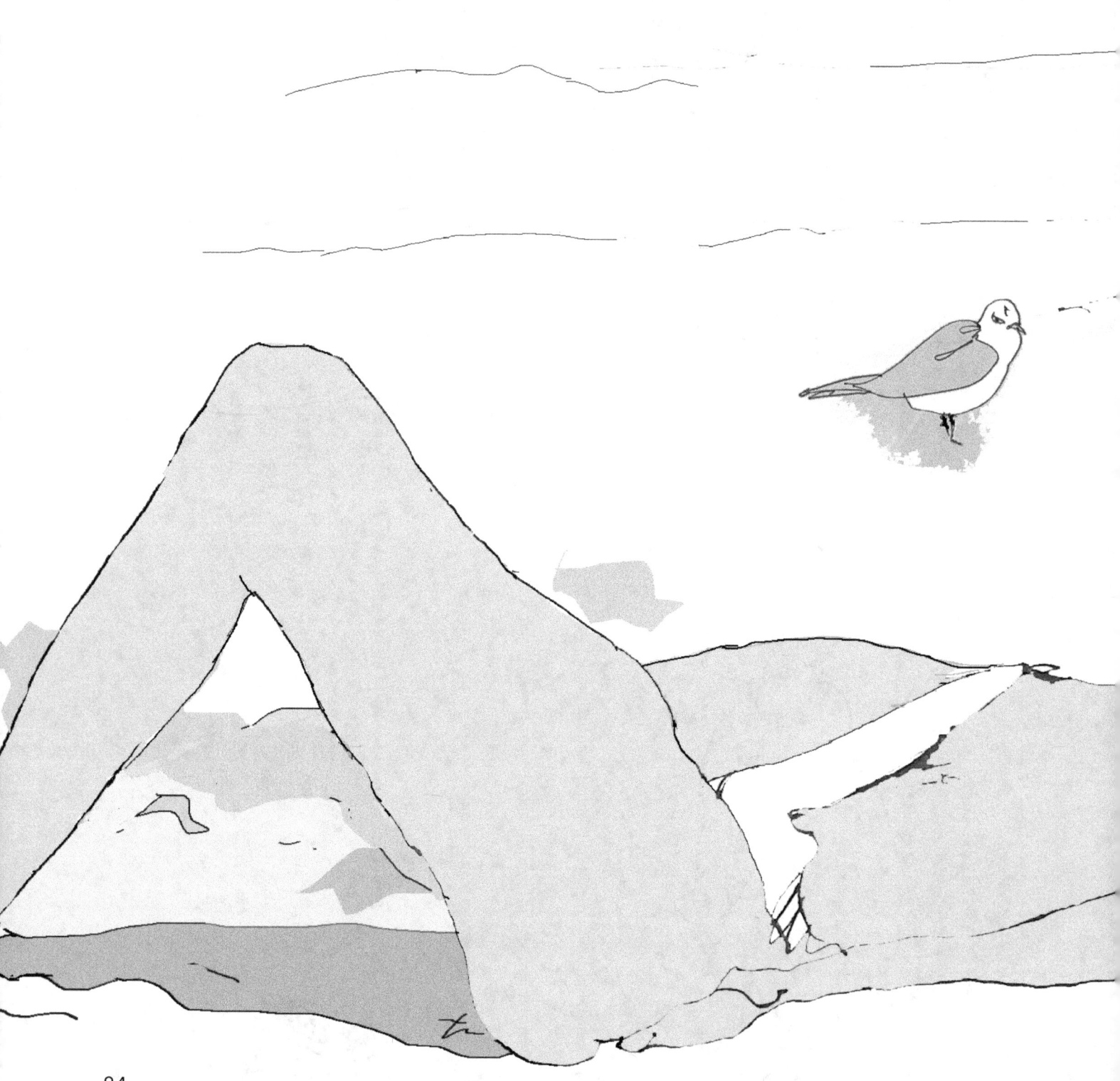

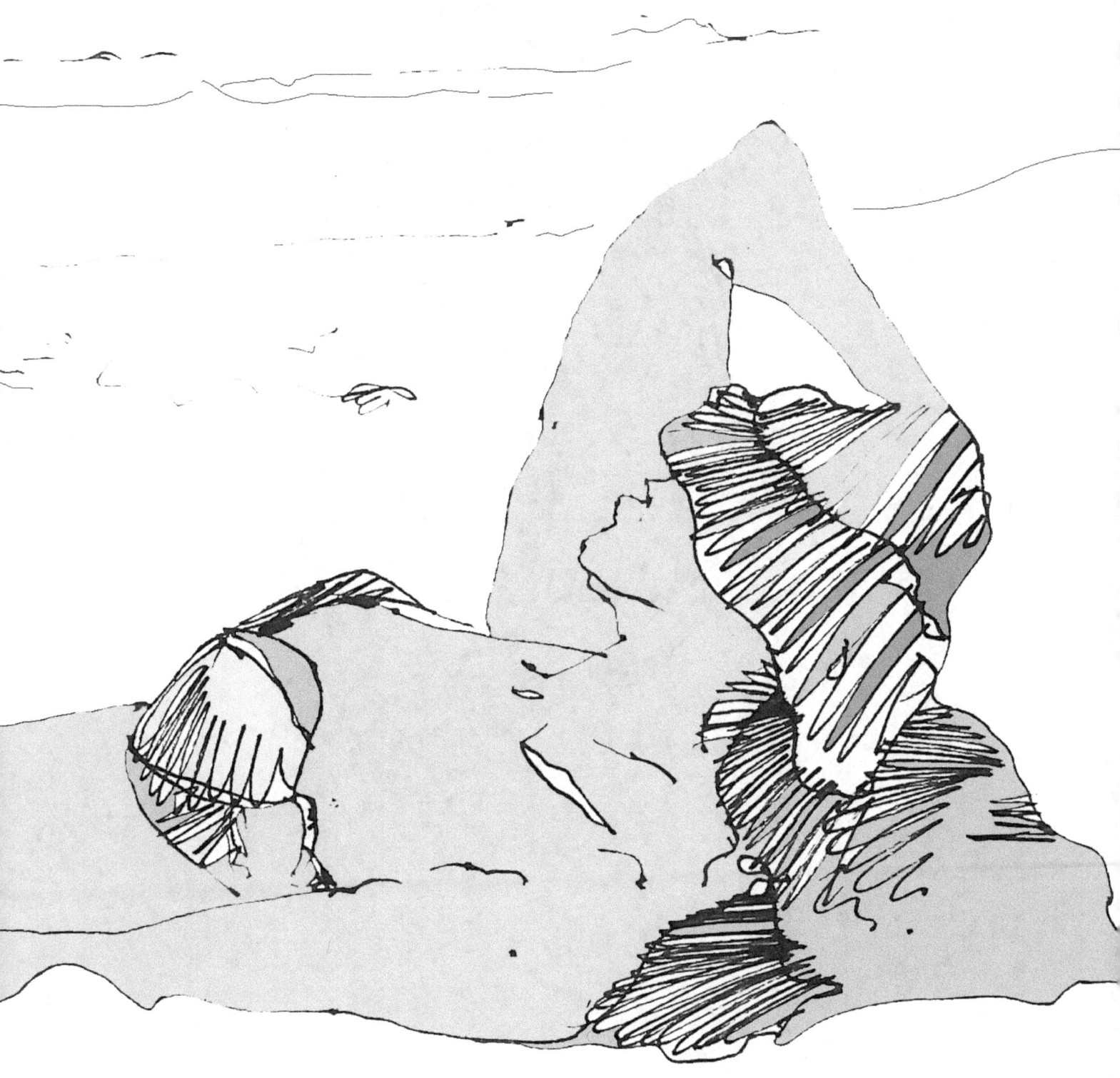

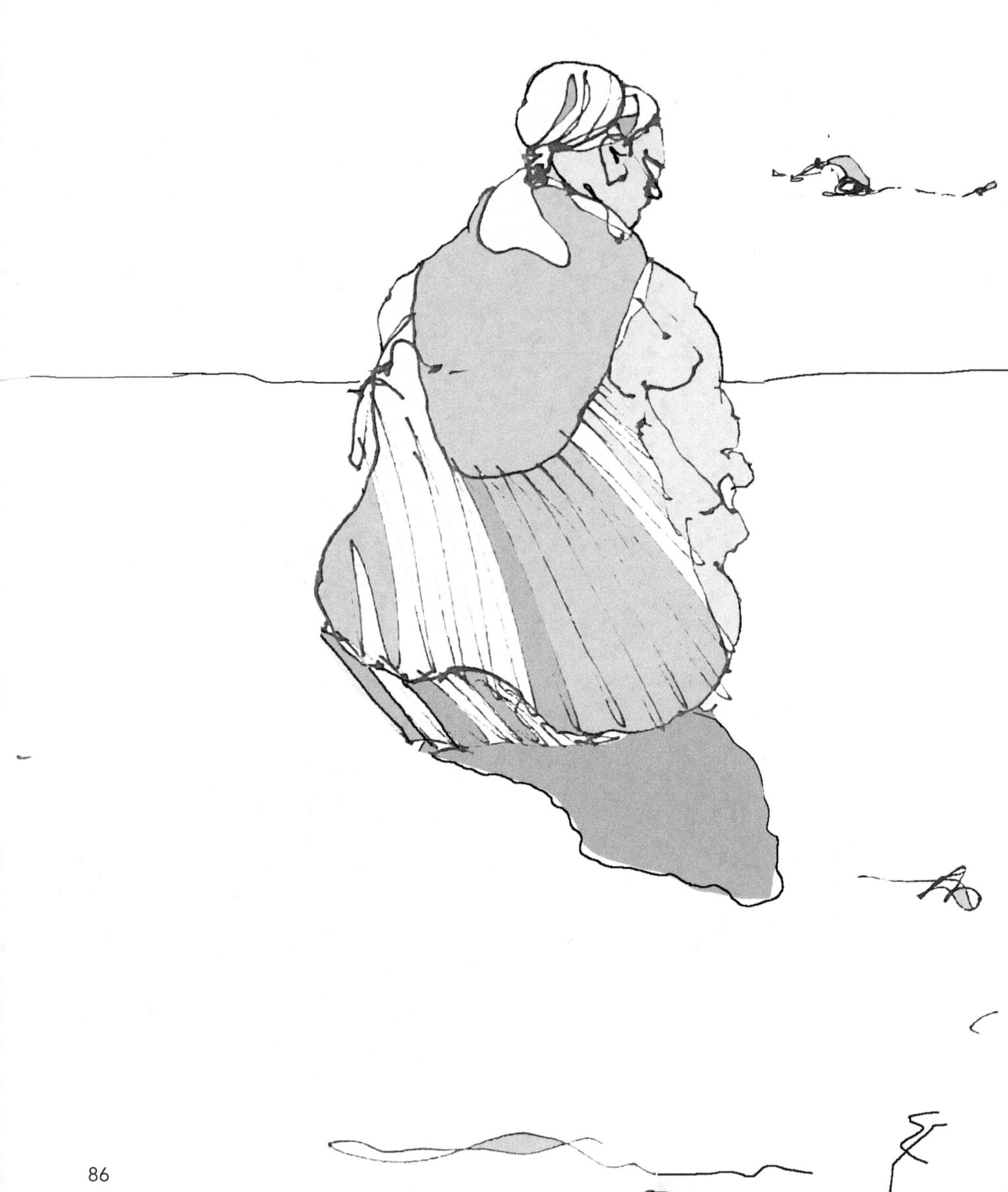

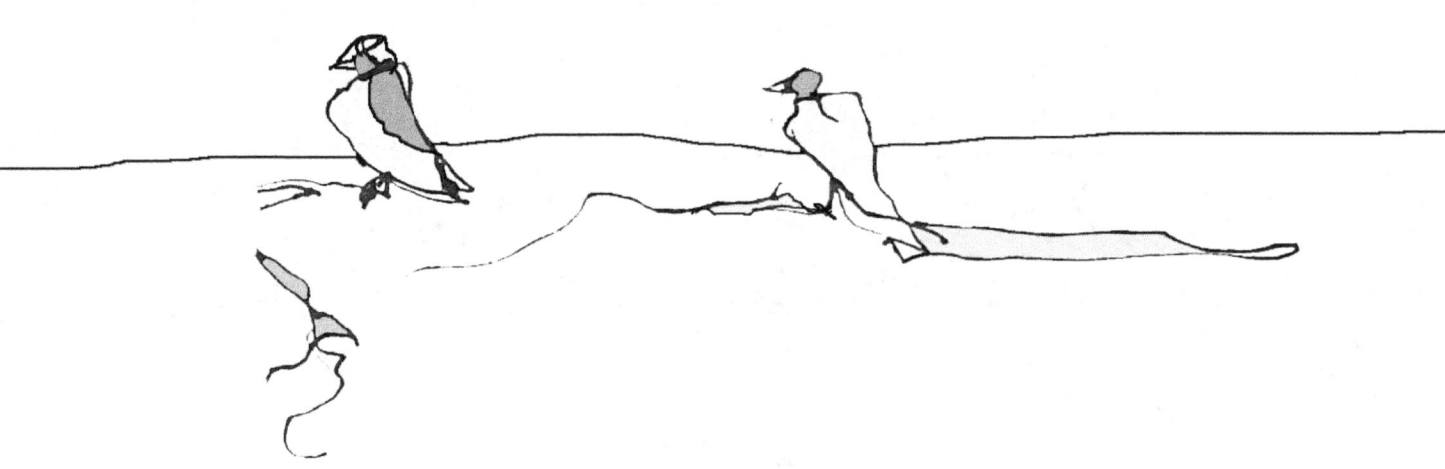

TIPPING POINT

Laddled broth
Saffron rice, shrimp in fiscus
Filled to brink.

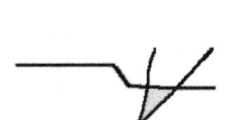
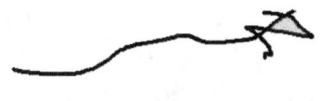

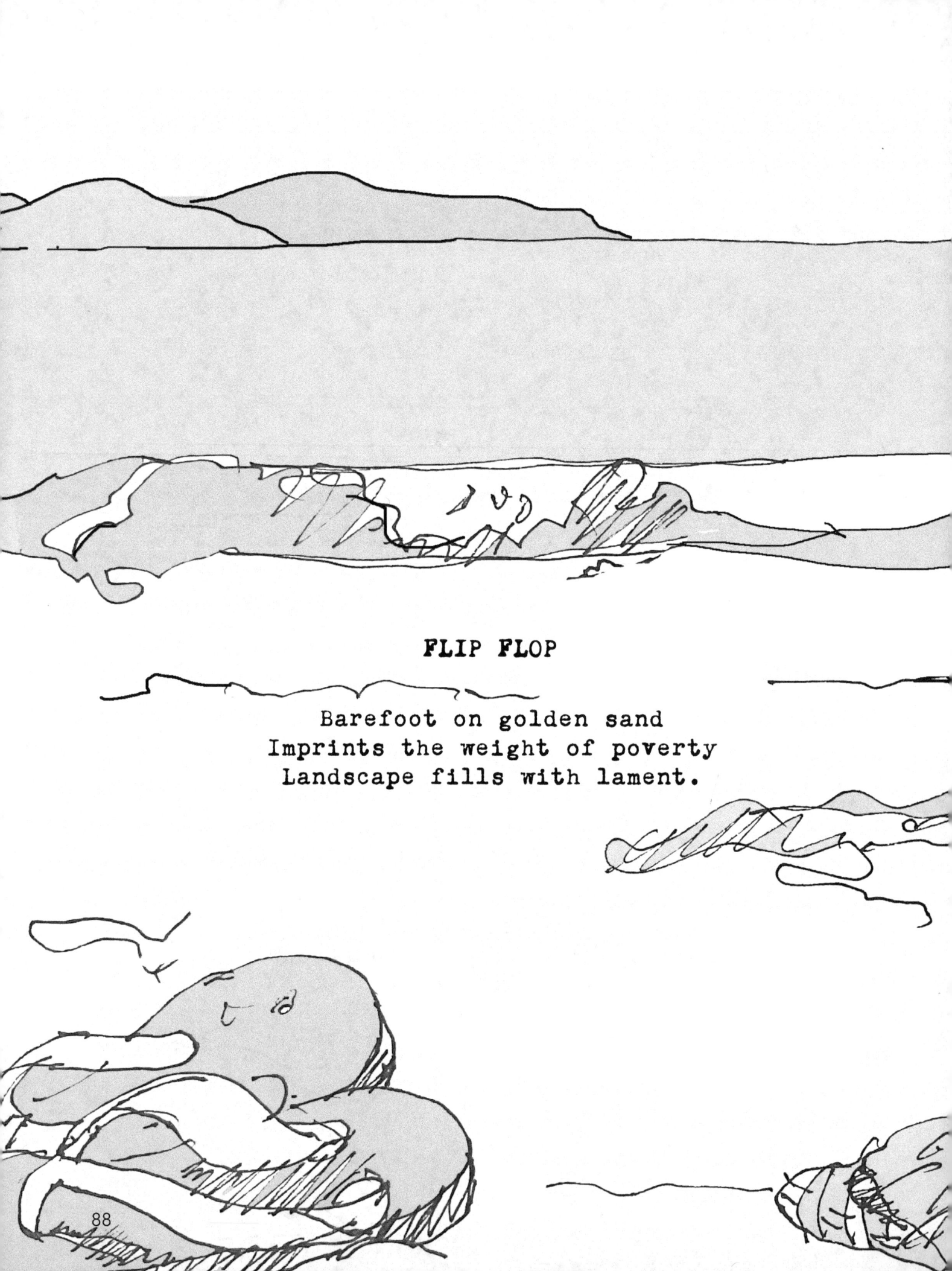

FLIP FLOP

Barefoot on golden sand
Imprints the weight of poverty
Landscape fills with lament.

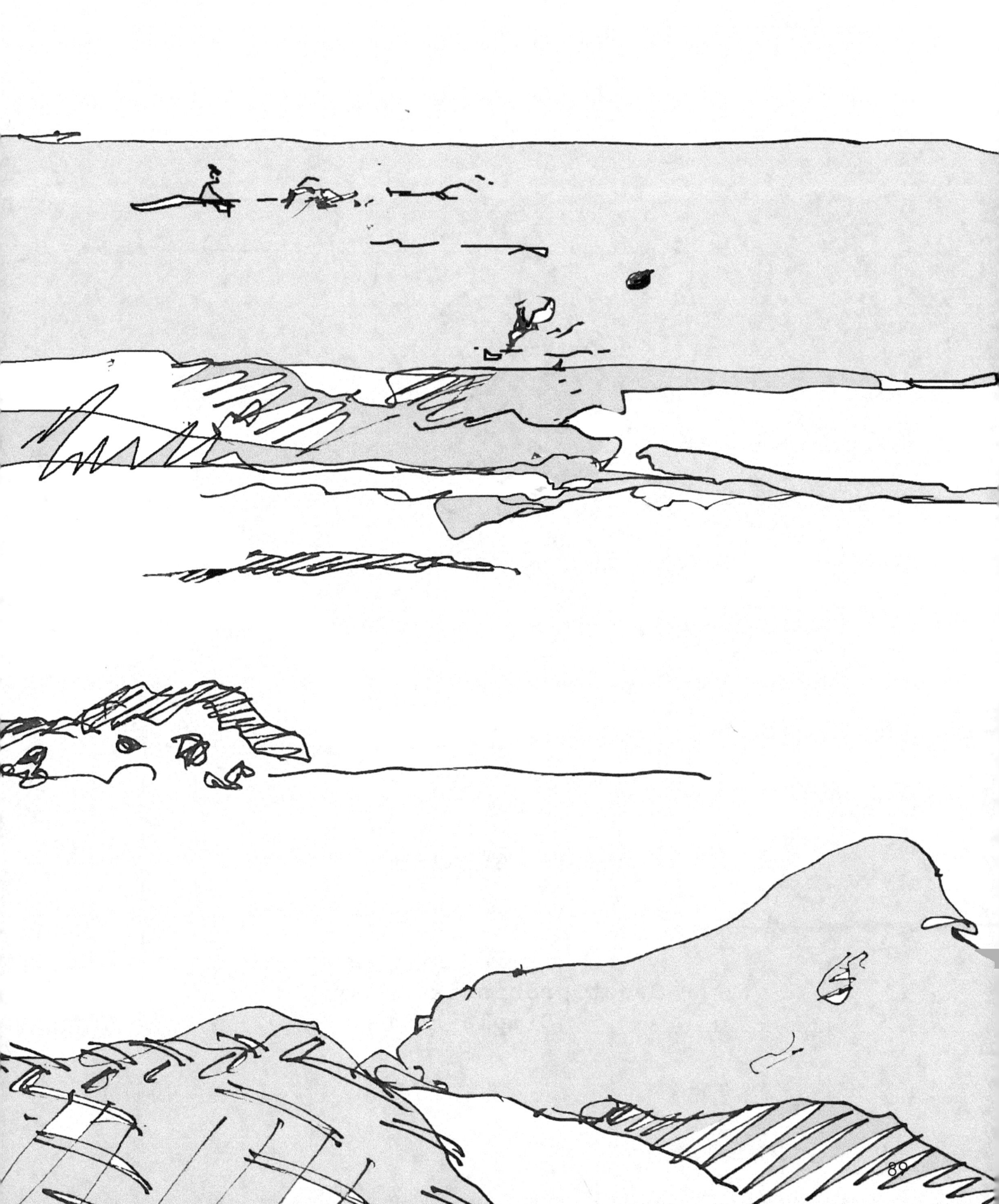

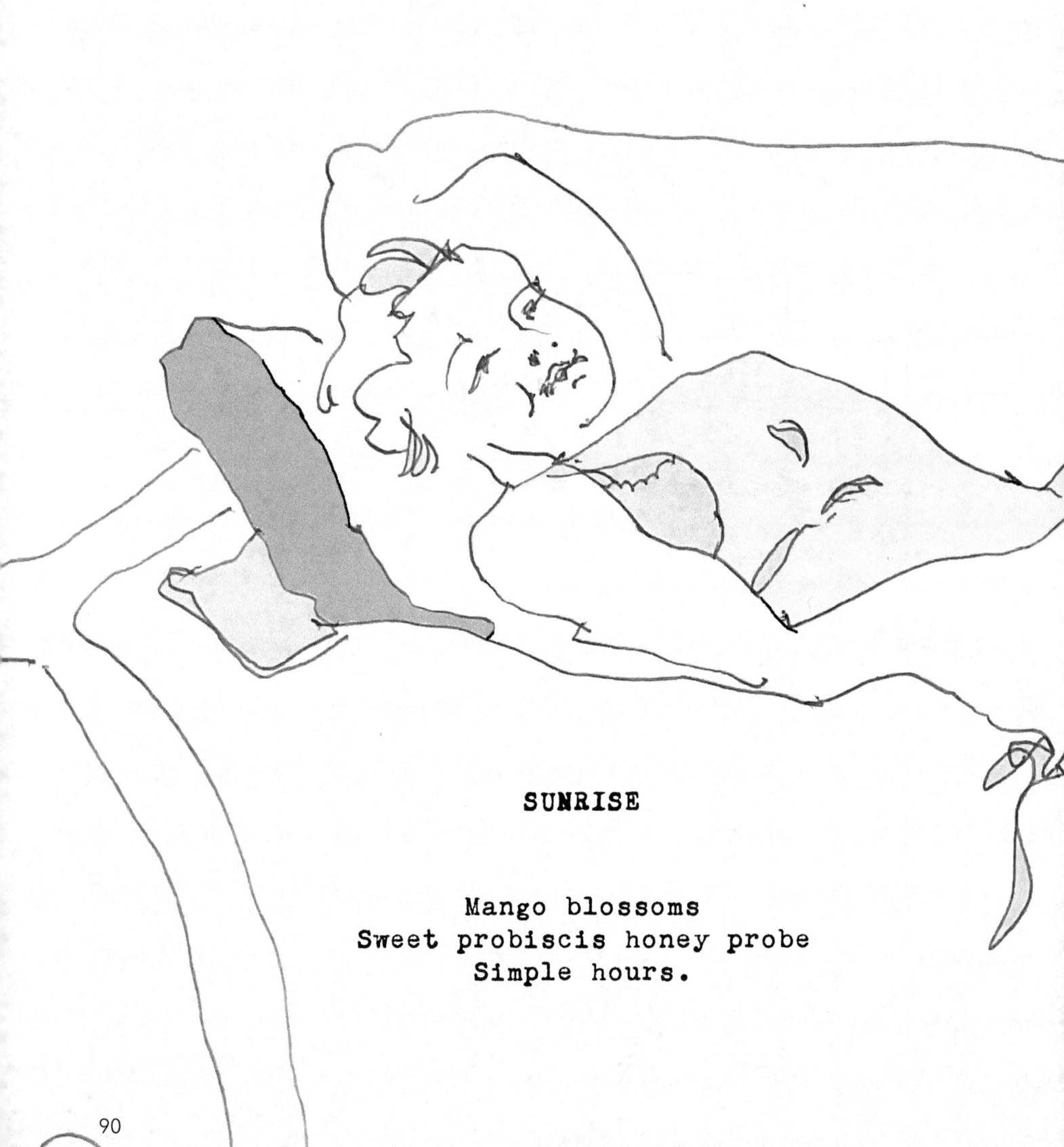

SUNRISE

Mango blossoms
Sweet probiscis honey probe
Simple hours.

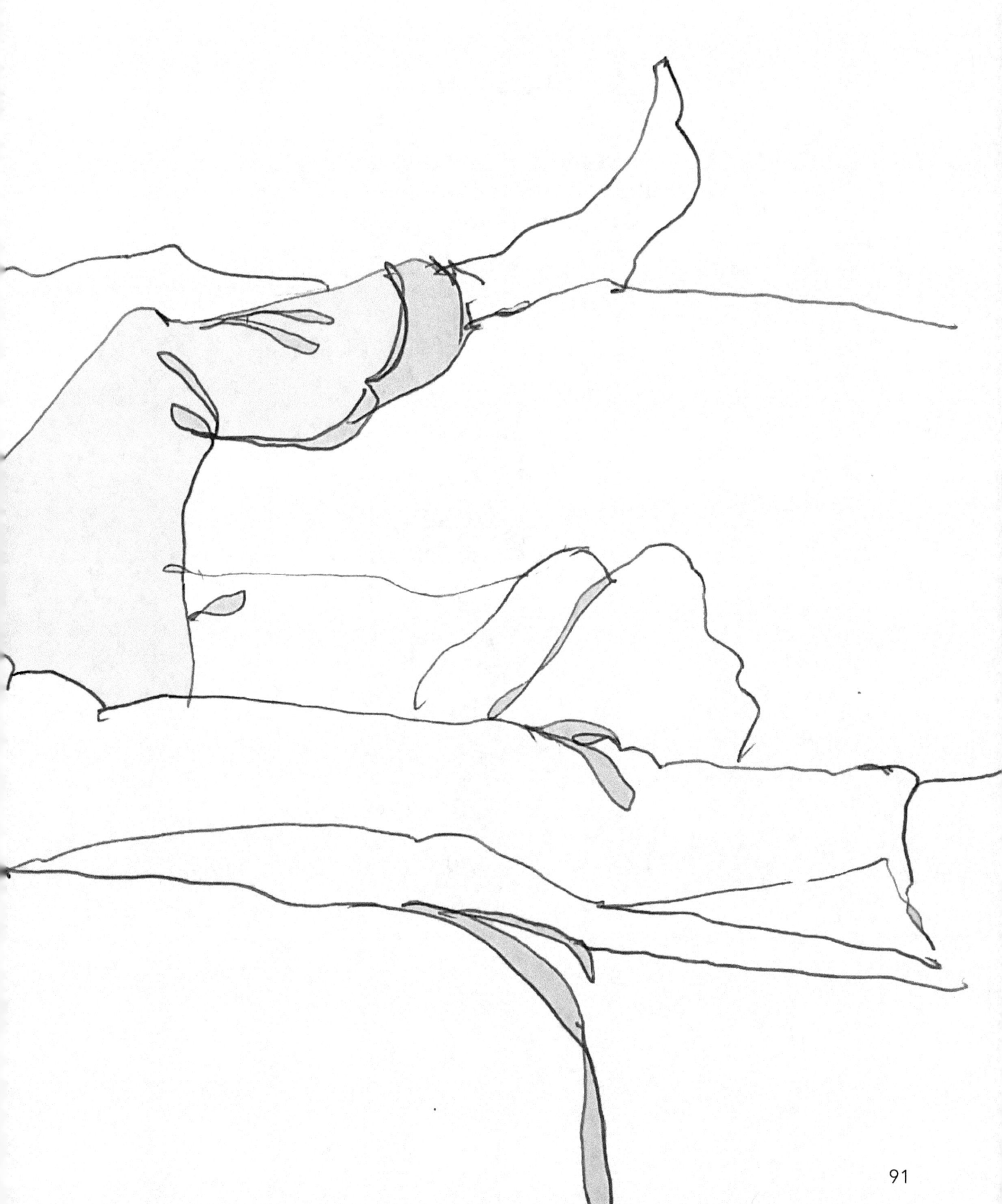

IRON BELL

Beneath the sands
Monks in monasteries chant
Prayer wheels turn.

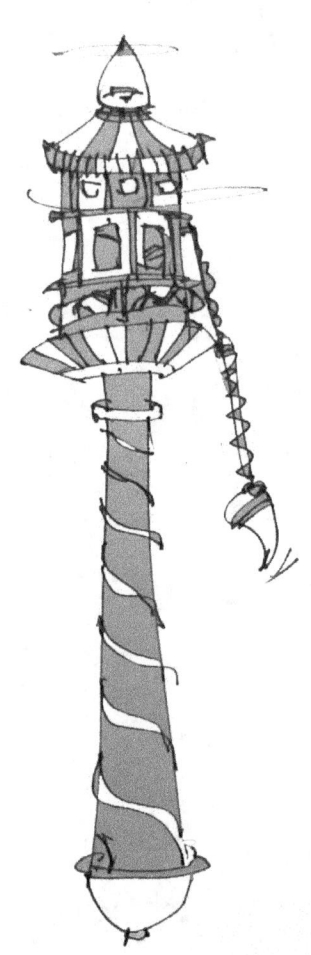

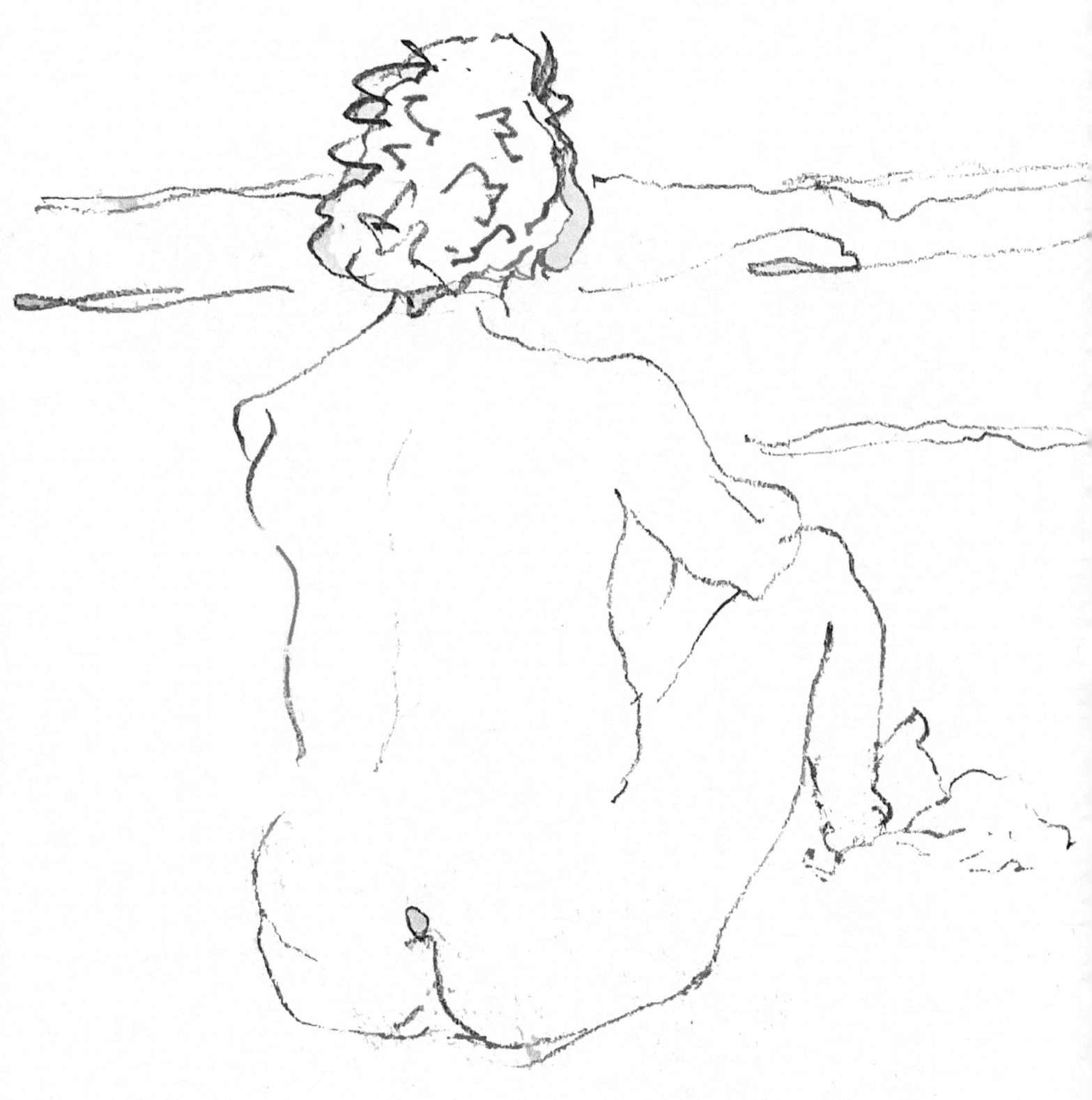

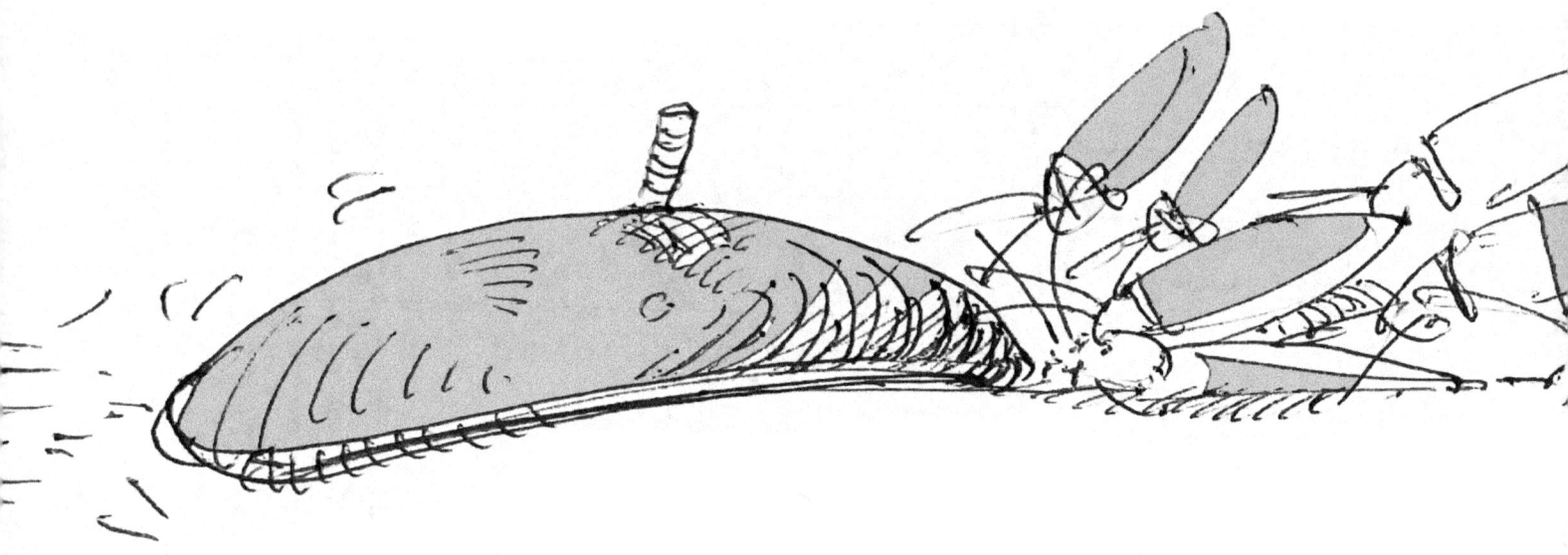

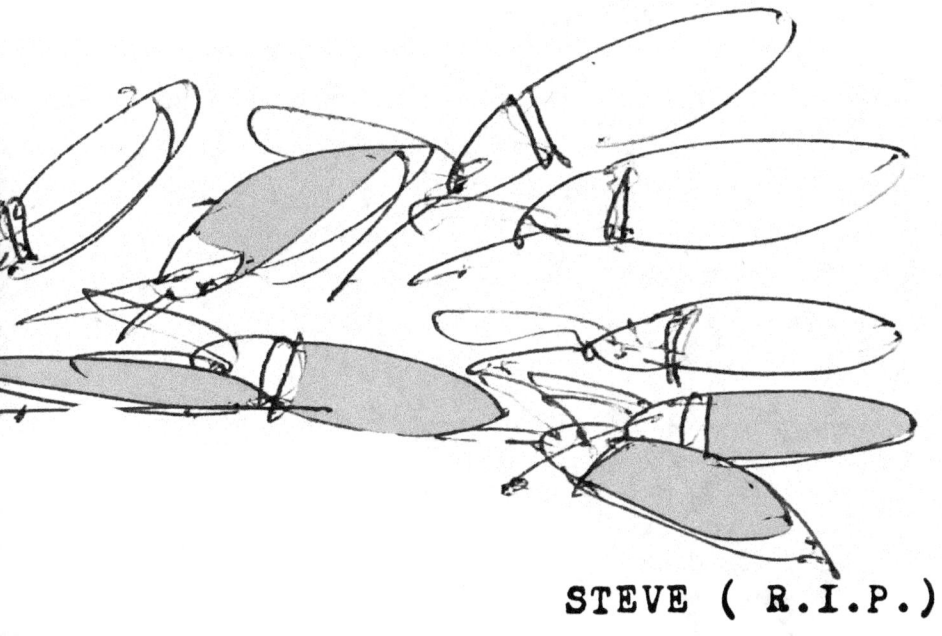

STEVE (R.I.P.)

"Had a beret once.
Cockroaches dragged it under the fridge.
And ate it."

PARK

Pigeons nod and coo
Look for hope in every grain of dirt
Flies search the concrete.

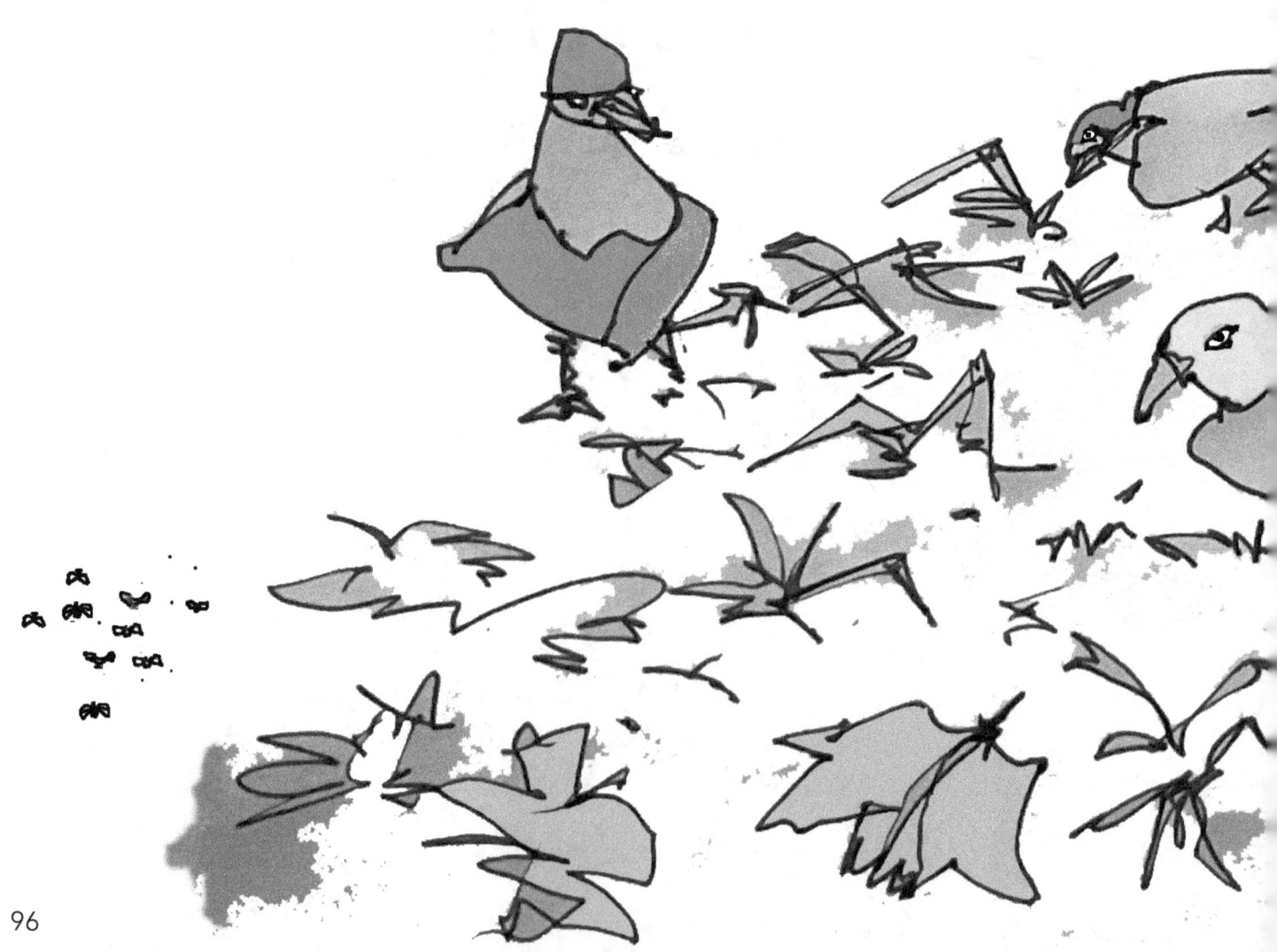

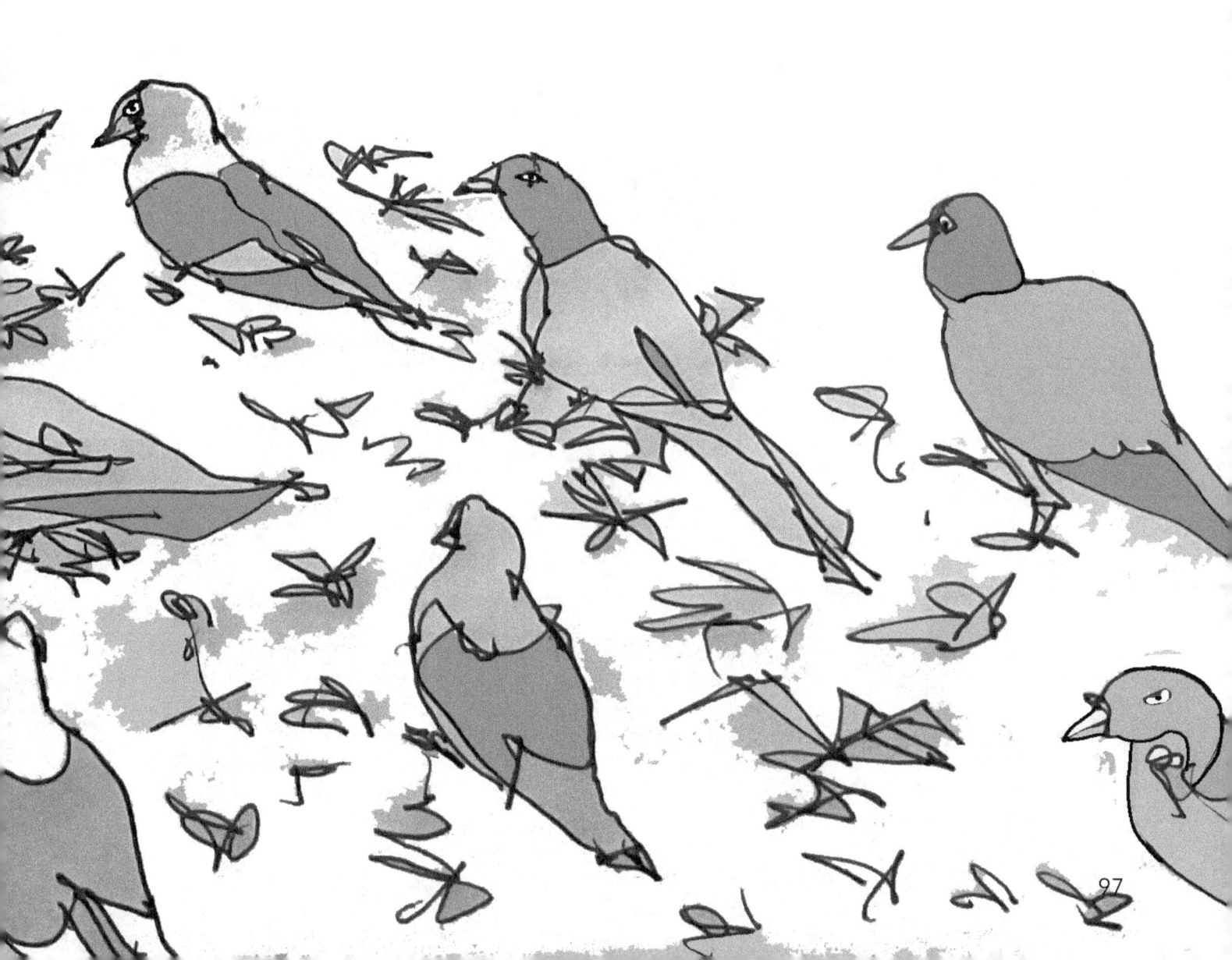

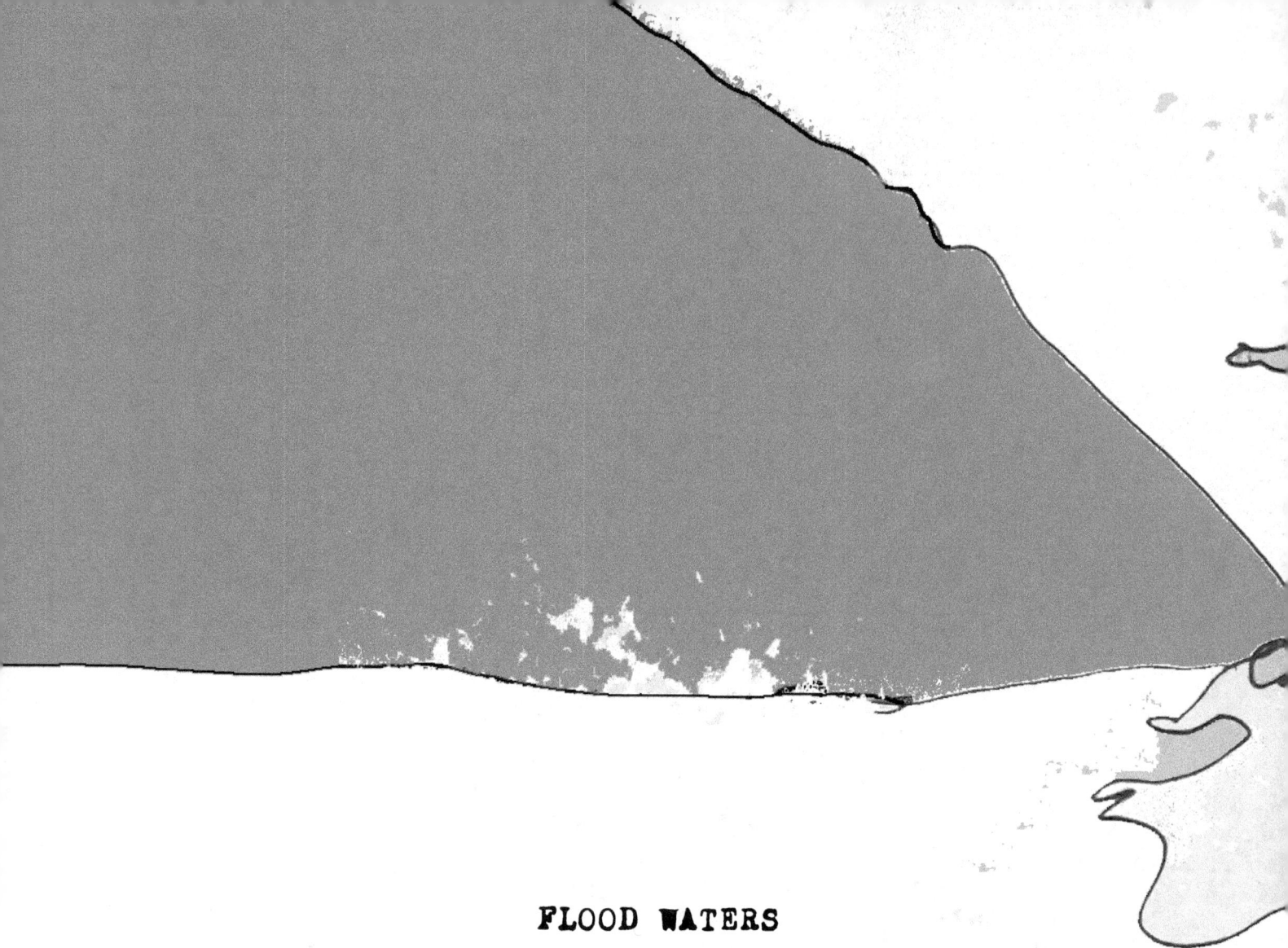

FLOOD WATERS

Seed pods split
Boy knee-deep in mangrove
Mud eels slick.

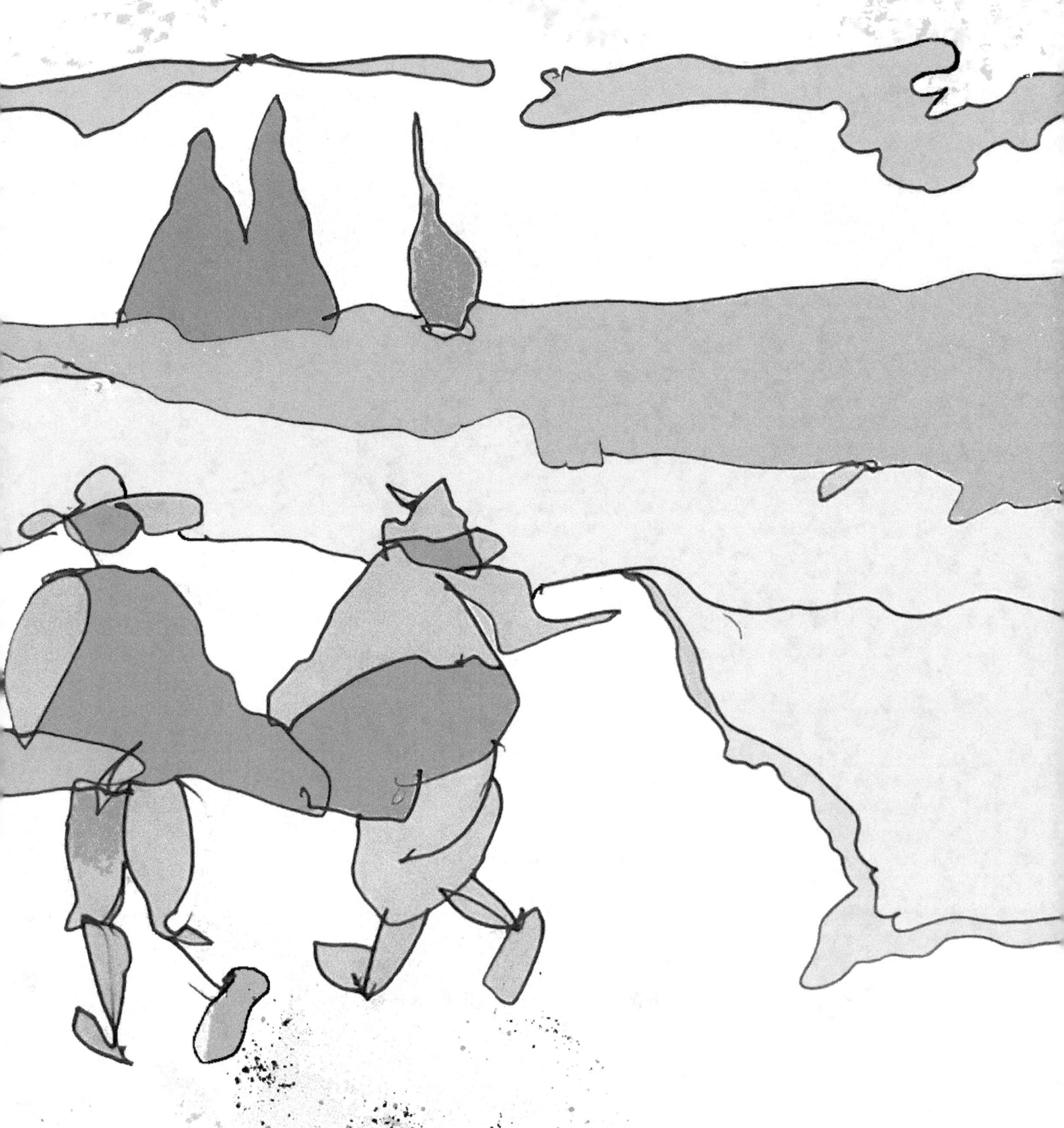

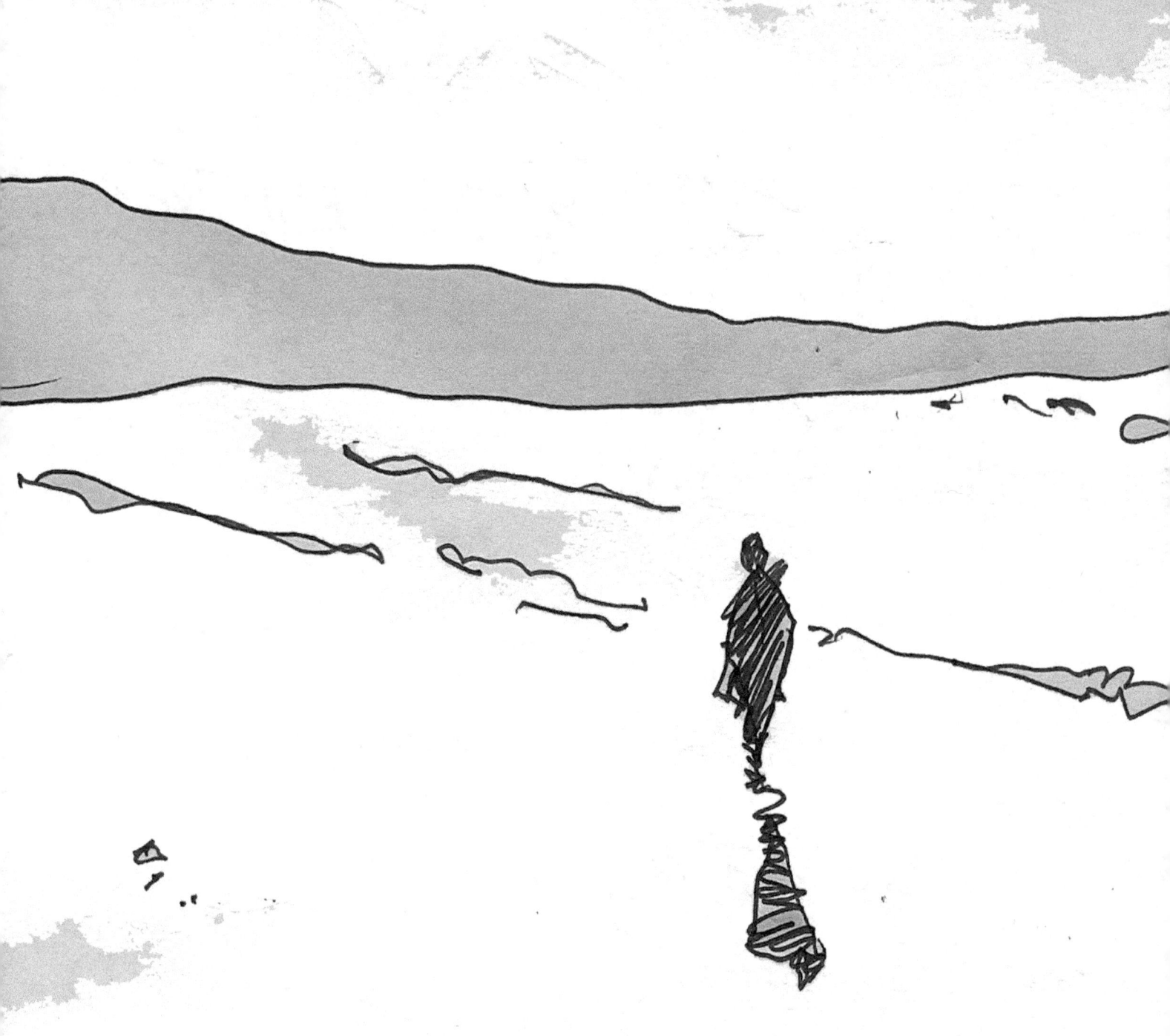

STREET CORNER

A woman beckons
Bread rolls born of brown sack
My mind unravels.

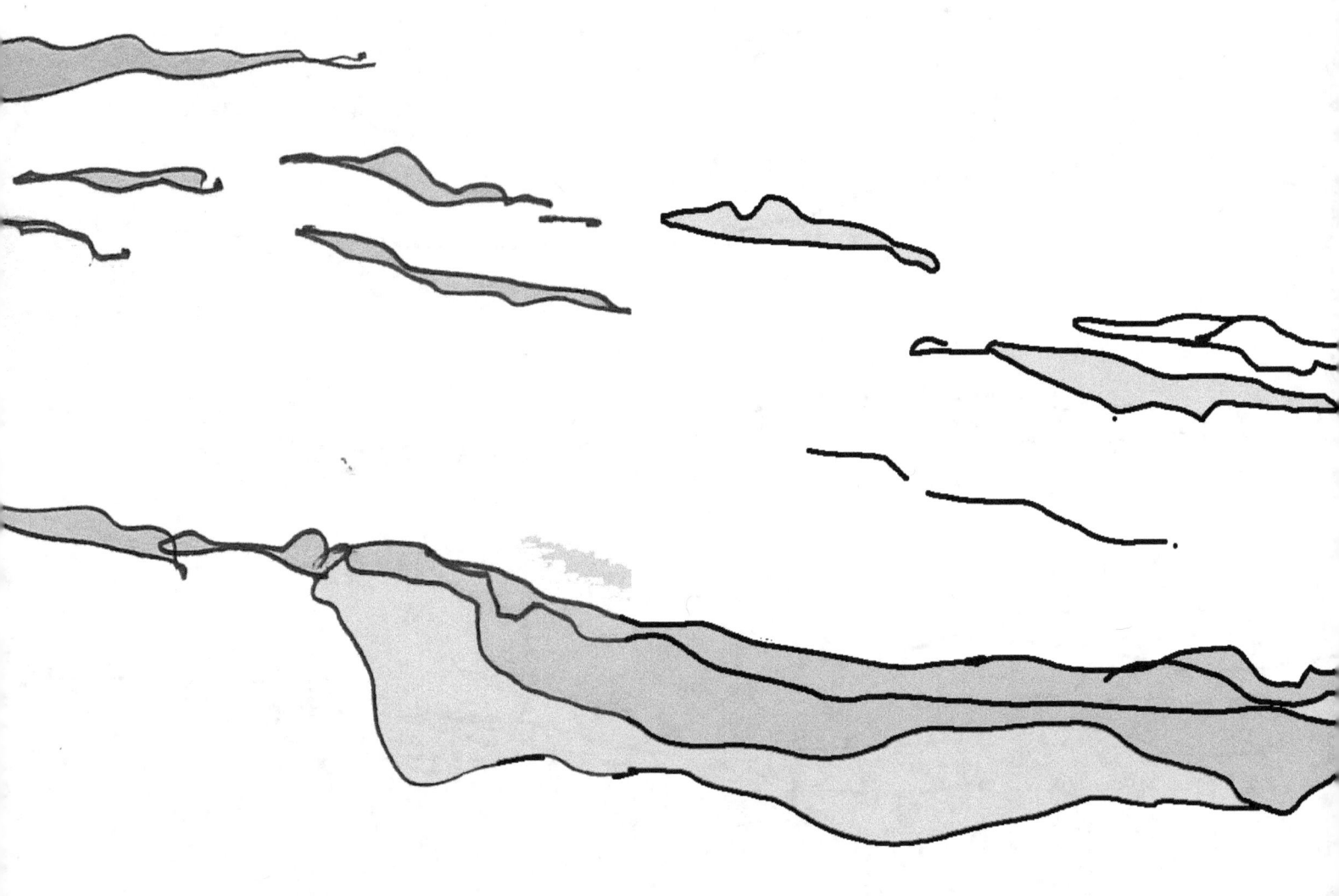

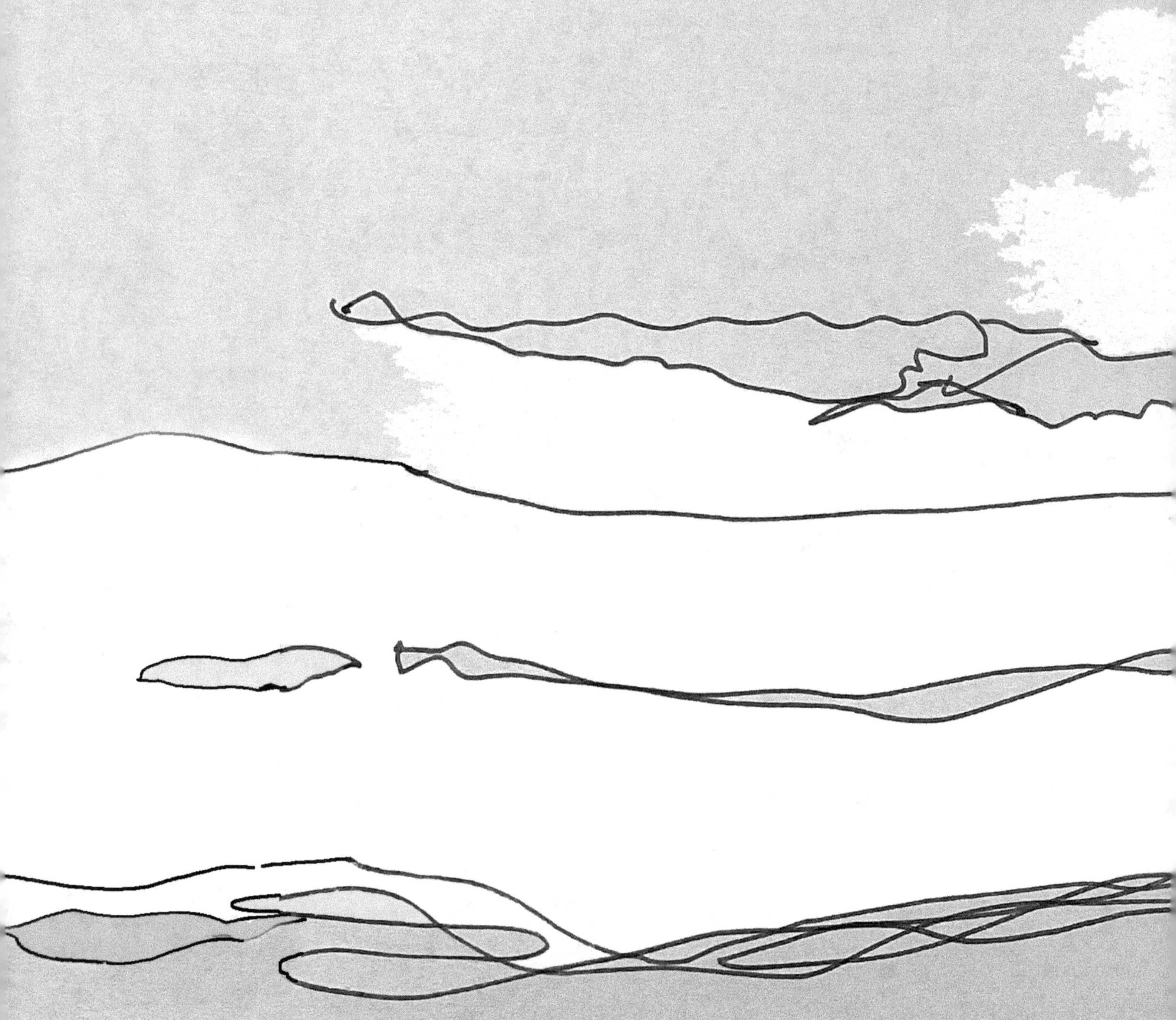

CONCRETE

Exhausted
Trapped in miasmic breath of urban heat
Birds fall silent.

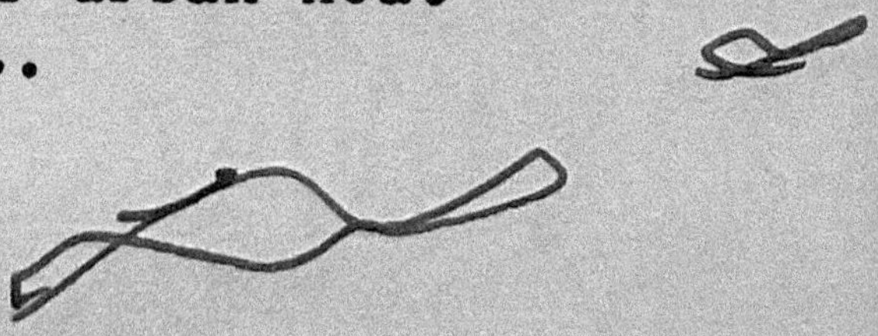

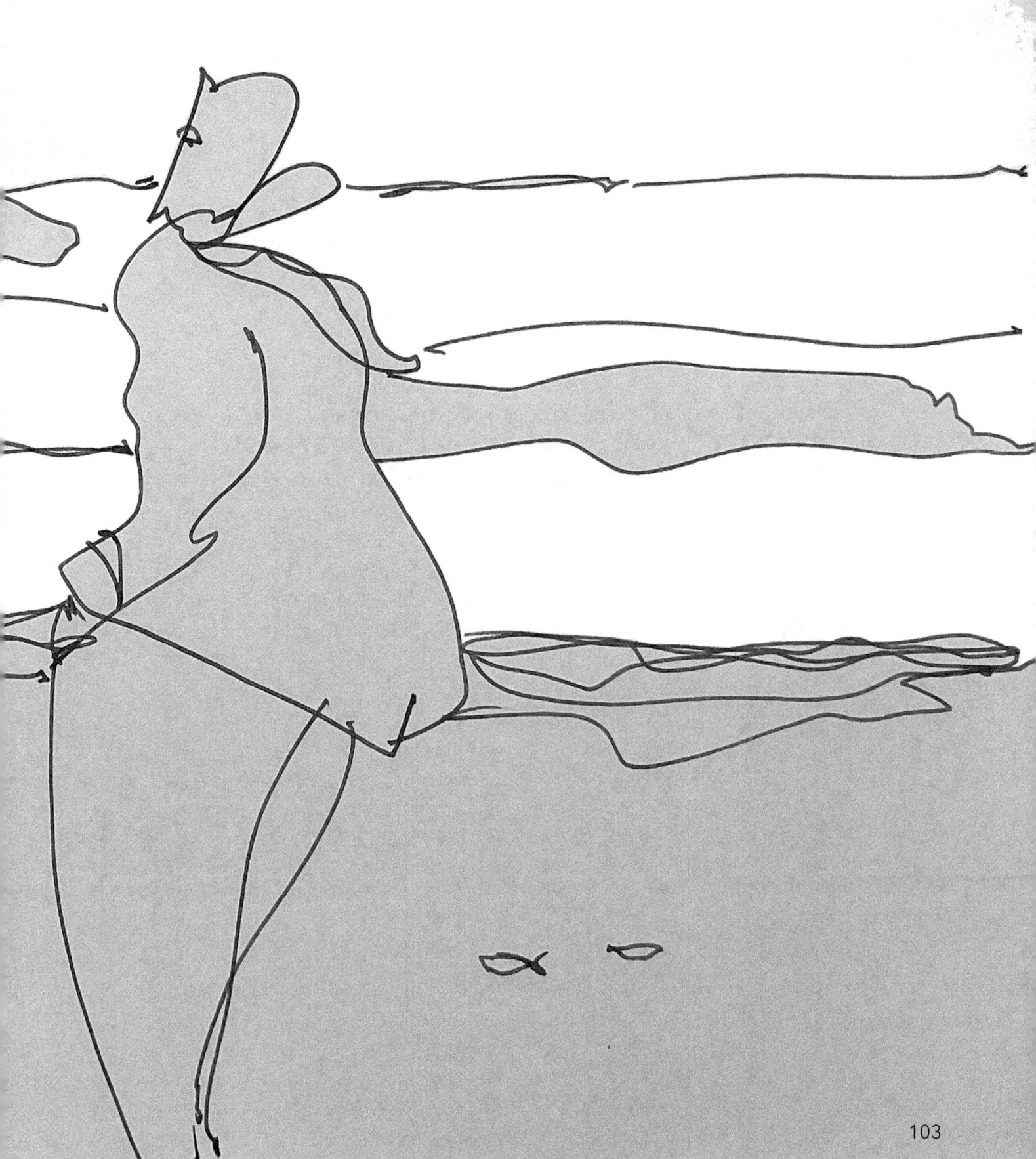

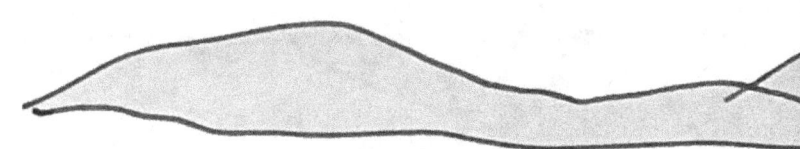

CRYING PATH

Barefoot on the track
Walk with purpose on shifted sand
Voyage of a fool.

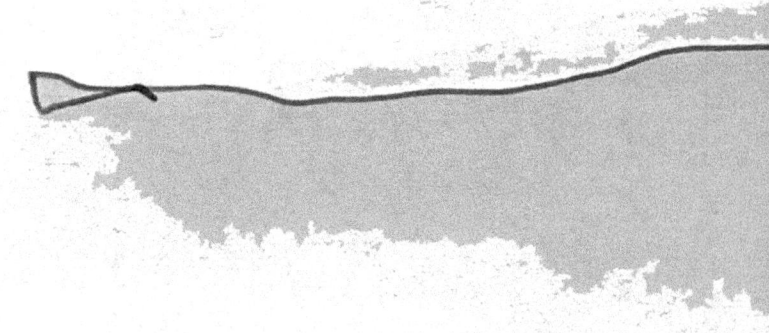

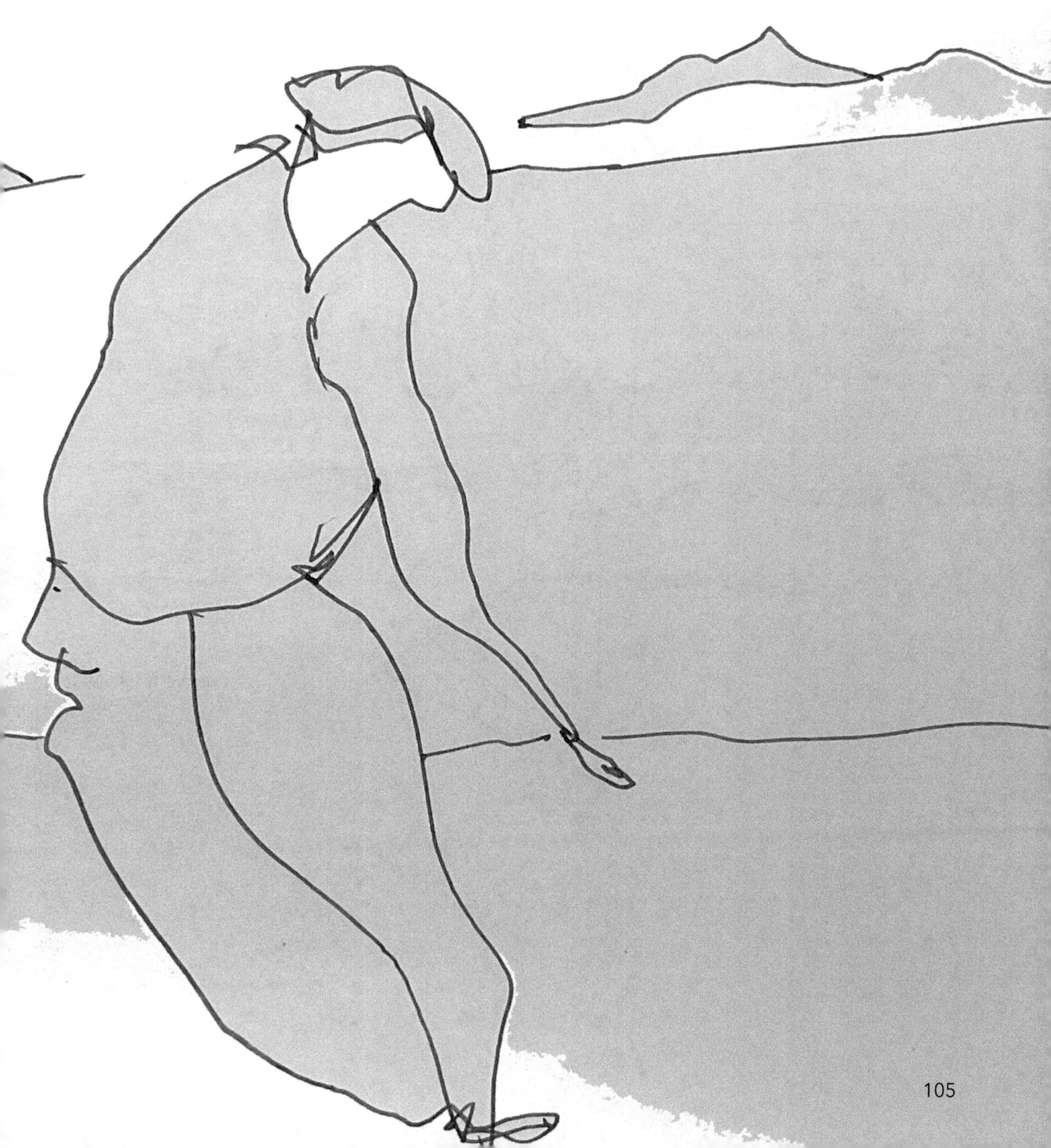

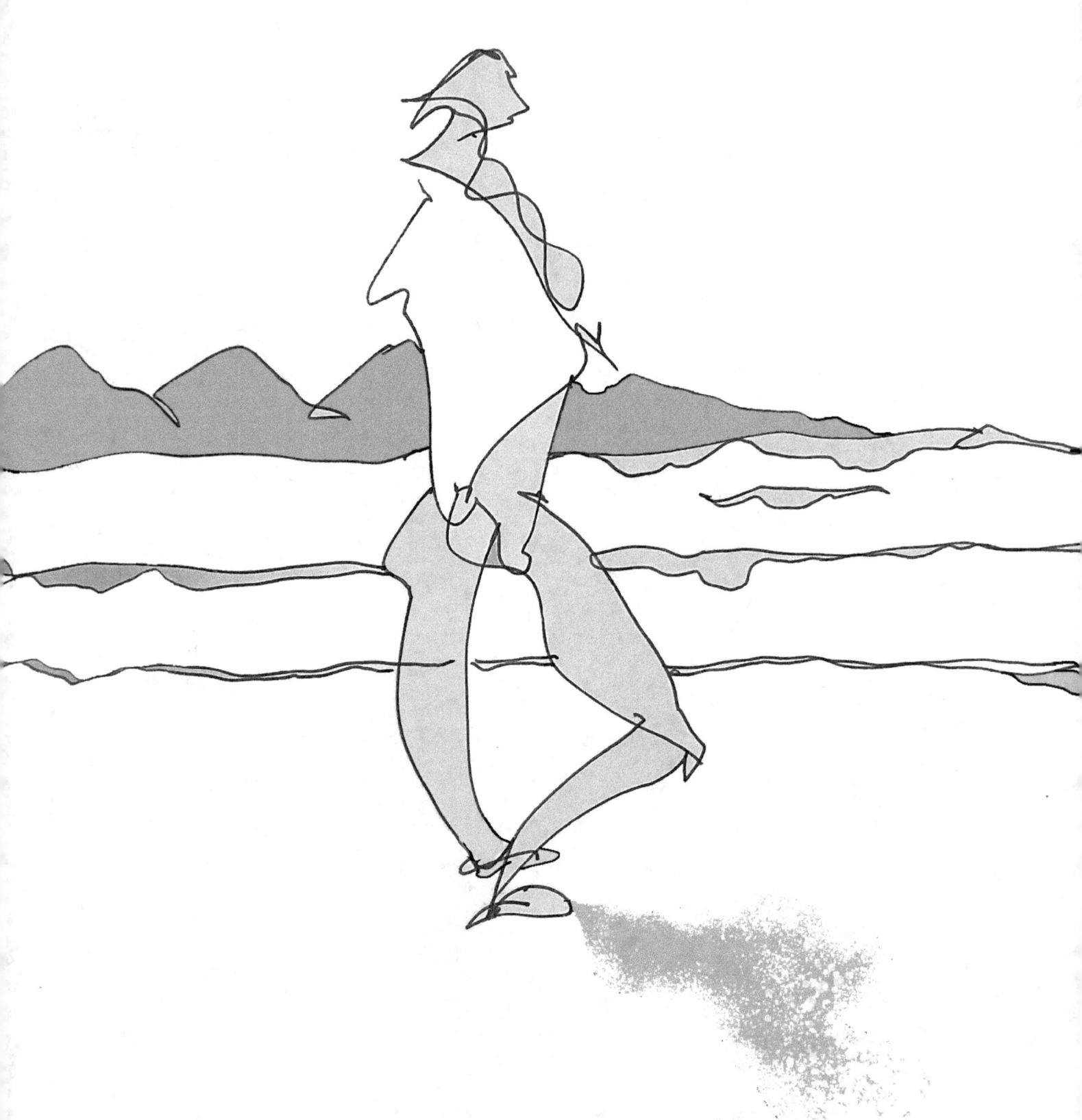

CHANGE OF LIGHT

Rooster crows
Slant of light over rising sea
Siliceous sand.

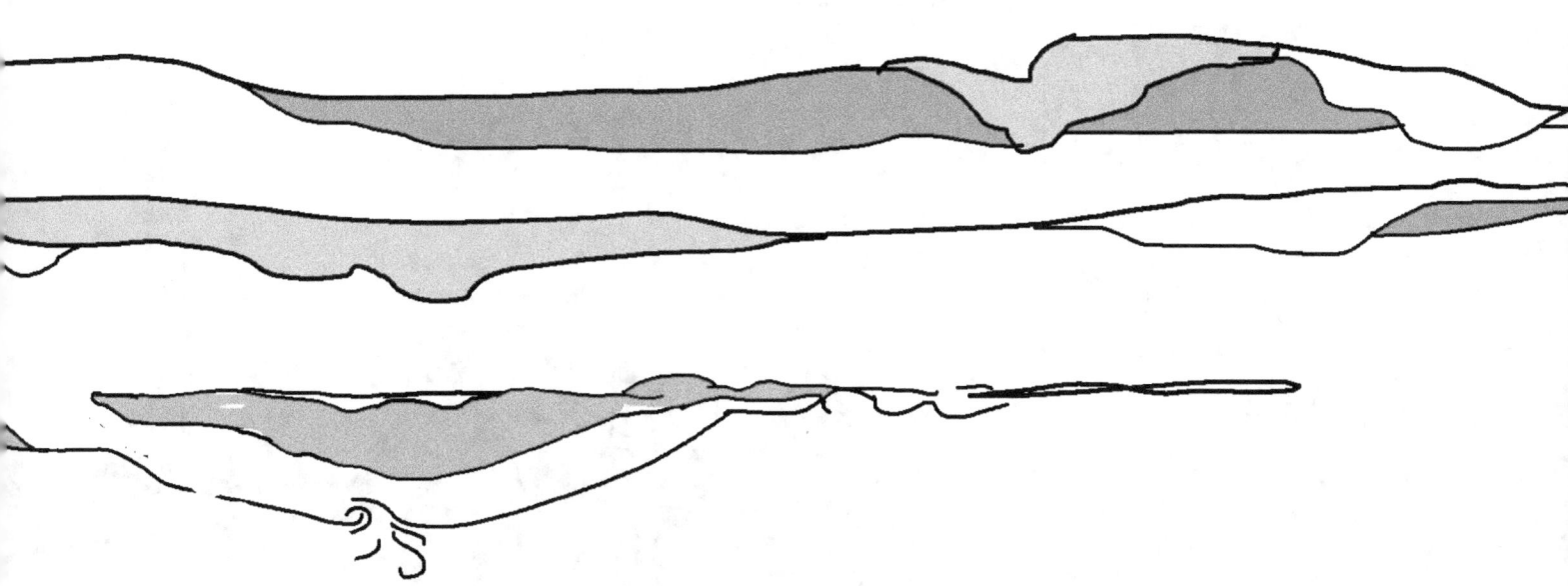

AMNESTY

Woman bent by war
Kitten clings to a quivering twig
Broken fingers curl.

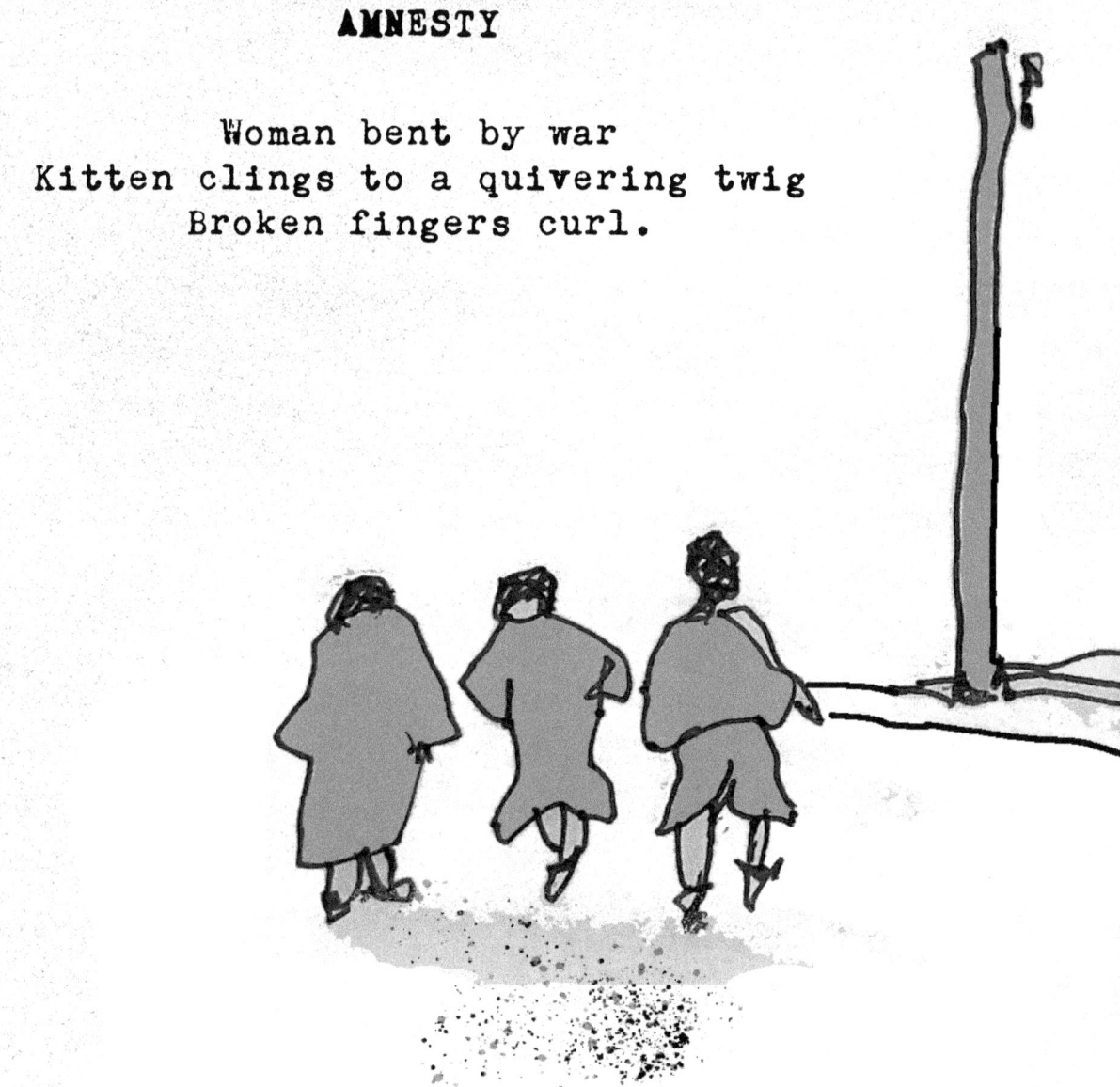

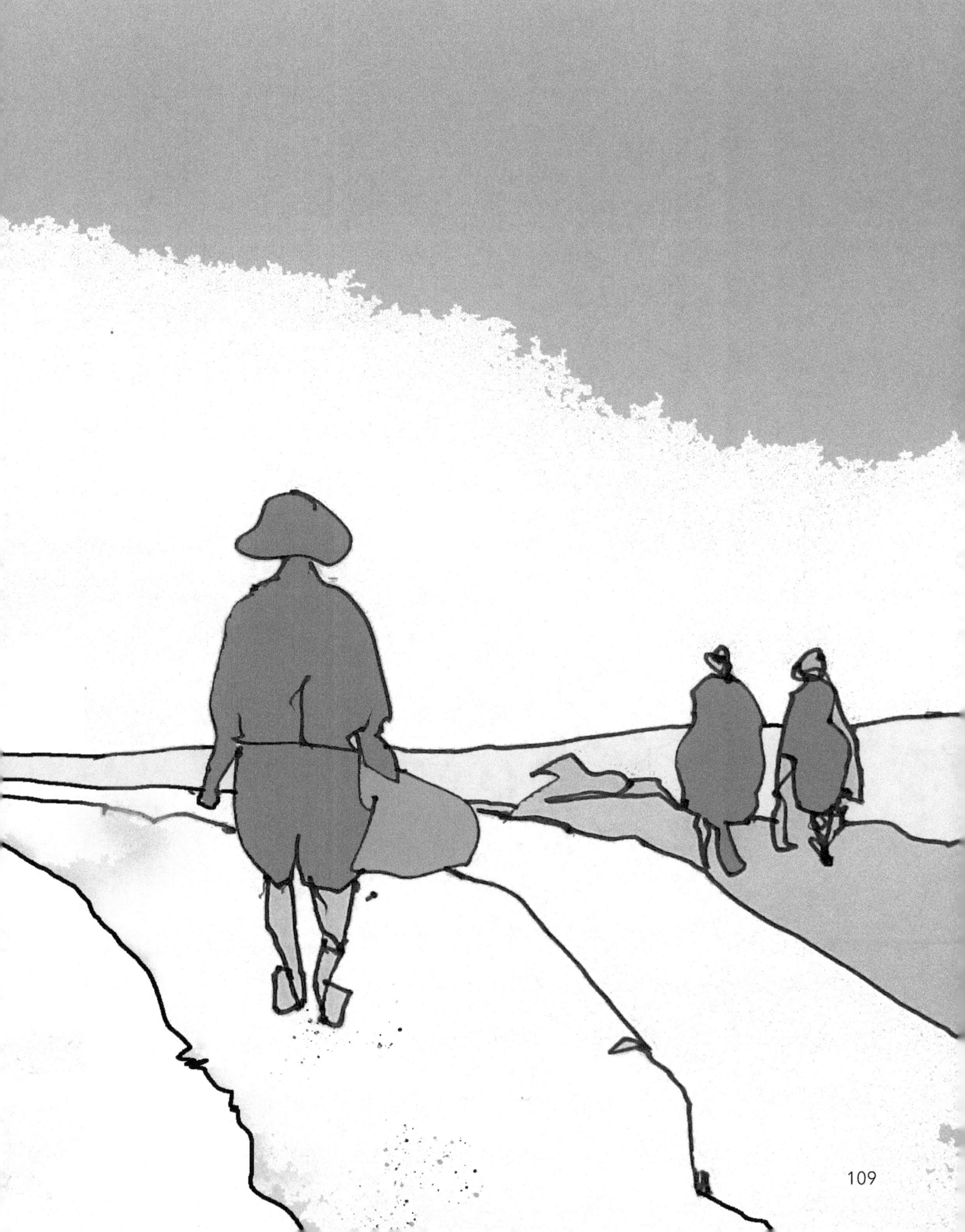

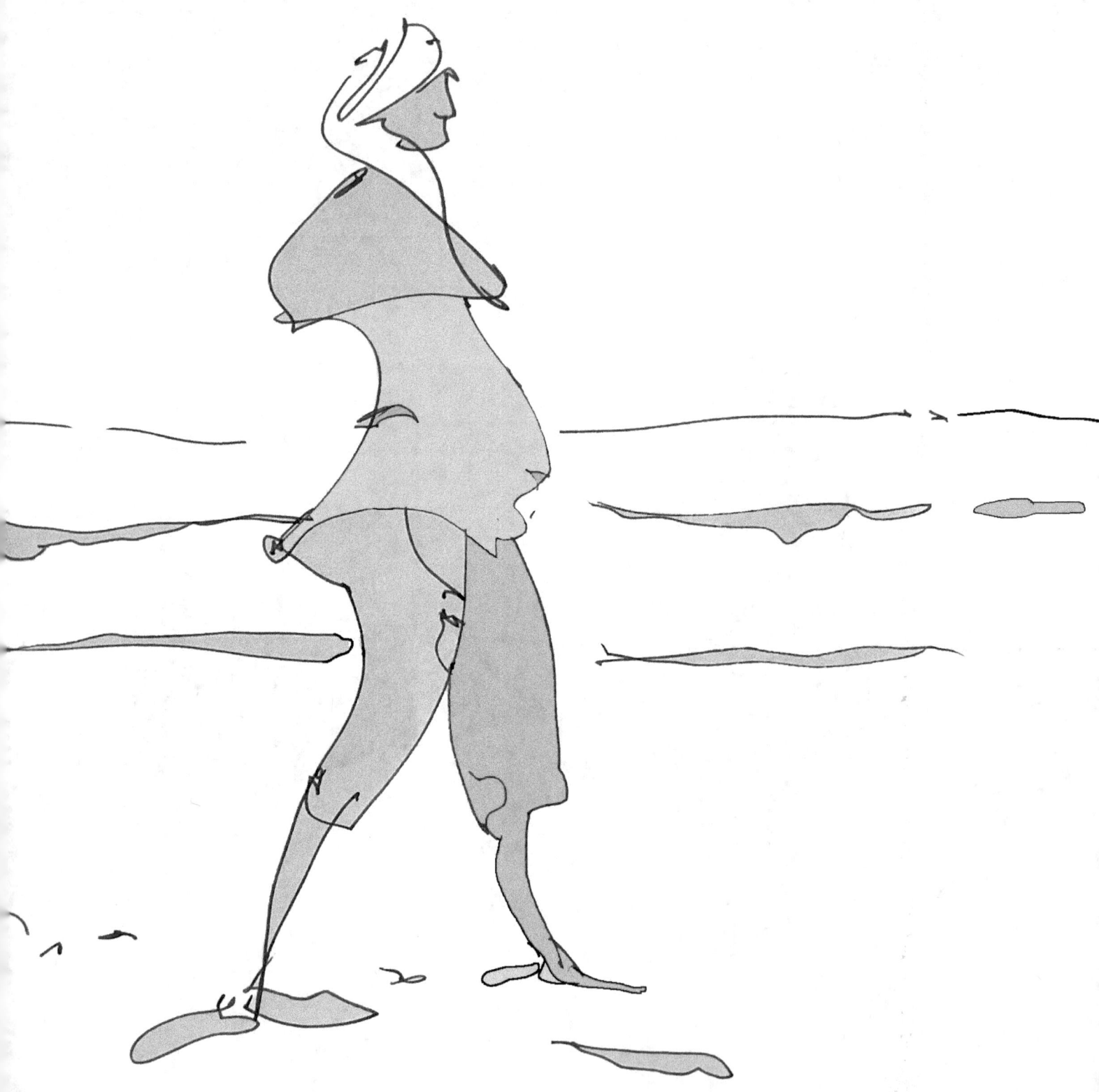

GROUND ZERO

Blocks of peat
Held deep in a fire's rage
Left to ember.

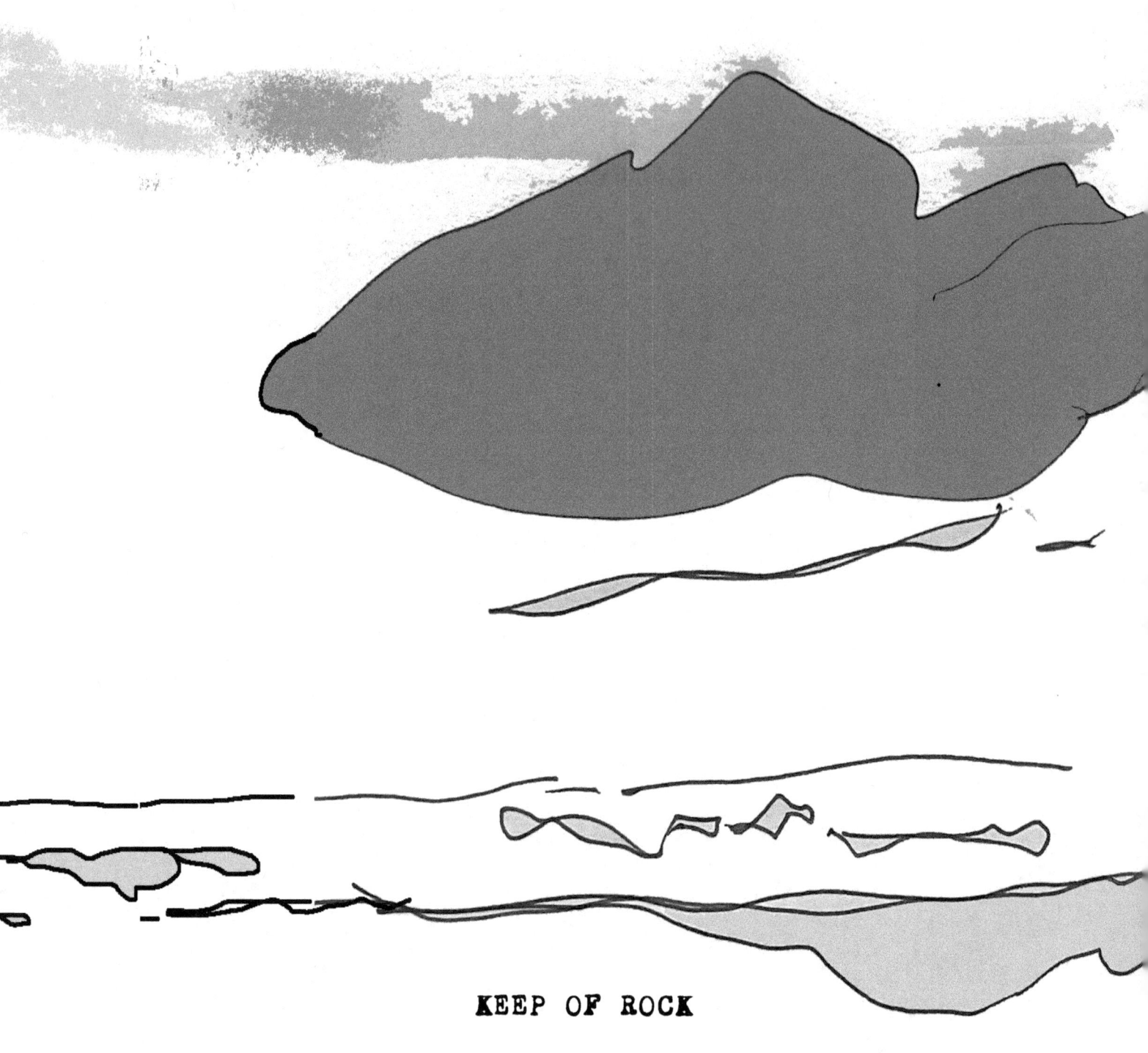

KEEP OF ROCK

Yellow roses red flecked
Man of age bends to tend the grave
As grass grows.

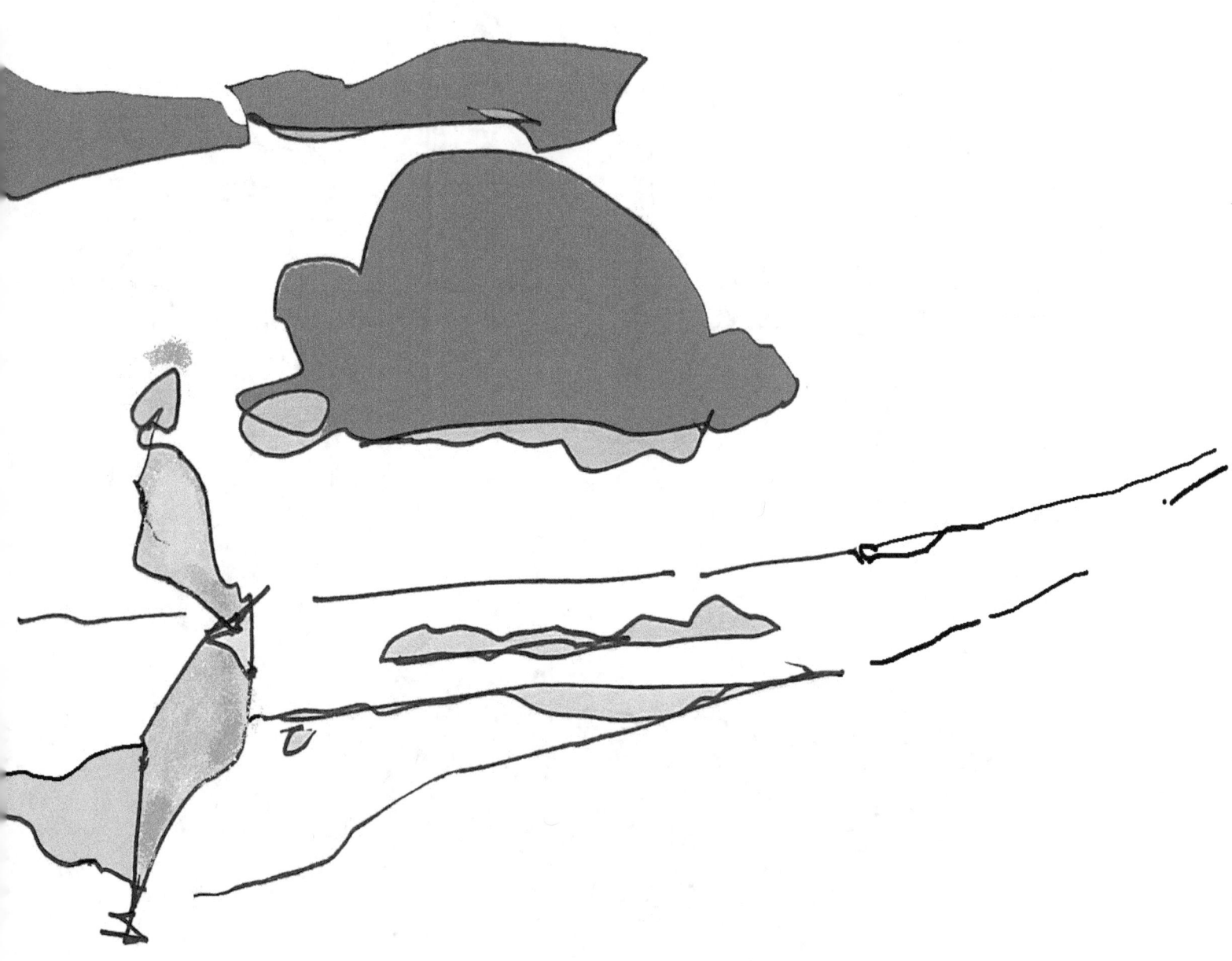

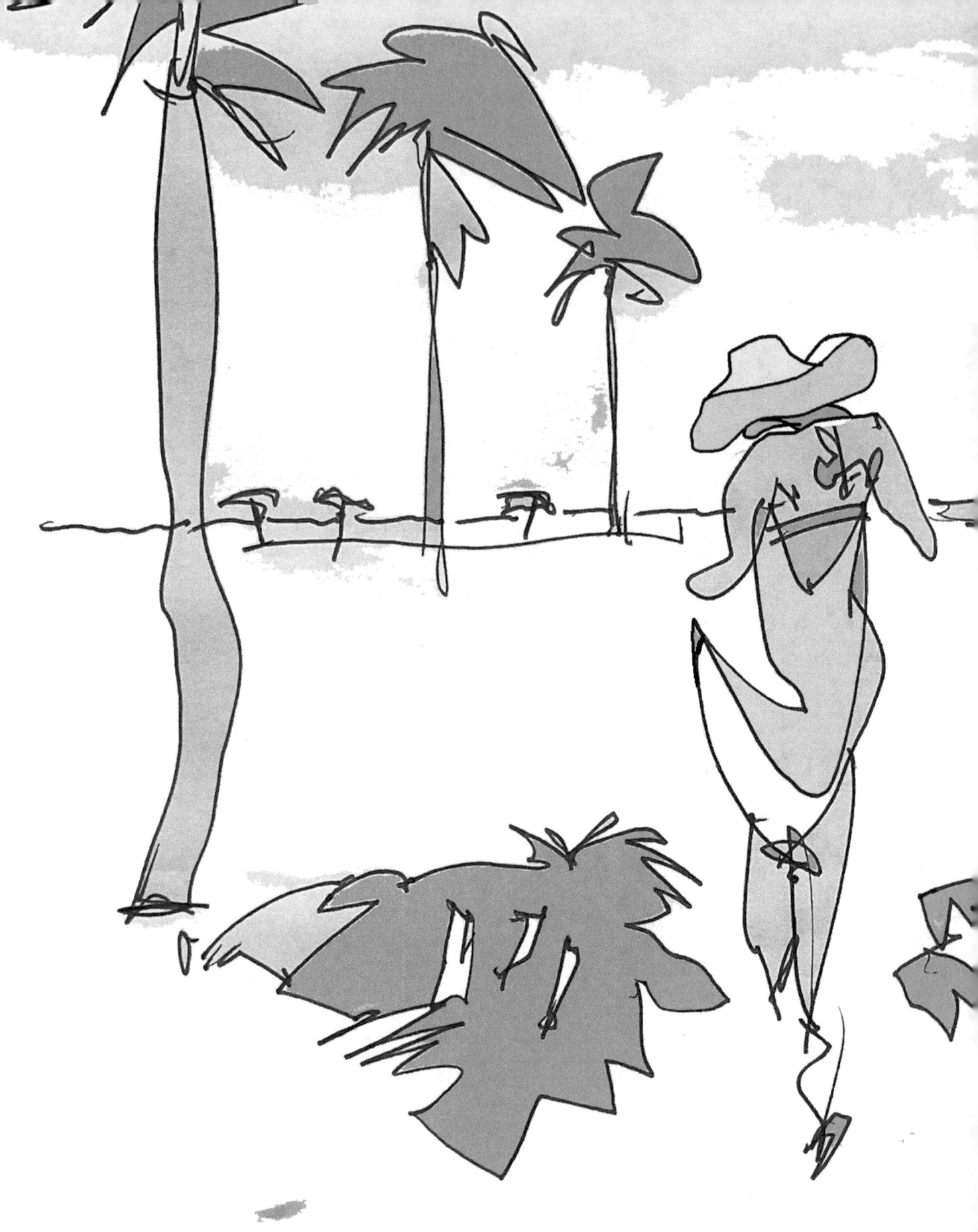

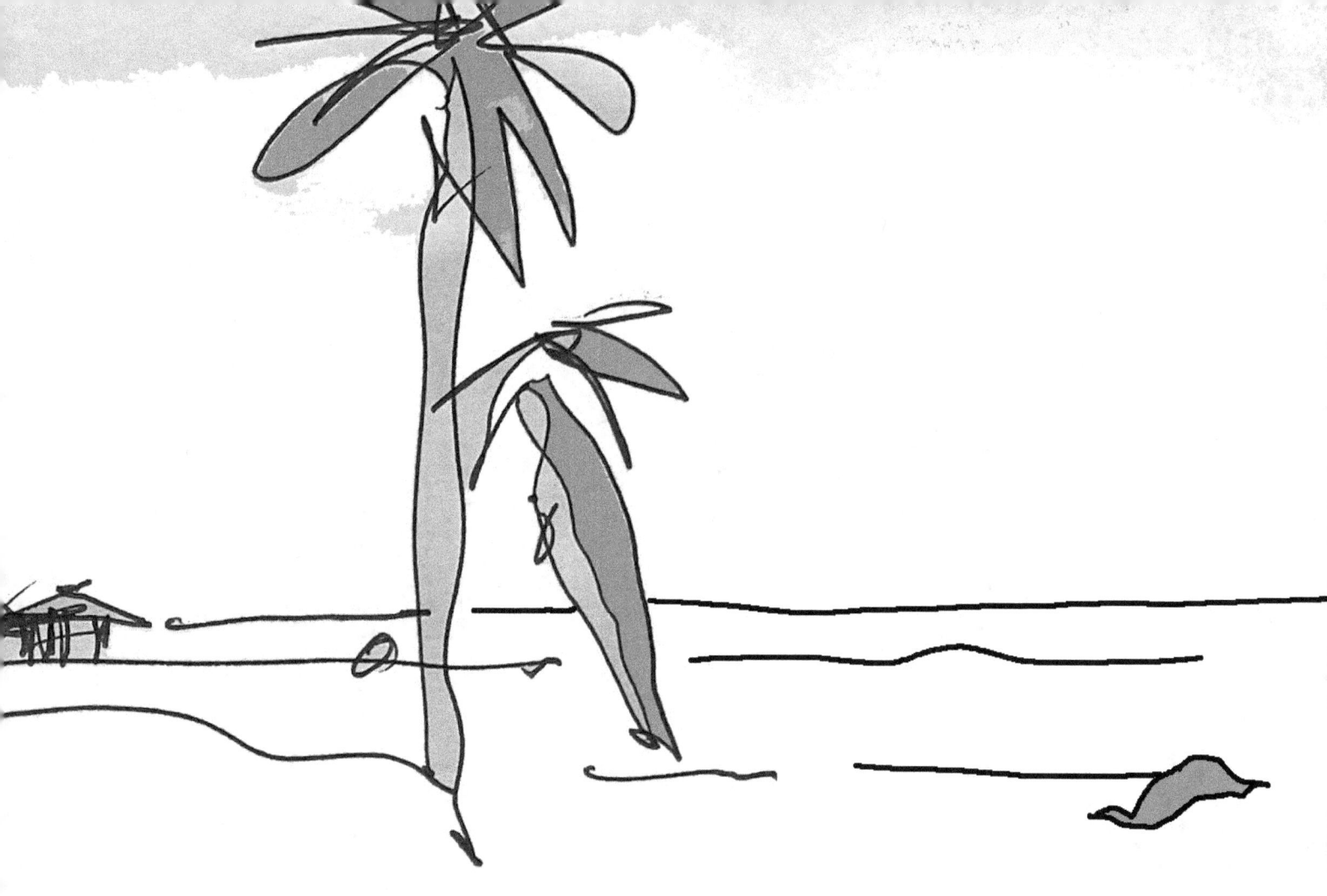

NIGHT WORK

Broom of split bamboo
Sweeps through sleep of night
By calloused hands.

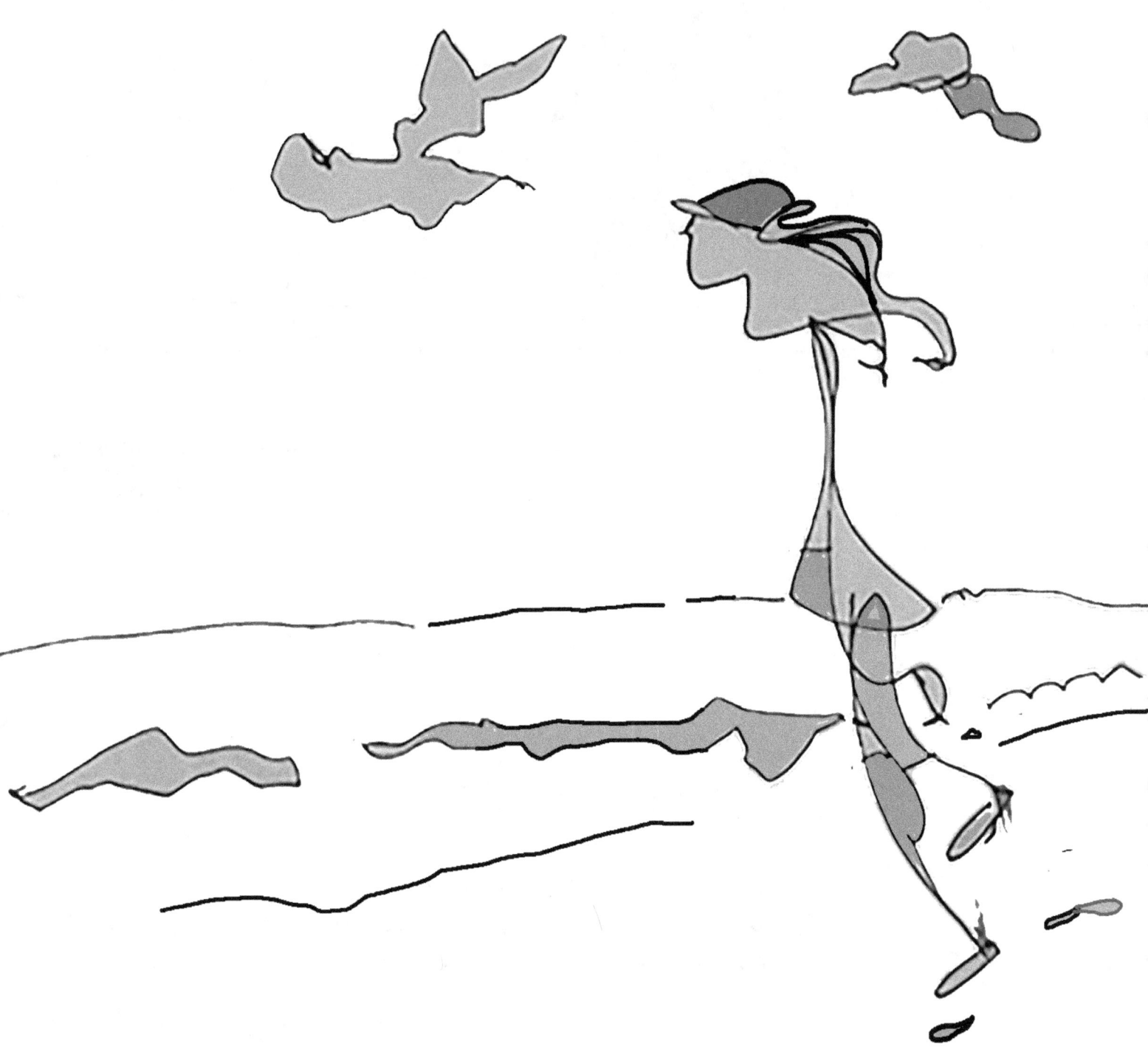

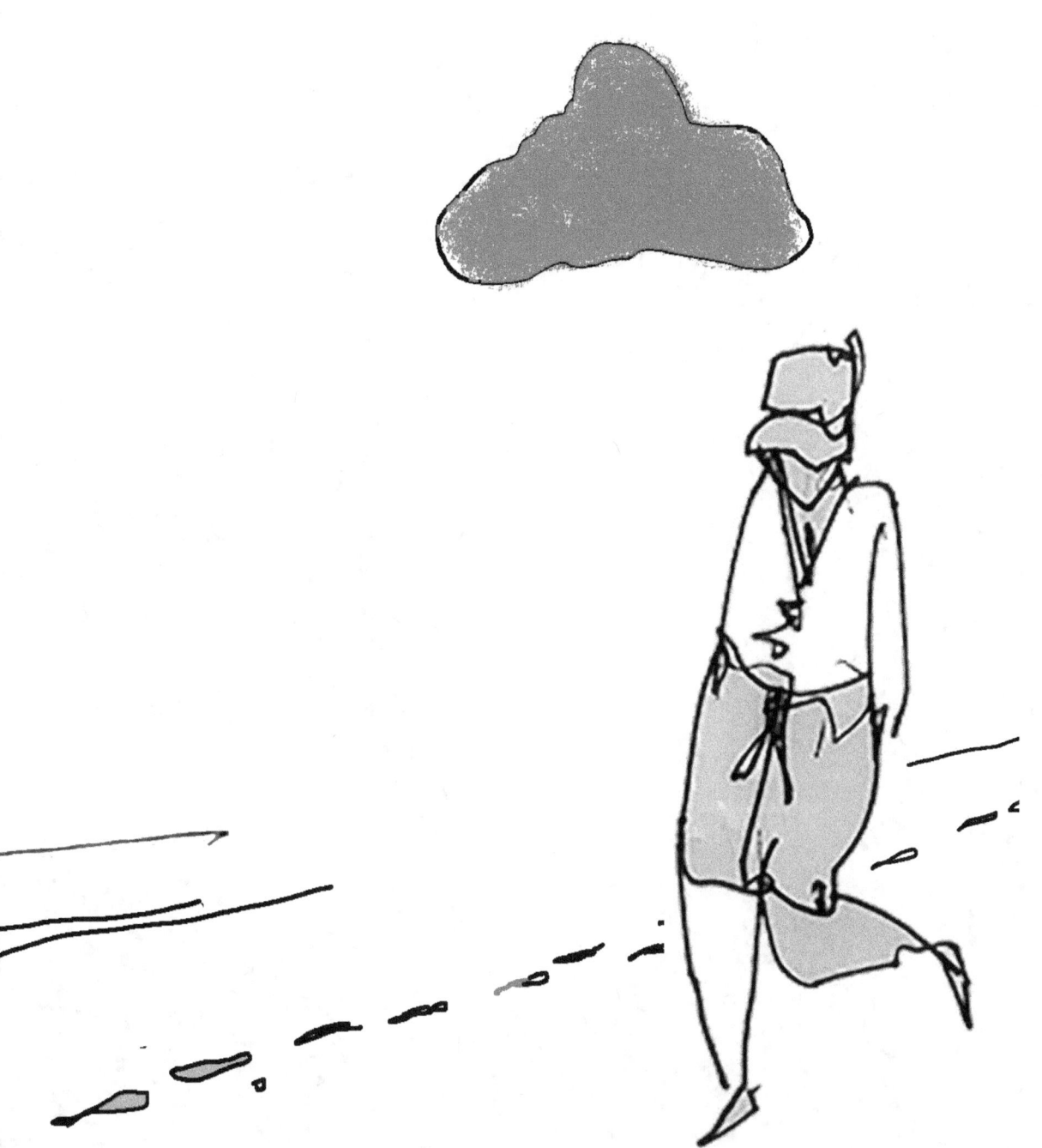

TRACKED

Which way
Sepulchral thrumming of ceaseless spectres
Don't look.

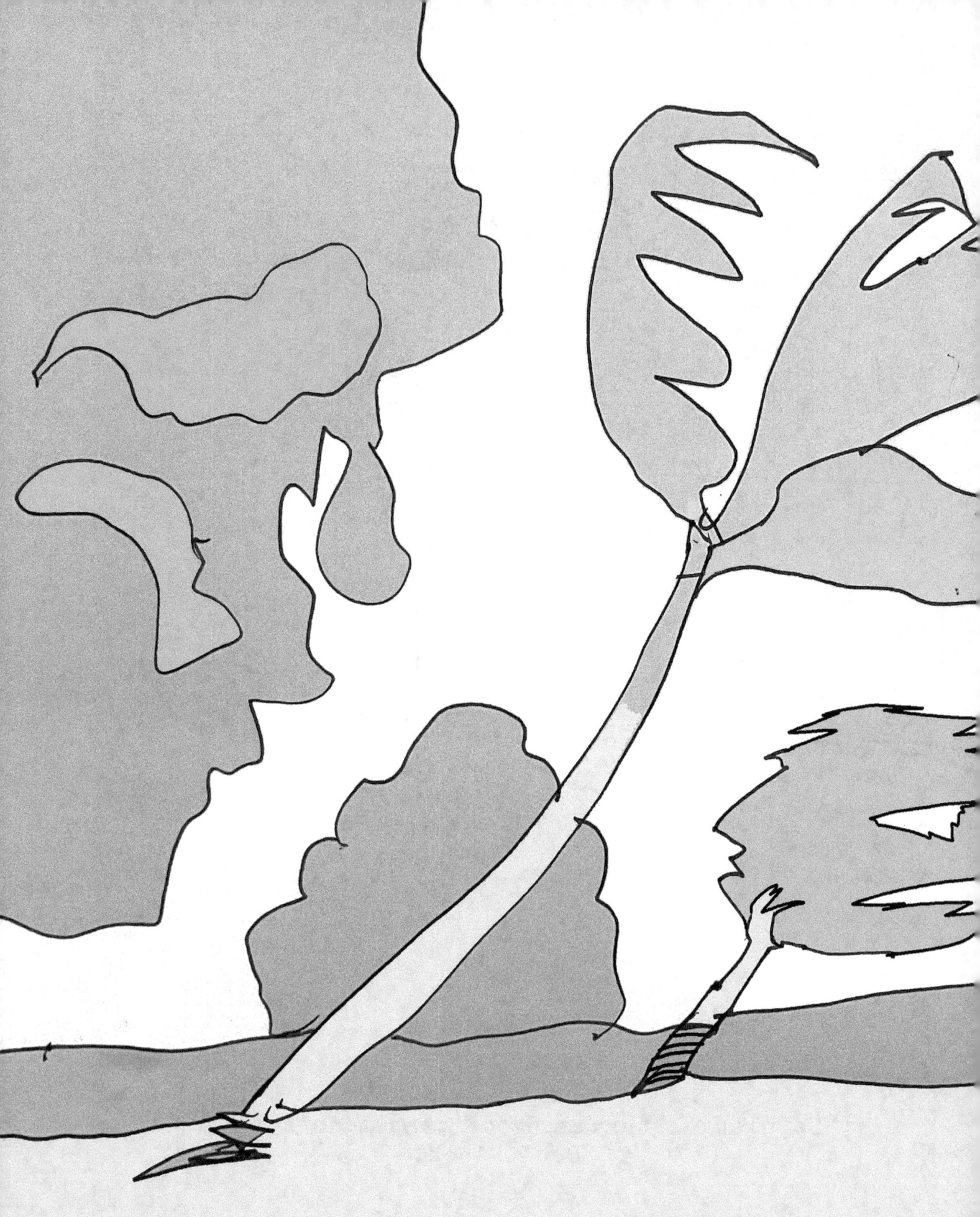

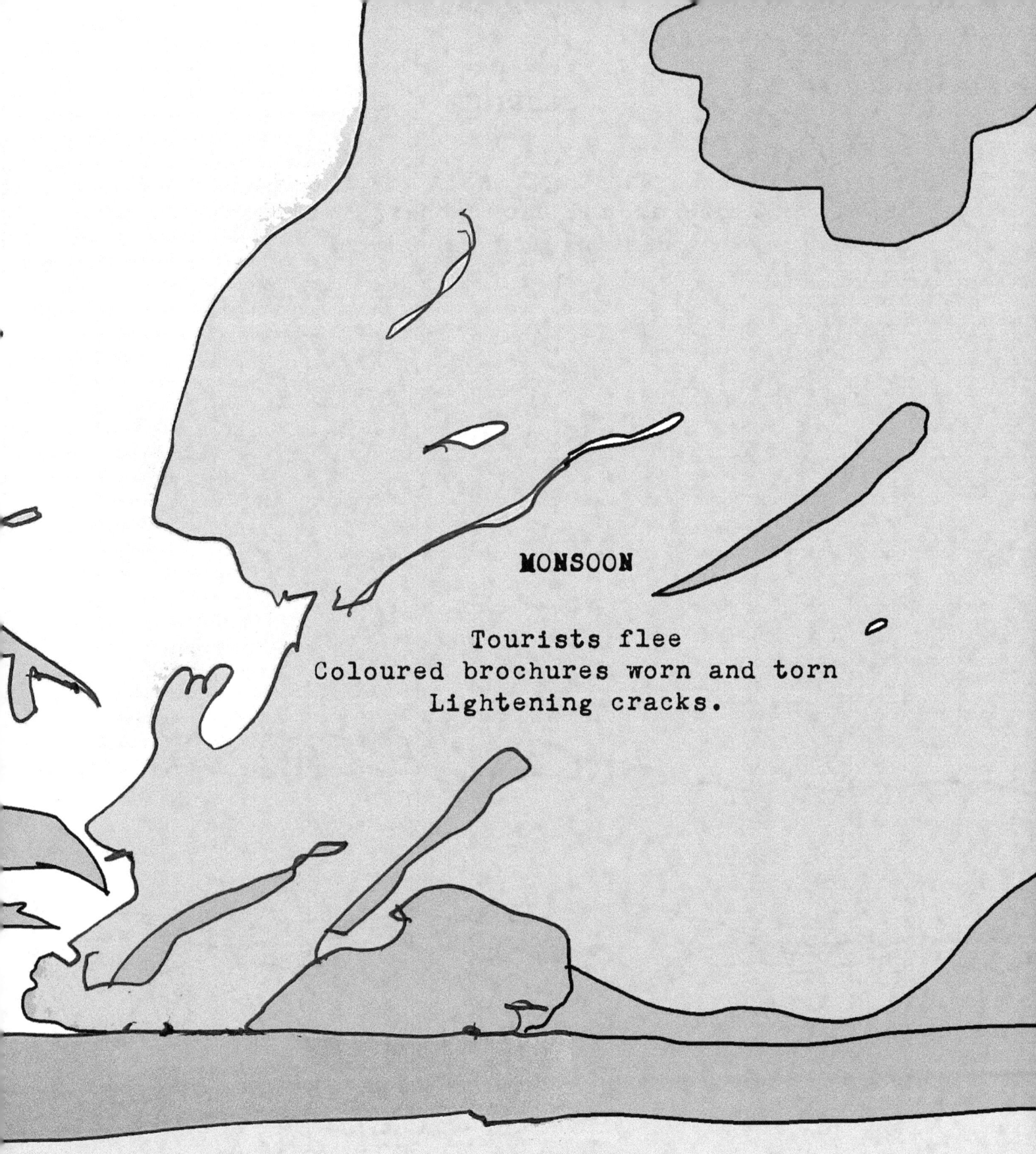

HOLIDAY

Three girls in arms
Close around each other's waists
Waiting for pancakes.

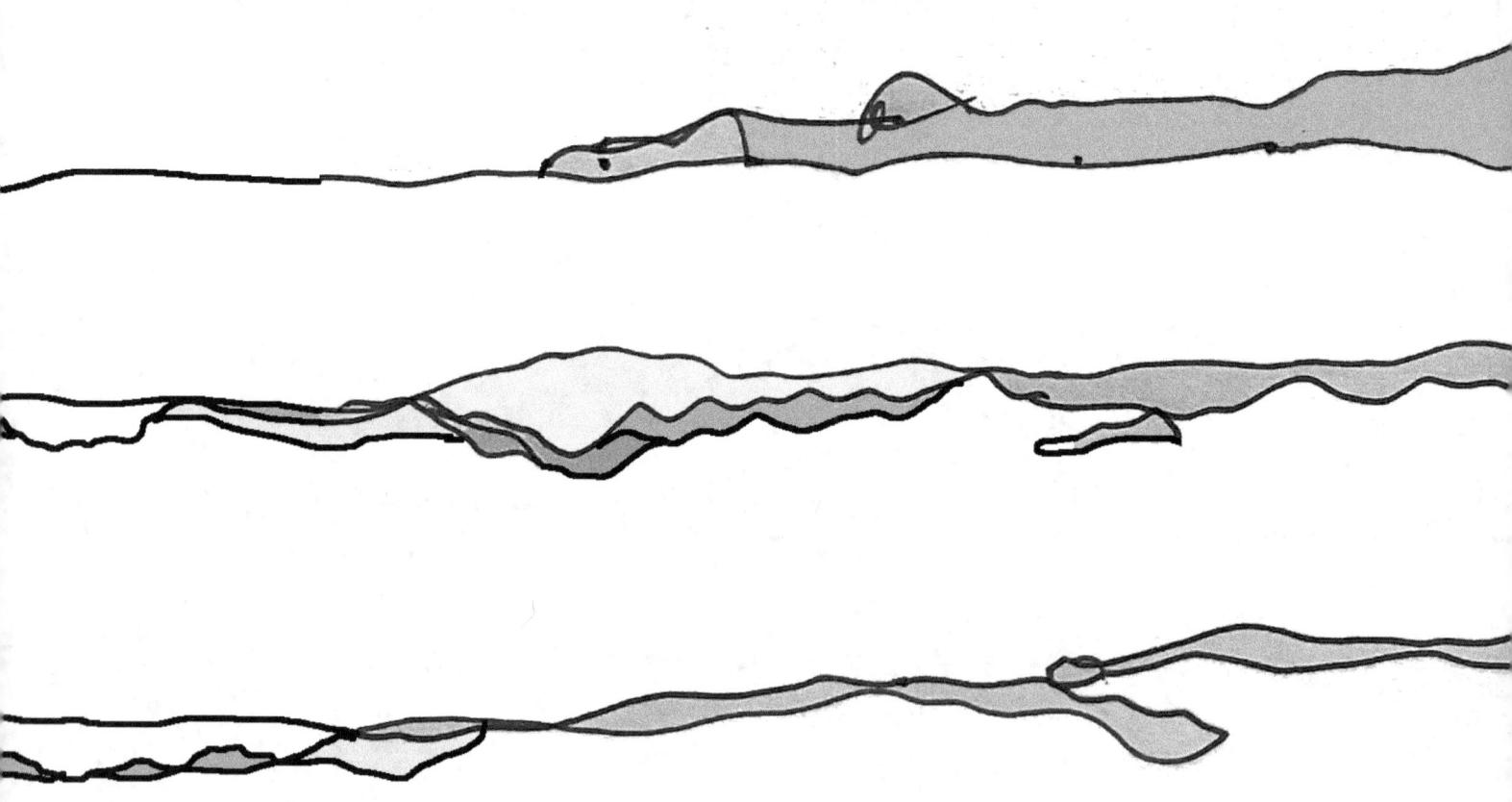

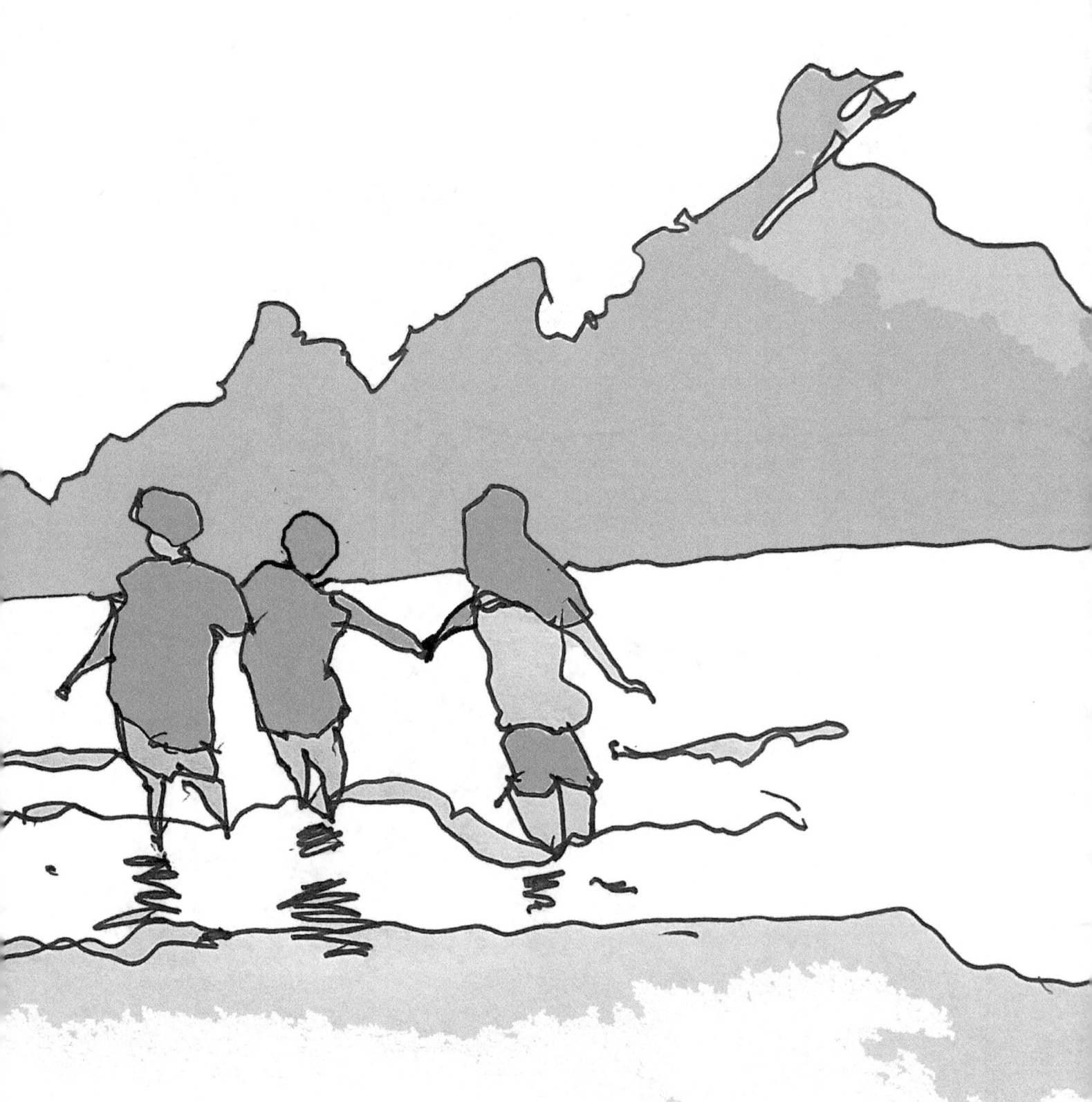

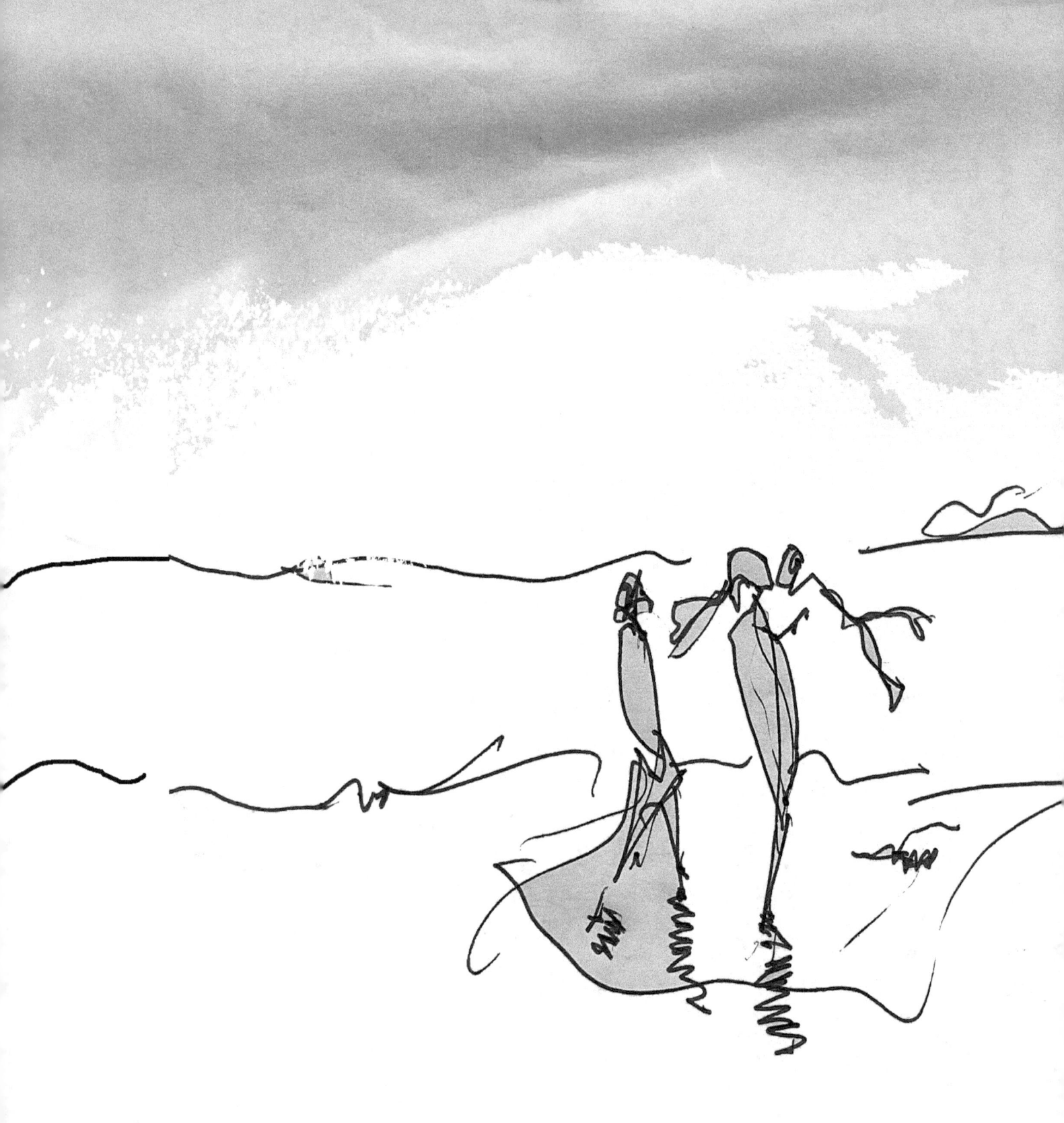

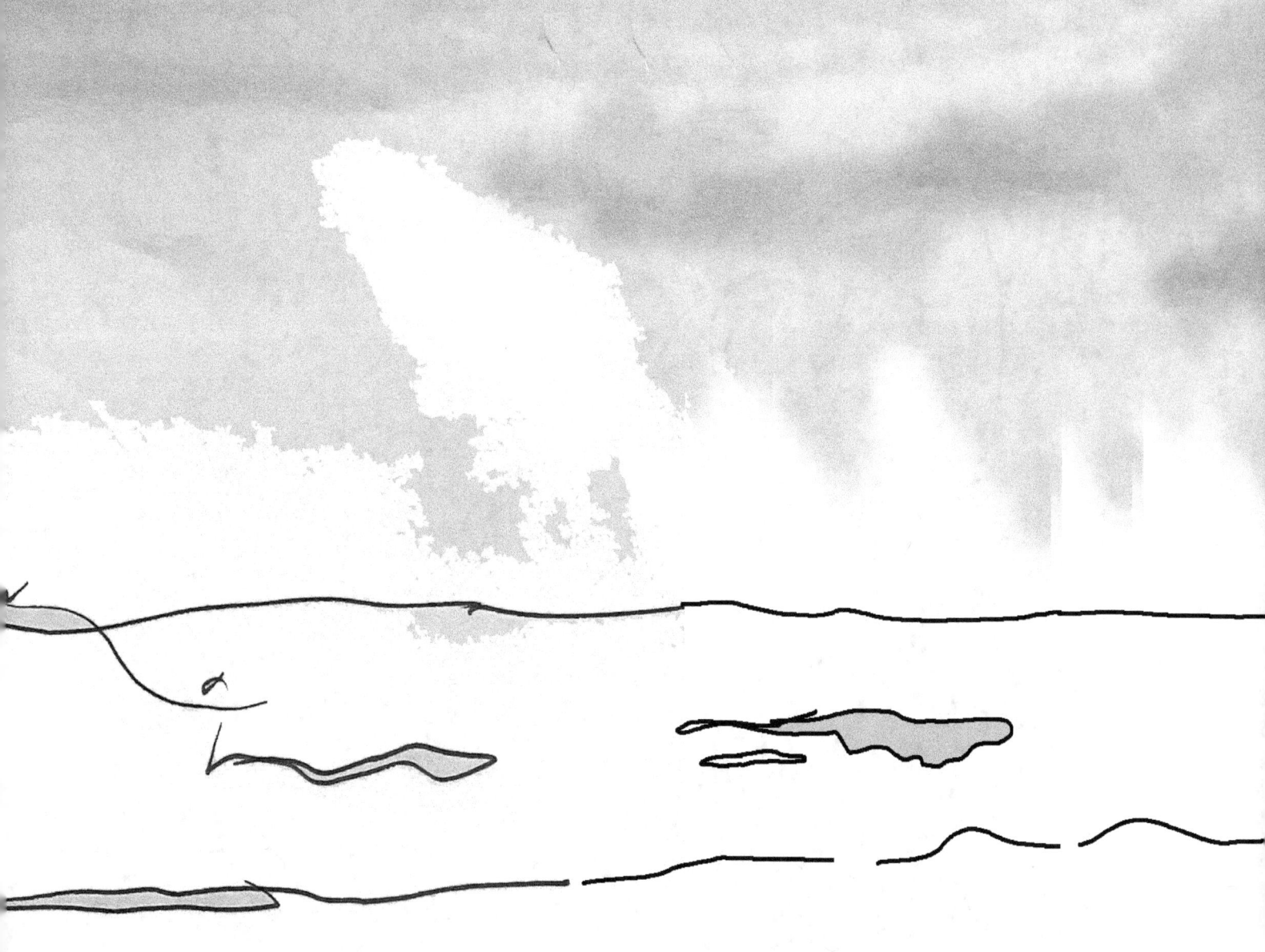

BLIND MAN BLIND WOMAN

Tap along alleyways
Hold sticks of tinkling silver bells
Jangle of trust.

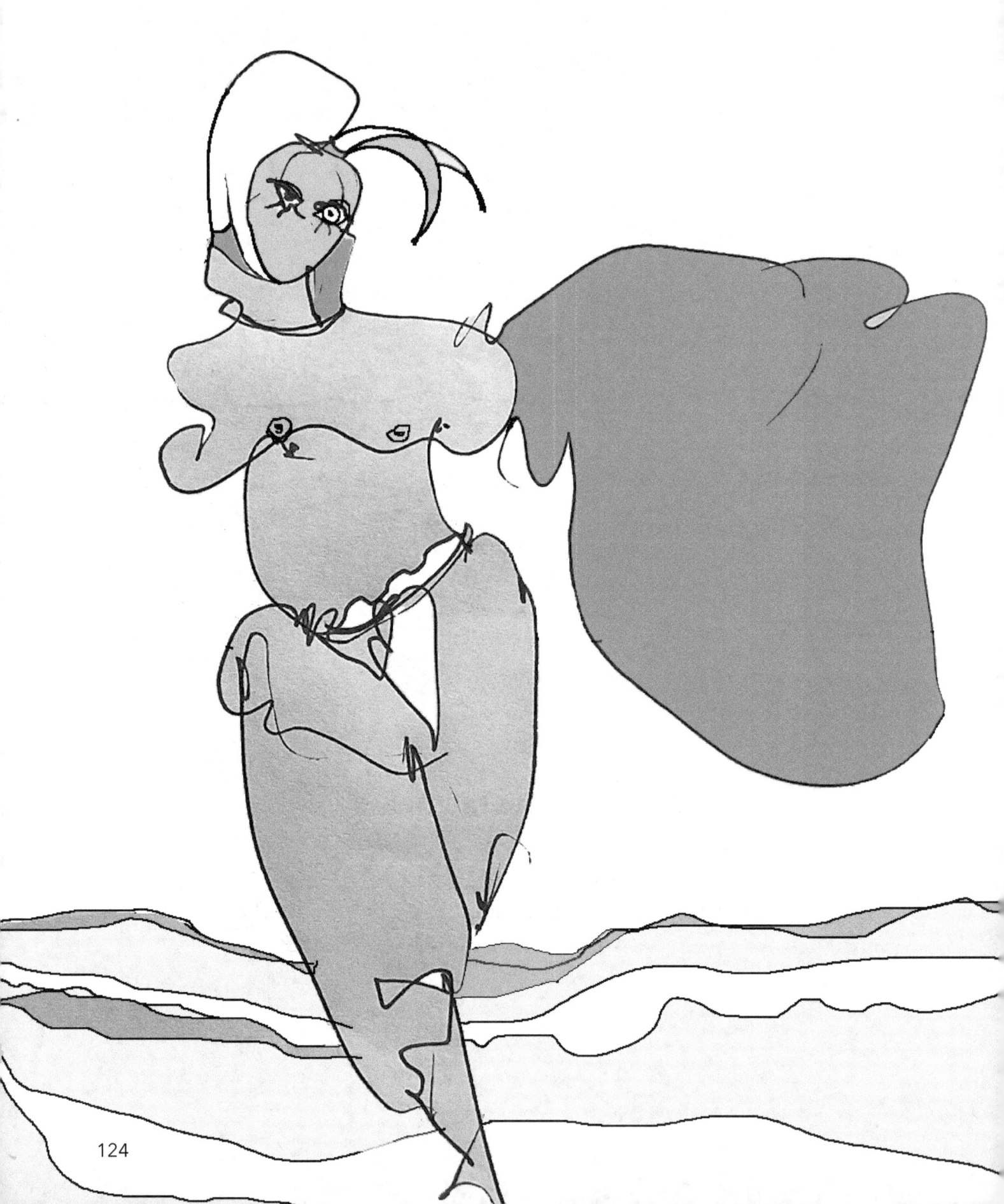

BANYAN TREE

Leaves fall
Paper prayers in temple's fire
Orphans wait.

STUDIO

Midsummer evening
Burning haze of rice fires suffuse
Walls in whitewash.

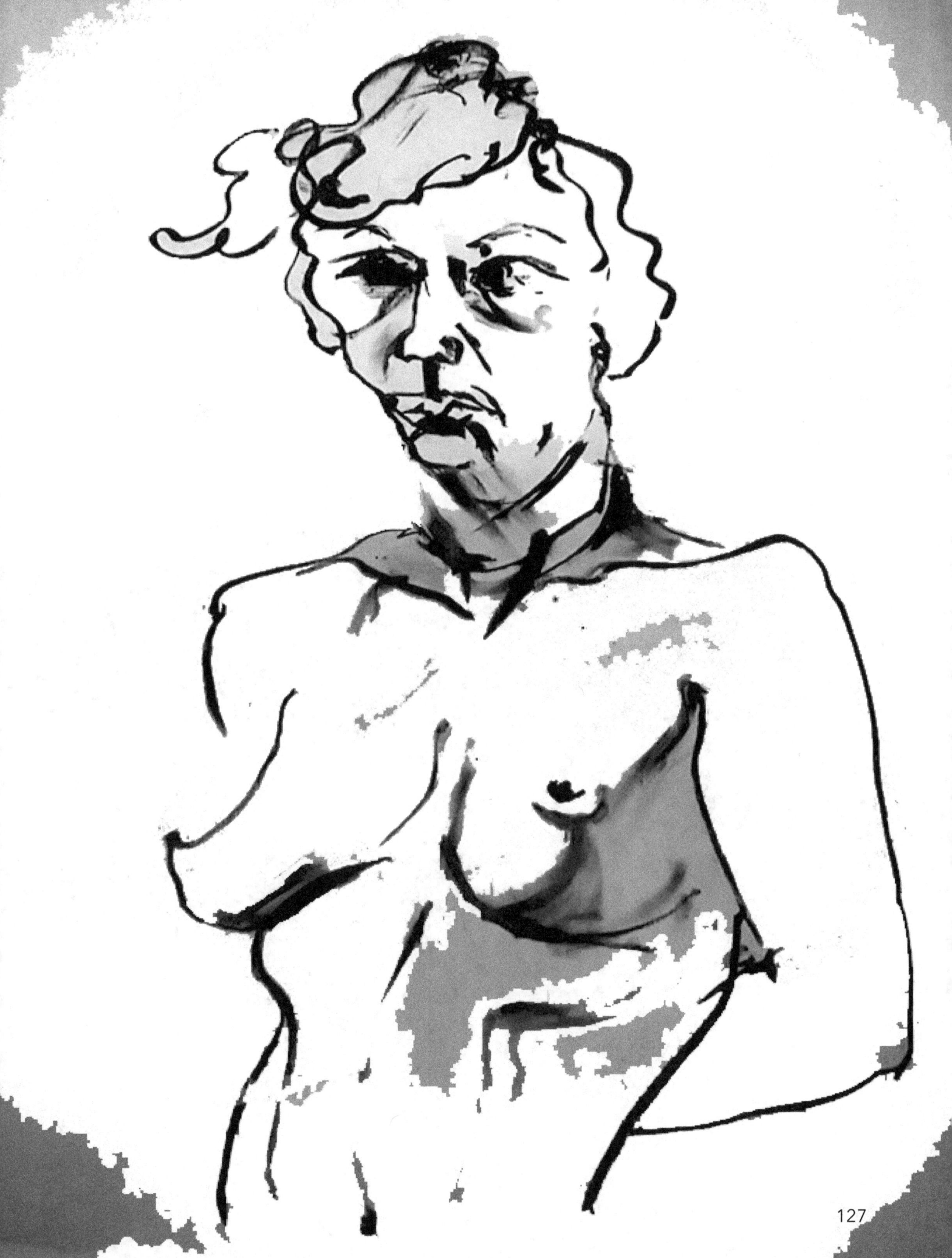

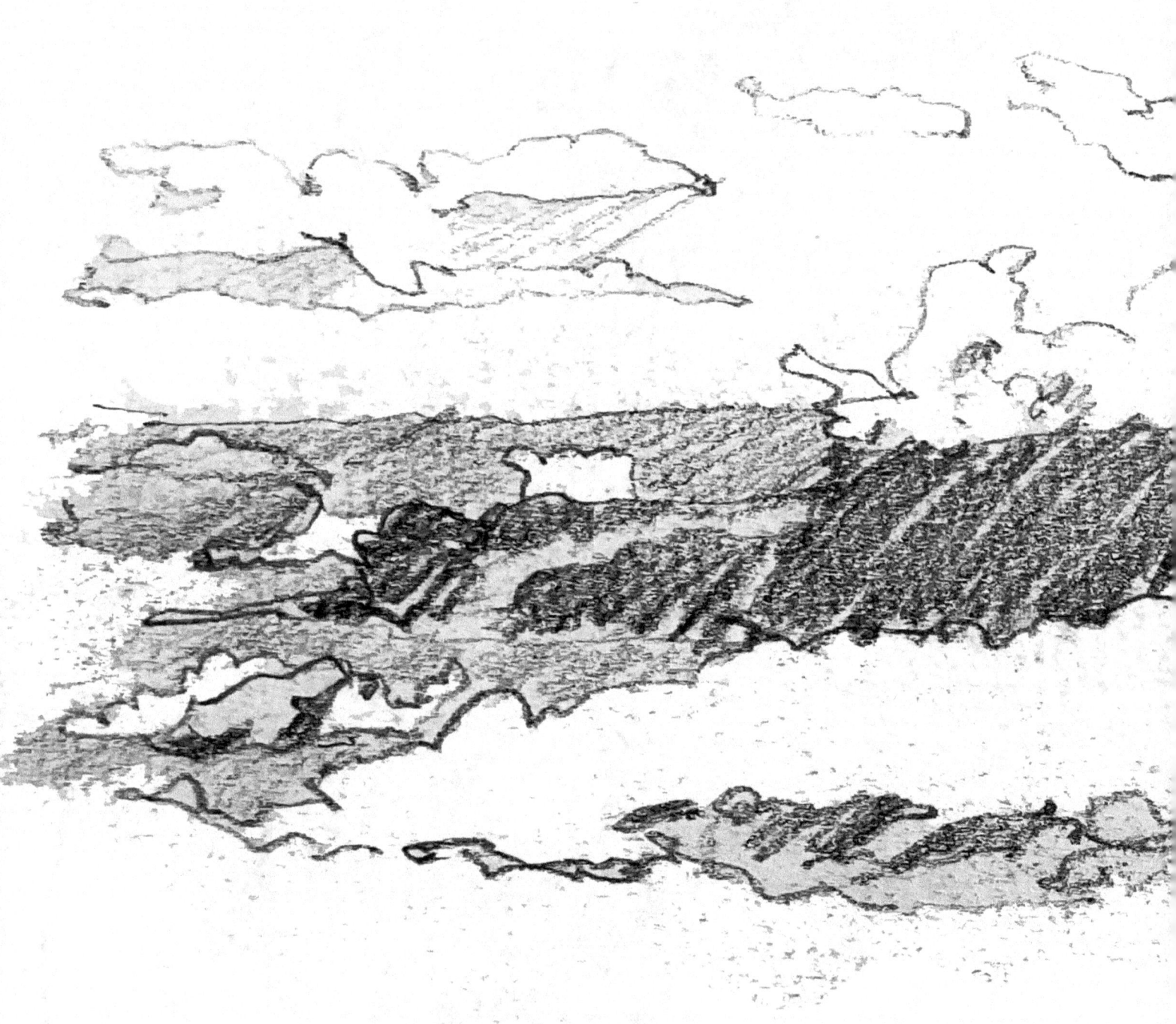

SEA BIRDS

Feathers arrowed
Gulls face the after-breeze
On the ledge.

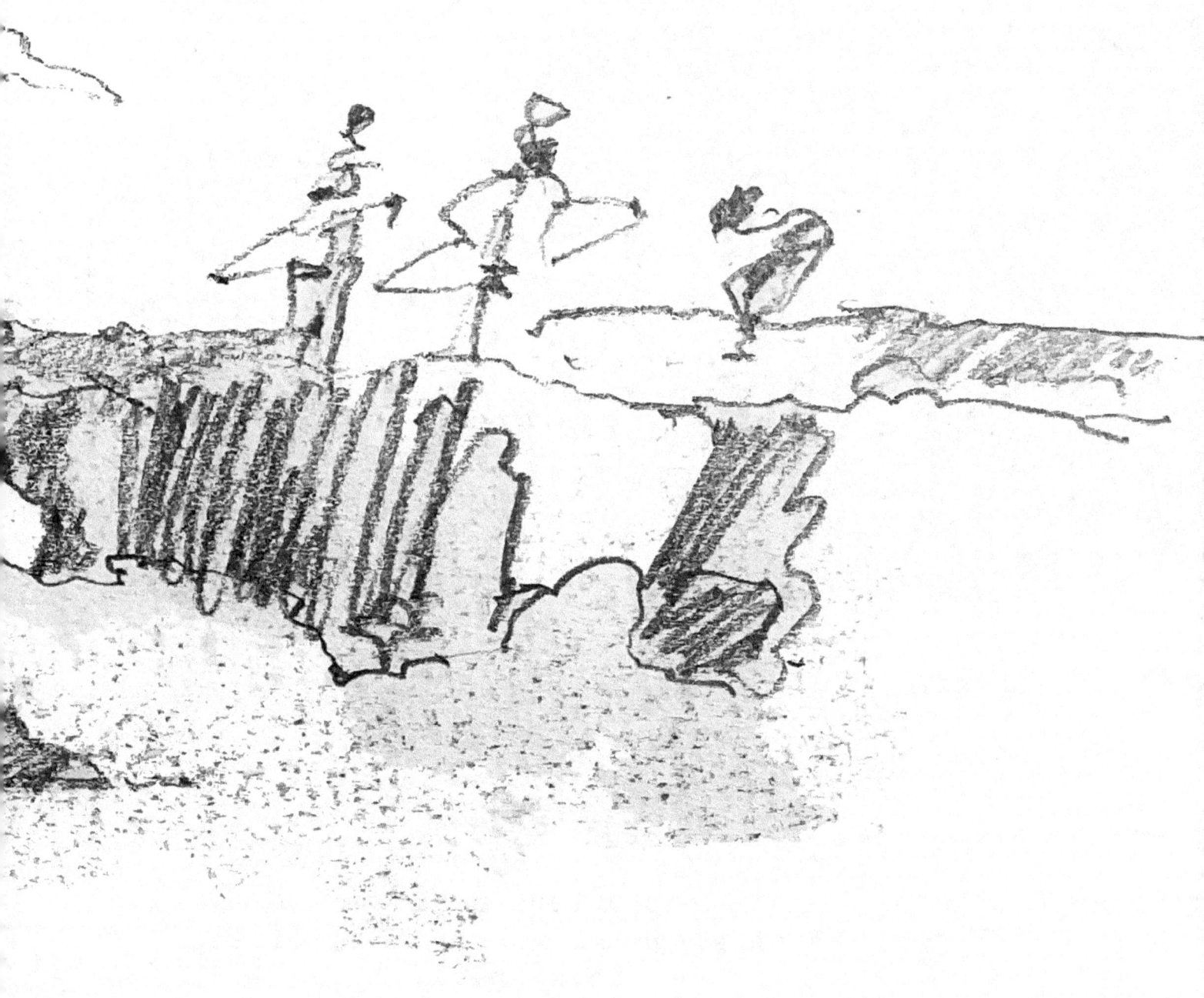

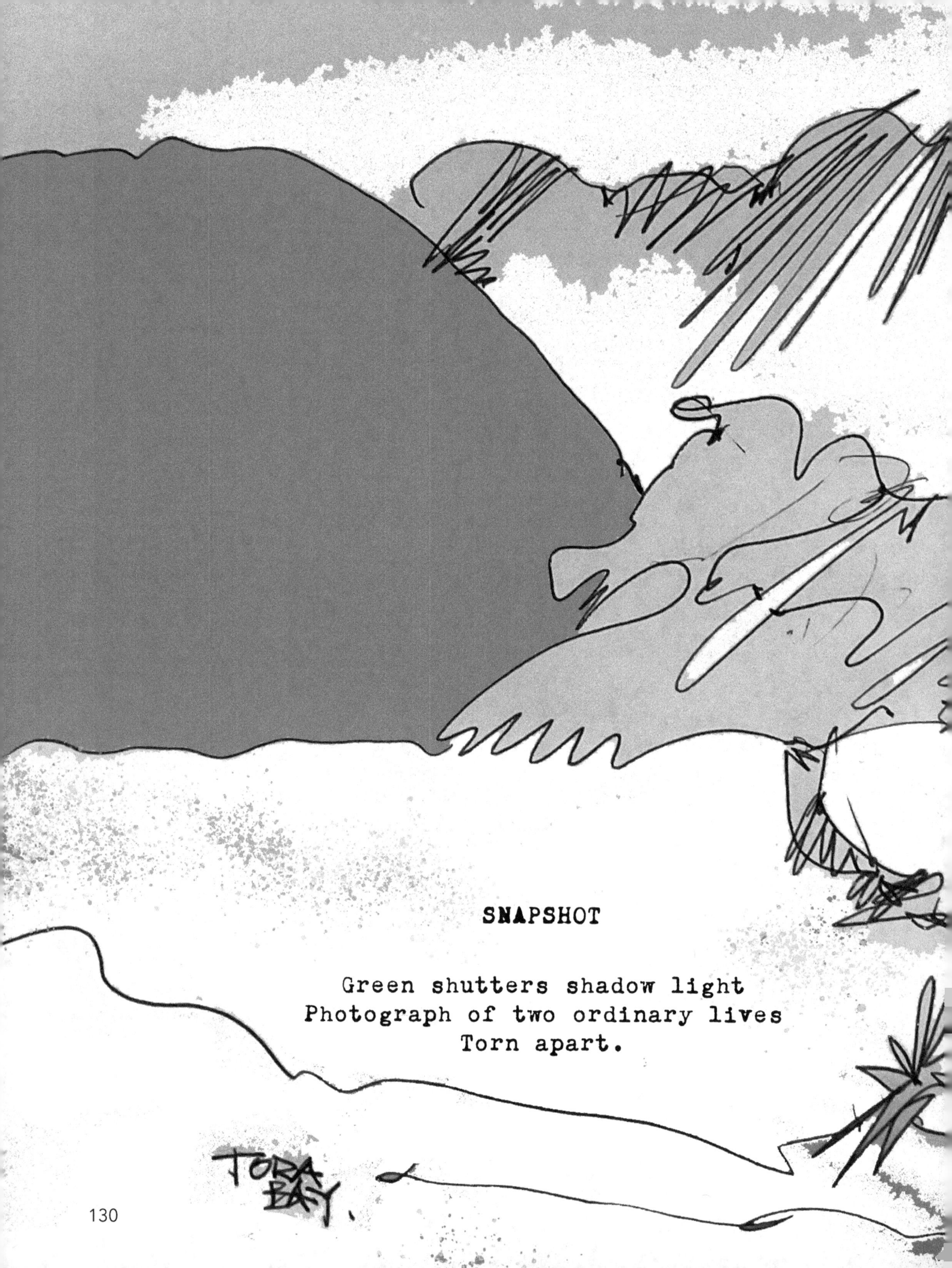

SNAPSHOT

Green shutters shadow light
Photograph of two ordinary lives
Torn apart.

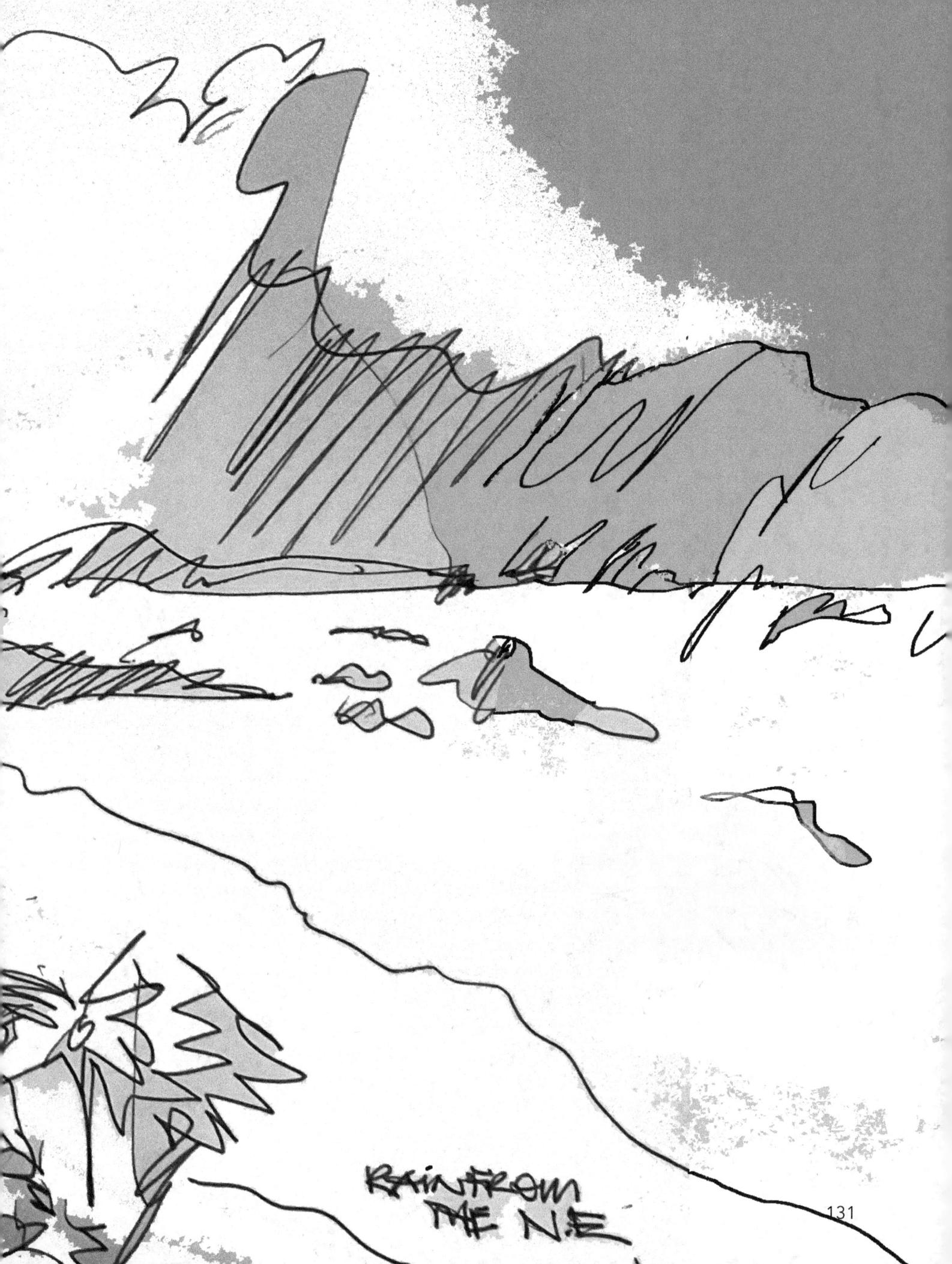

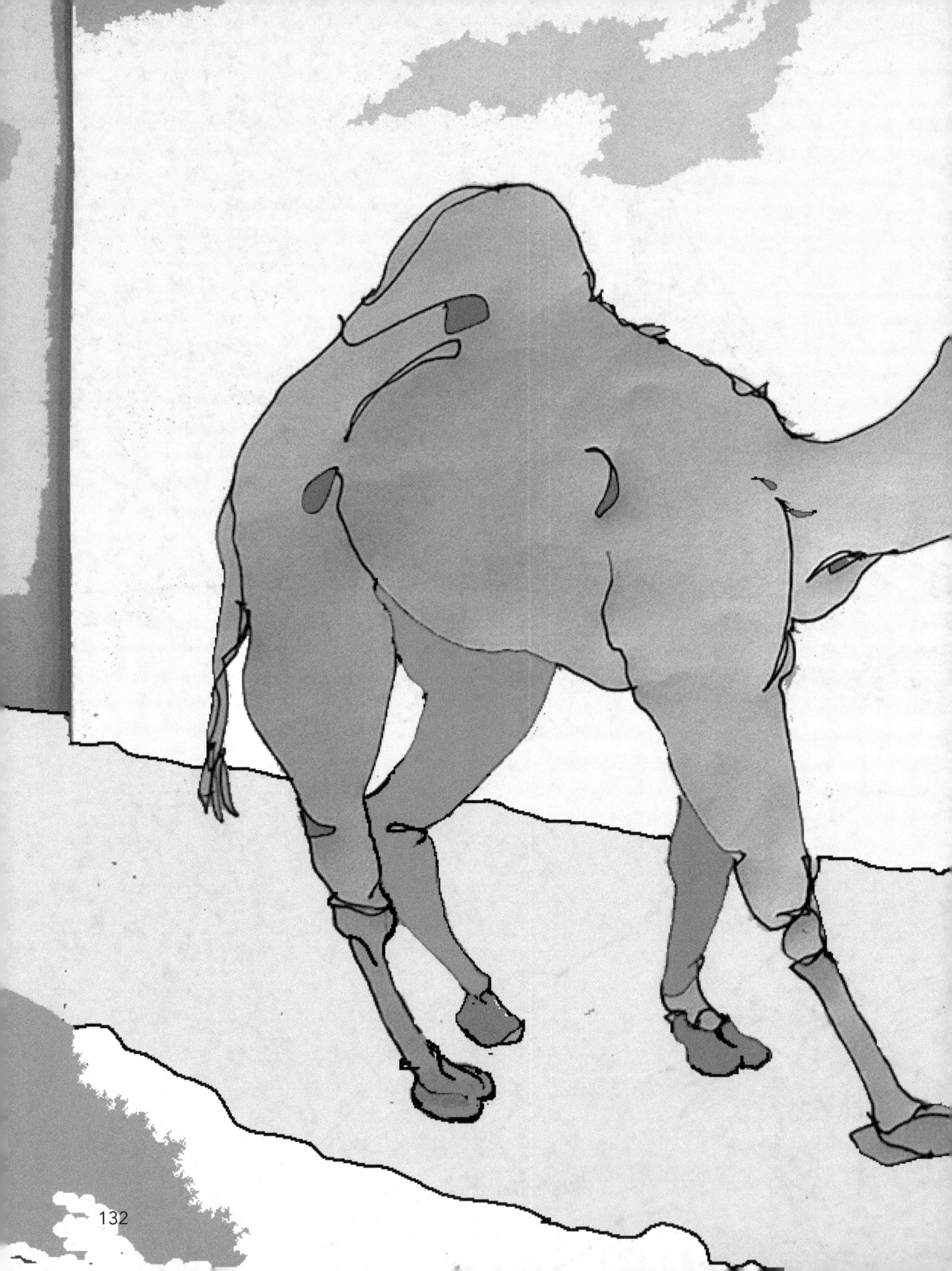

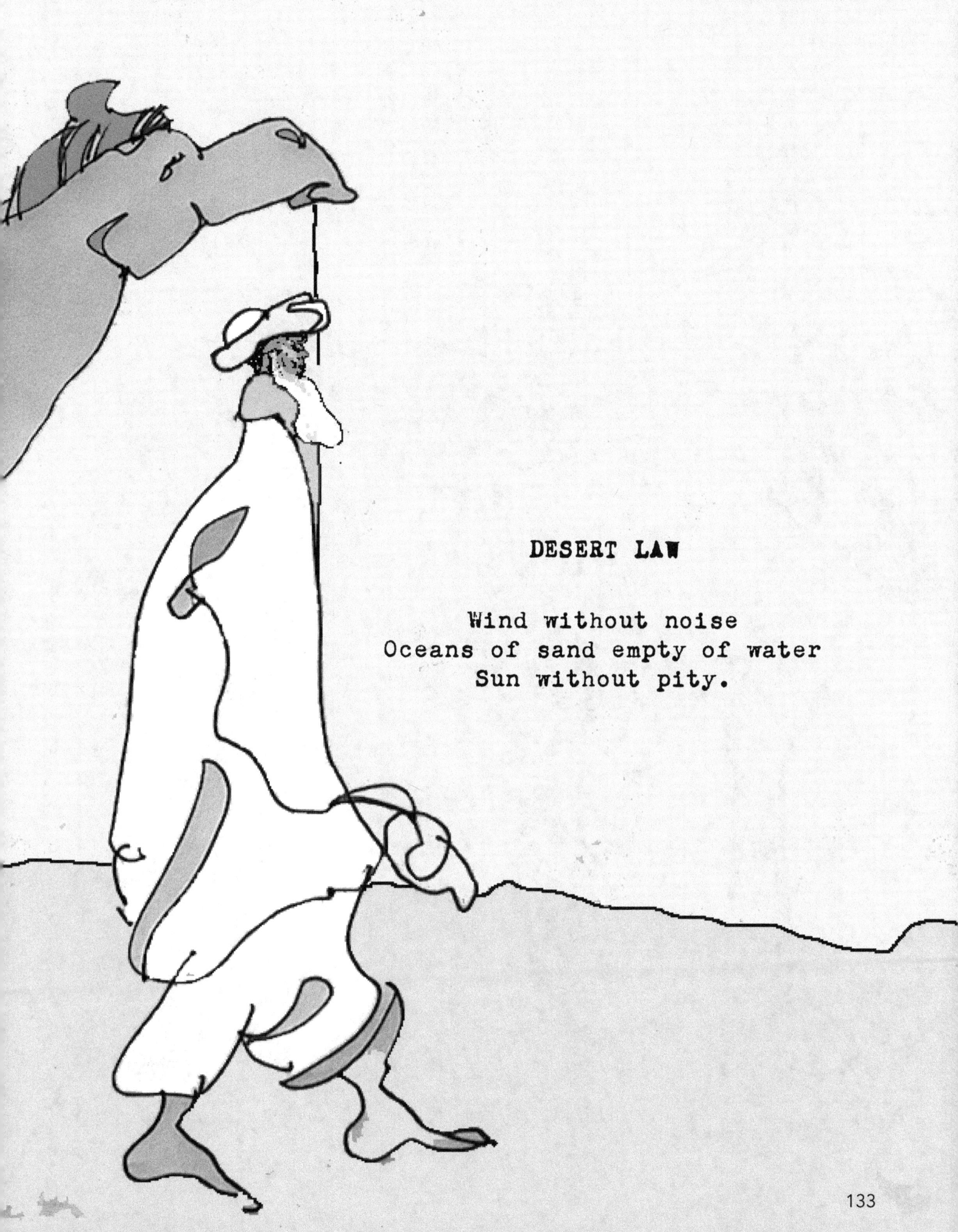

DESERT LAW

Wind without noise
Oceans of sand empty of water
Sun without pity.

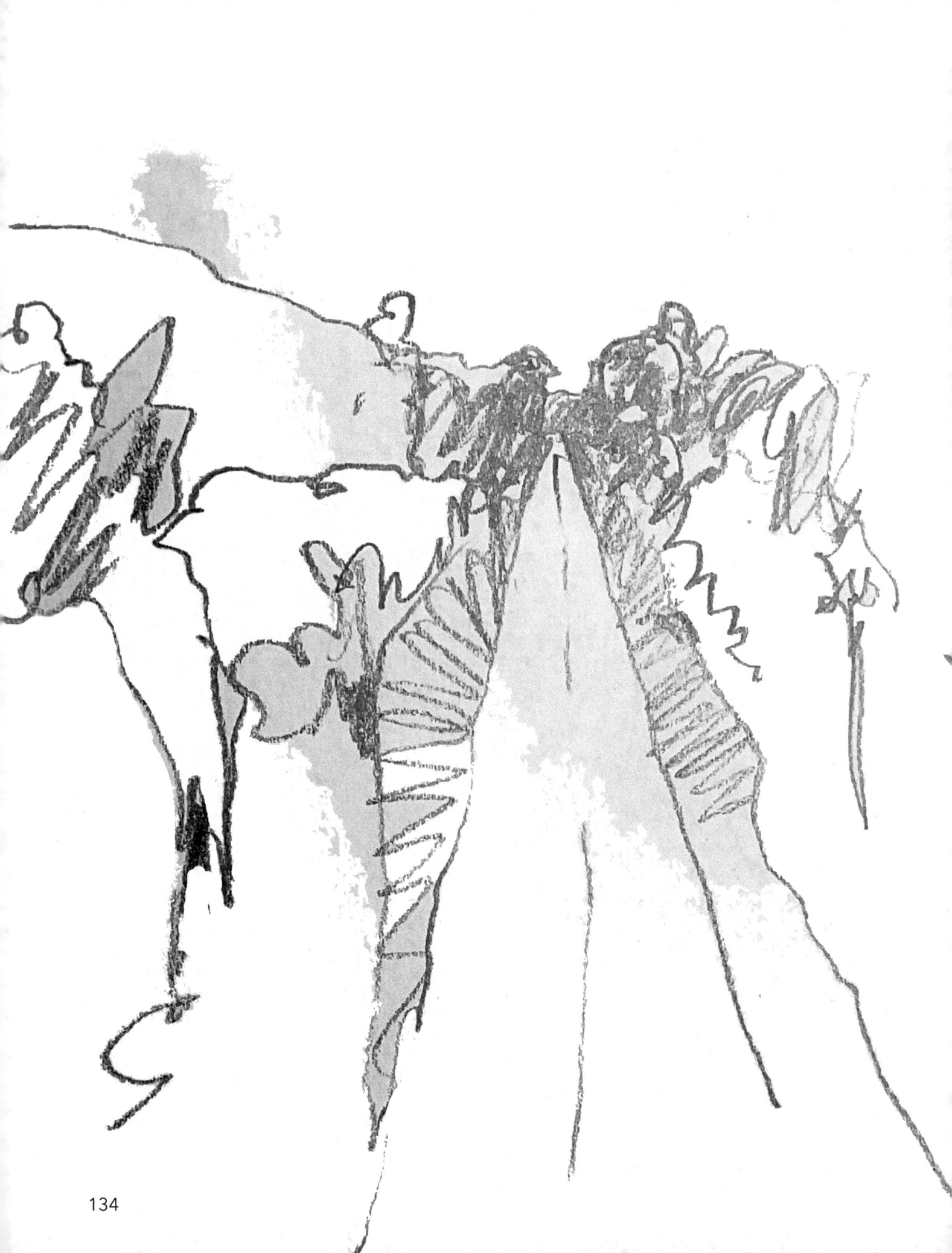

OPEN ROAD

Far north highway
Escape fetid breath of judgement
No shadow behind.

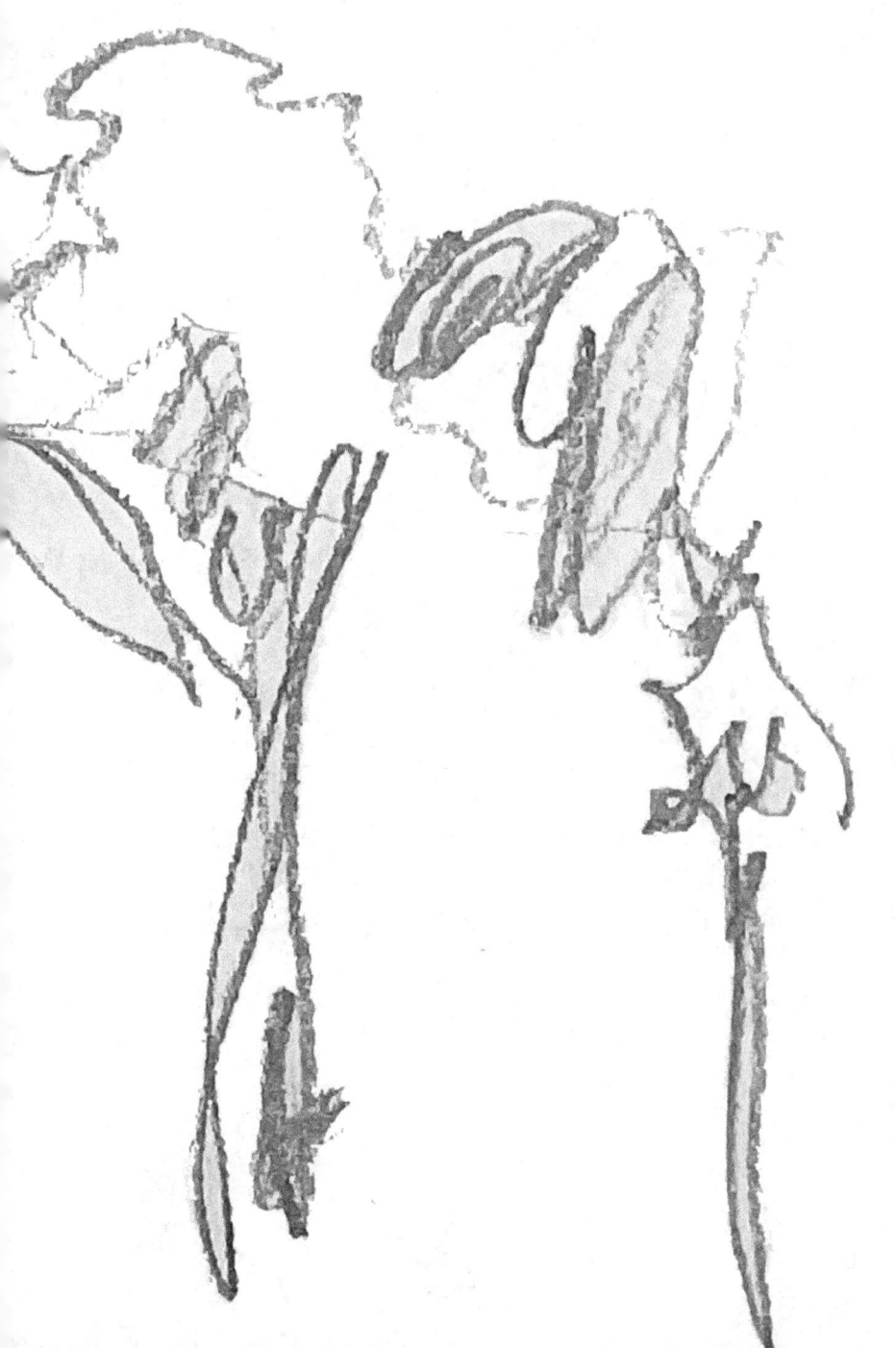

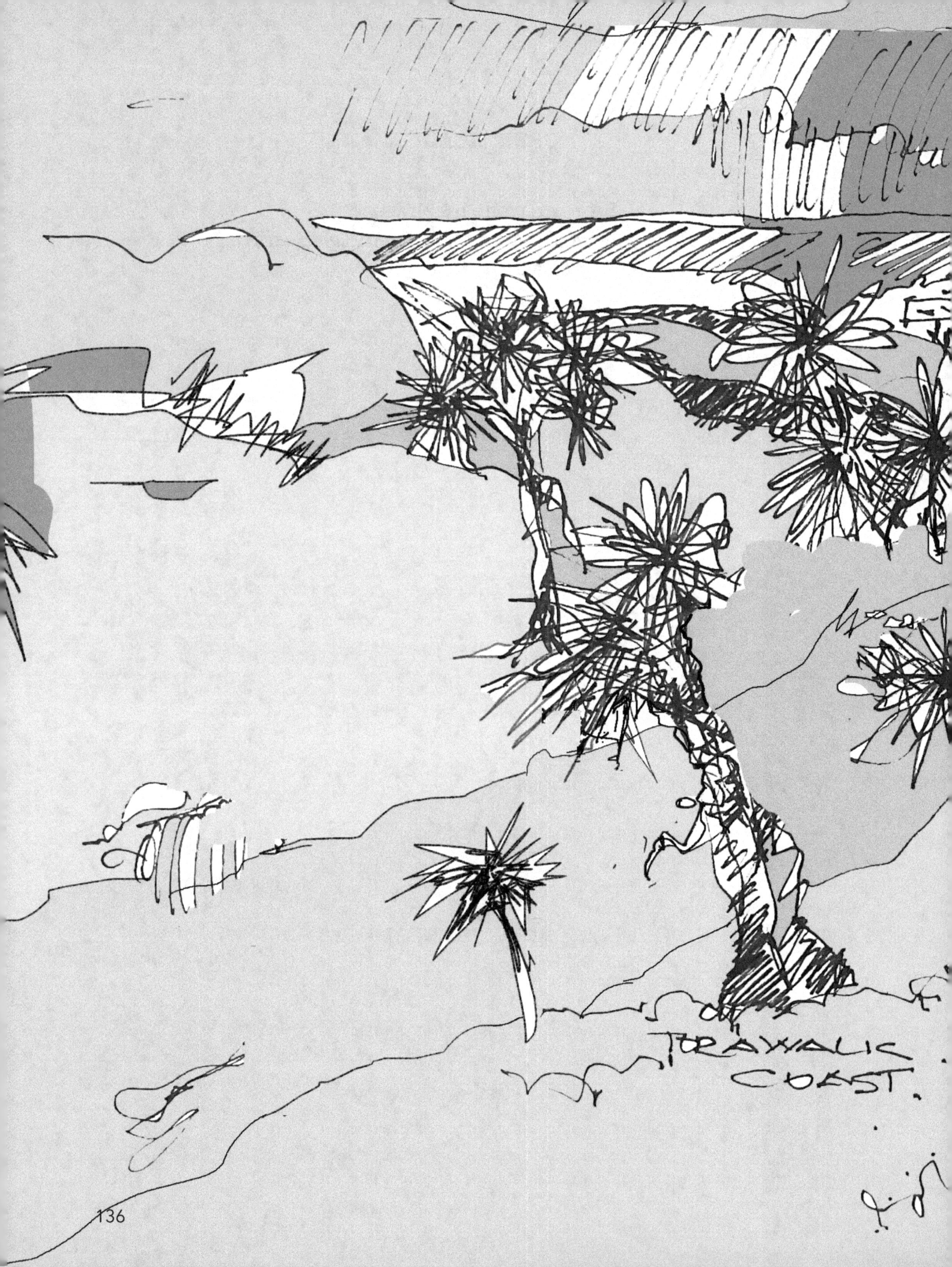

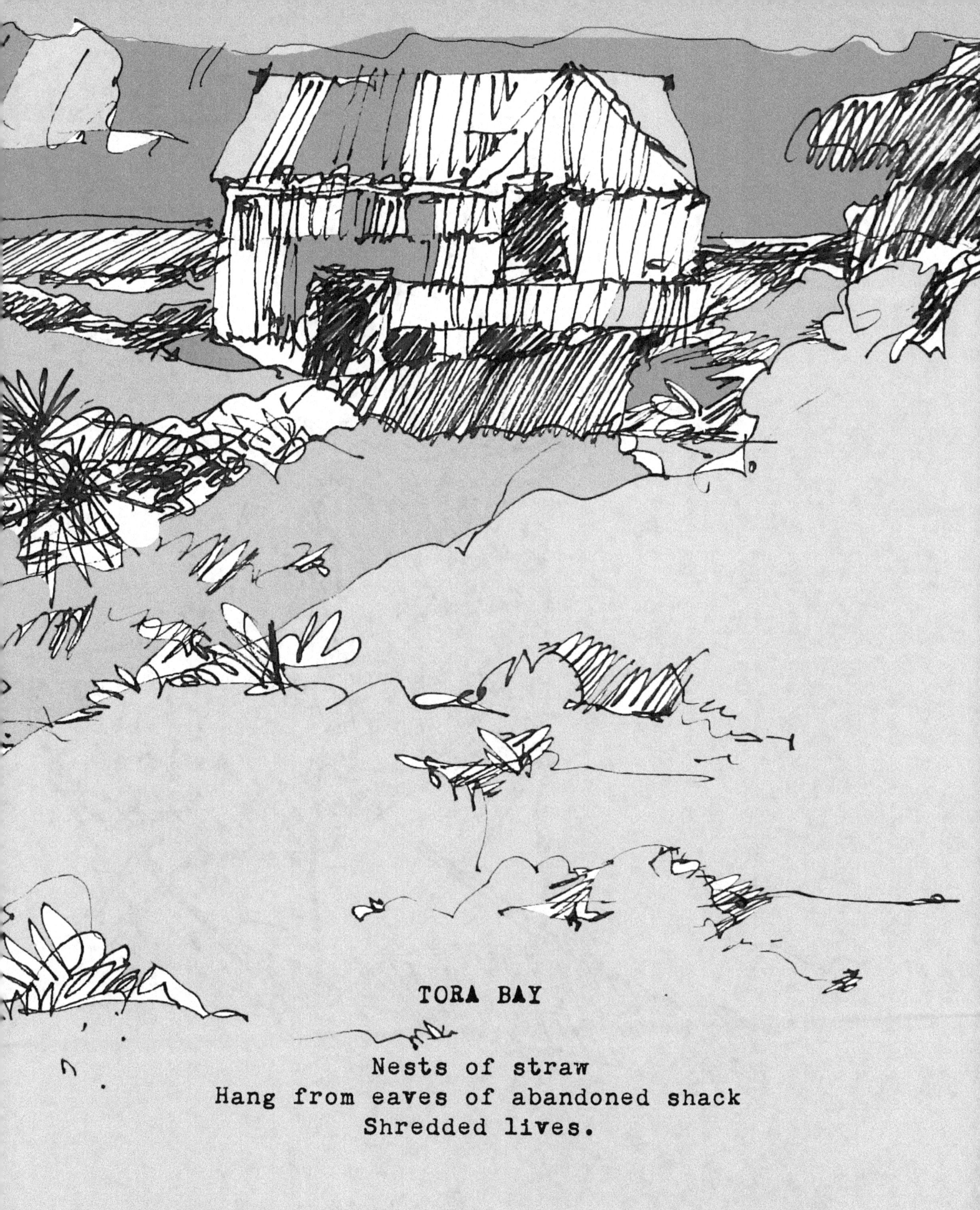

TORA BAY

Nests of straw
Hang from eaves of abandoned shack
Shredded lives.

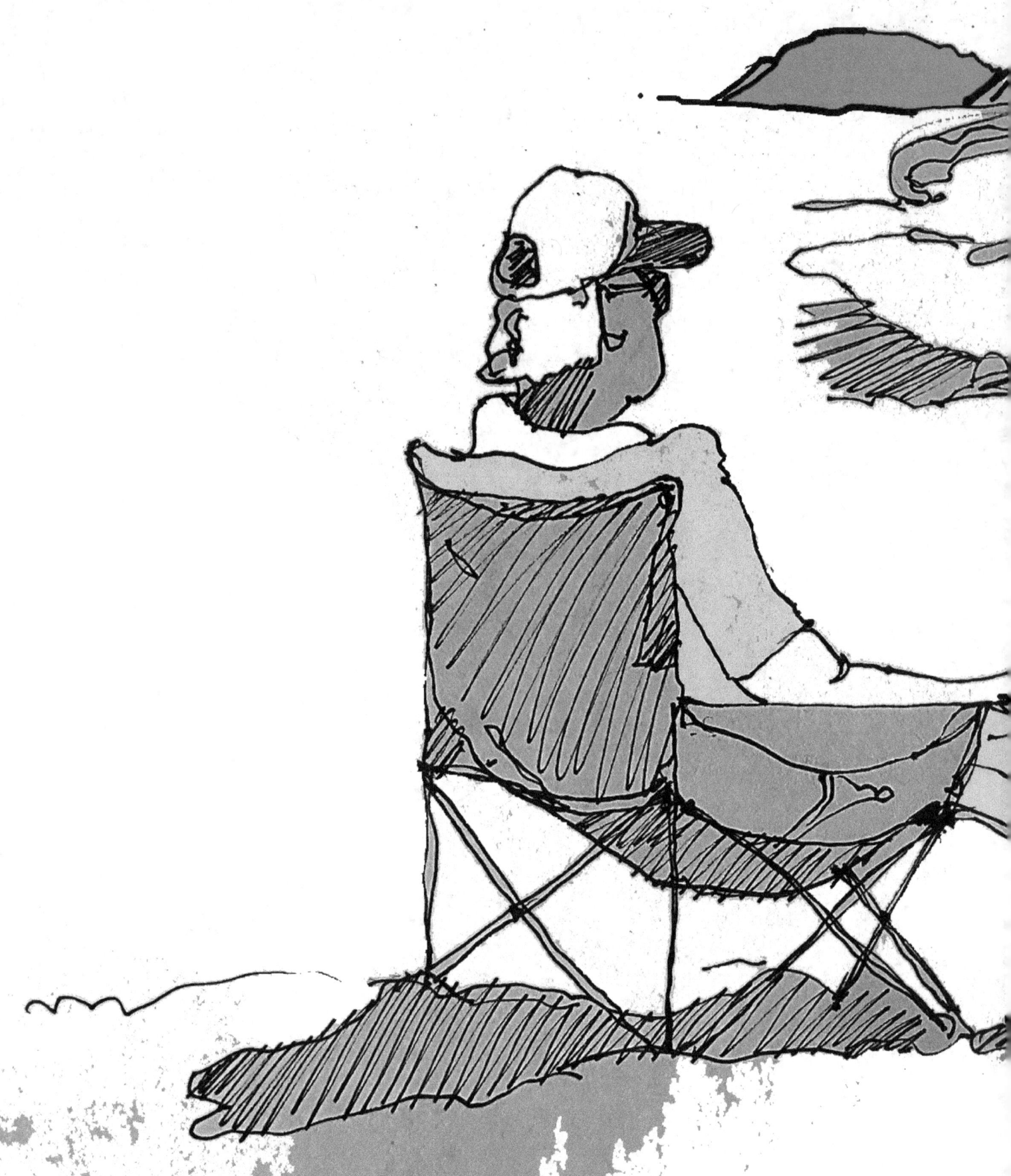

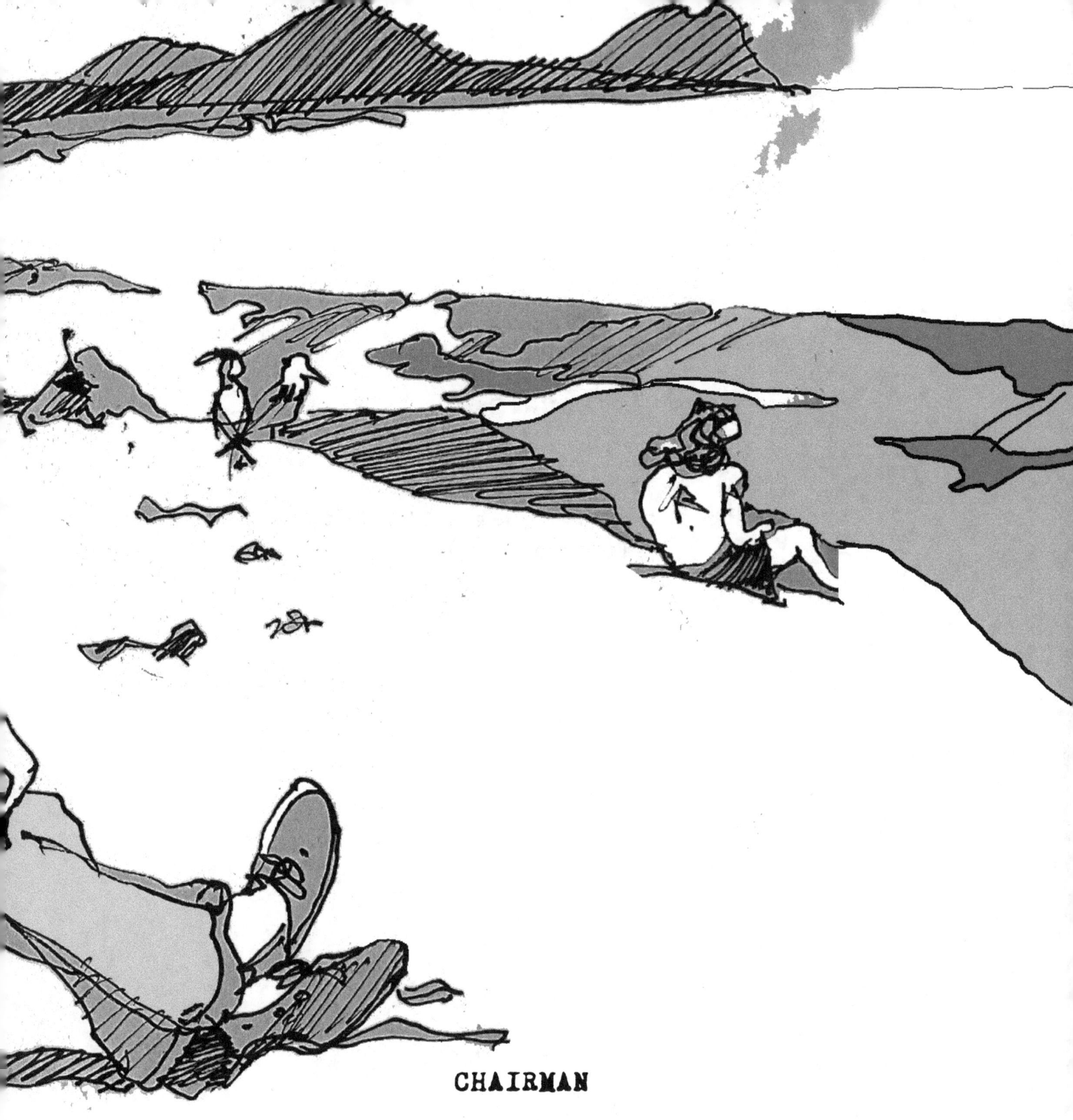

CHAIRMAN

Unfold a canvas chair
Make claim to square of land
In sinking sand.

BLACK SAND

Frenzy of crab
Hide beneath magnetic rock
Turn of tide.

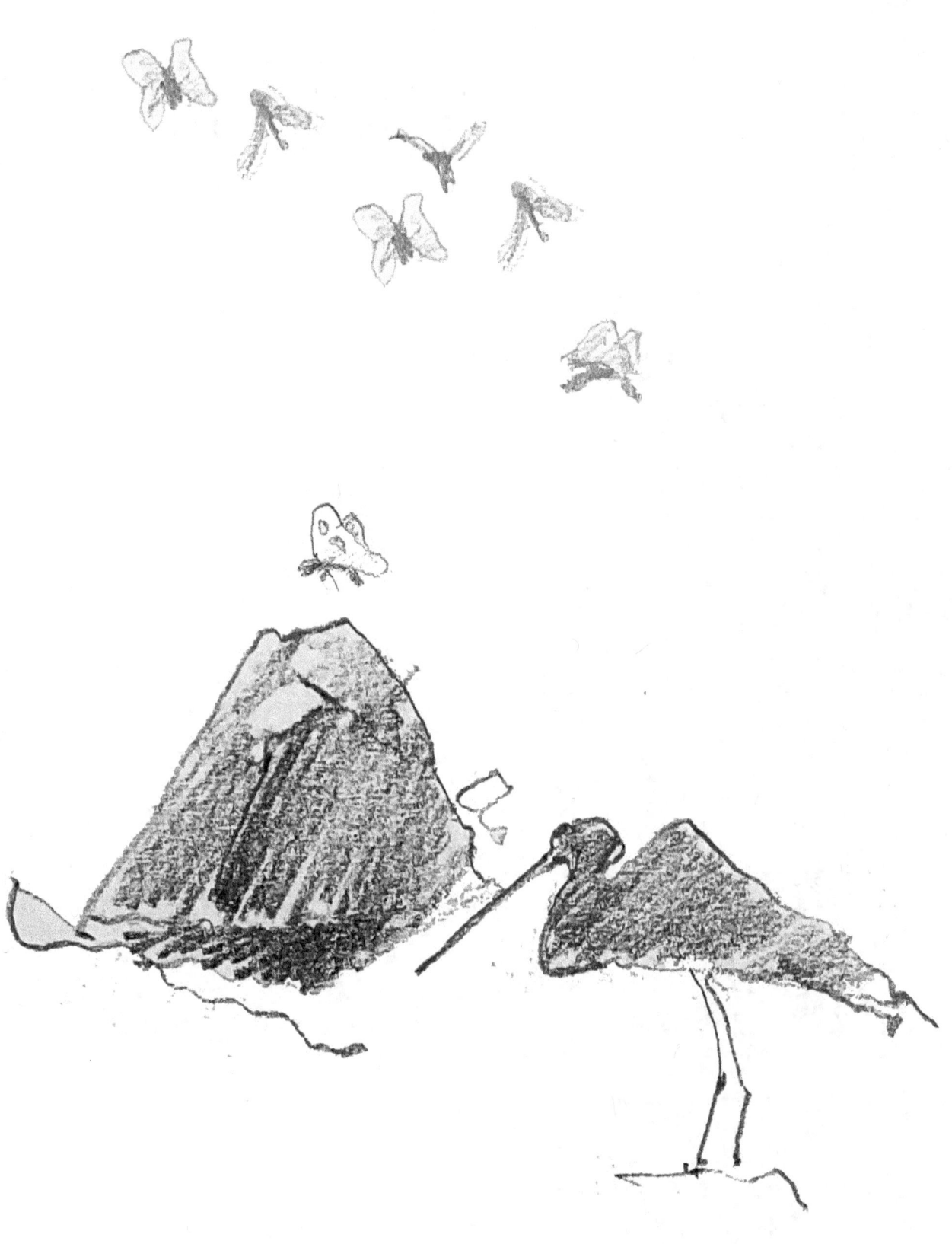

TALARIA

Steel wire strung
Foot fall over ocean of vanities
Two snakes coil.

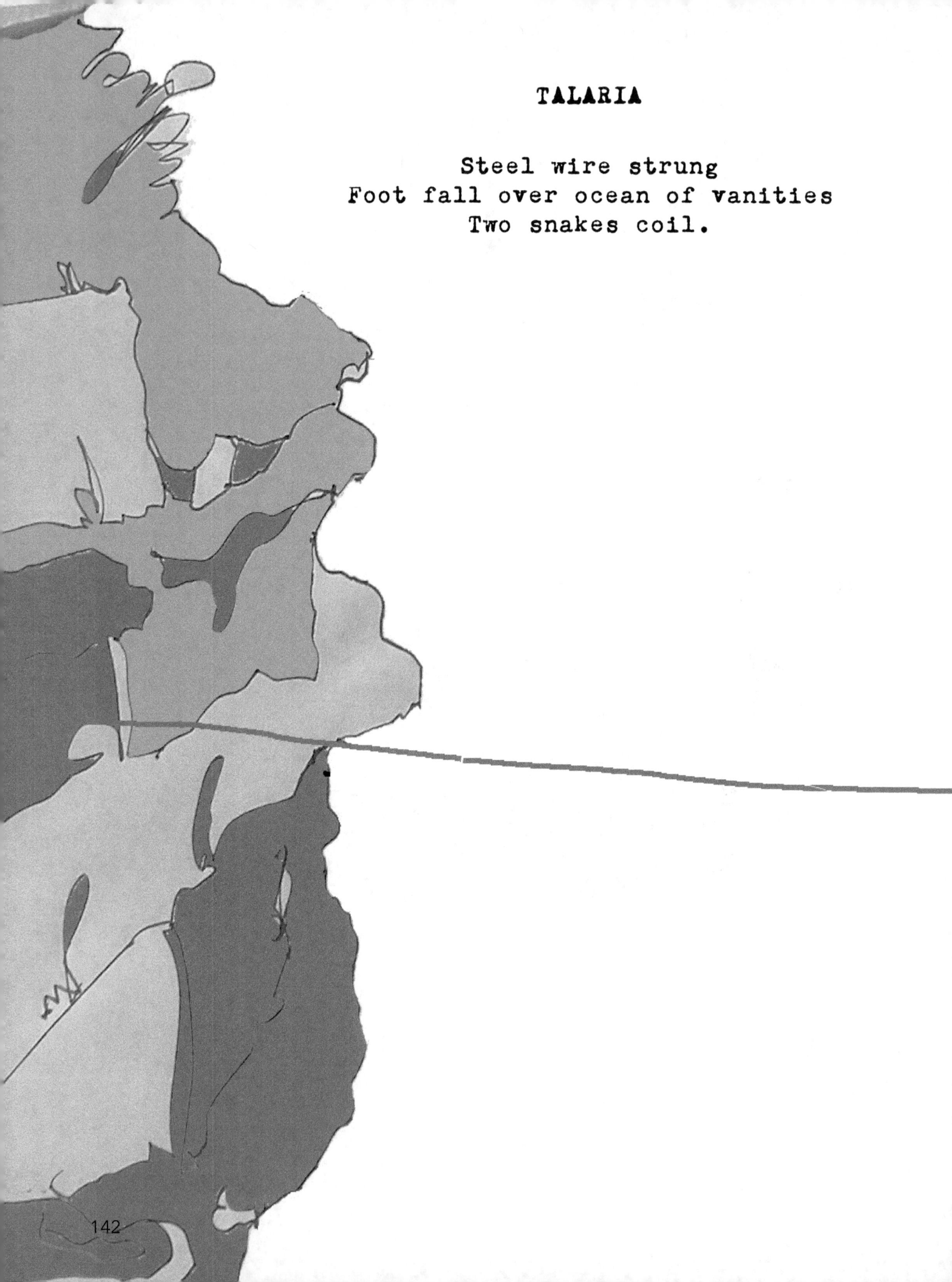

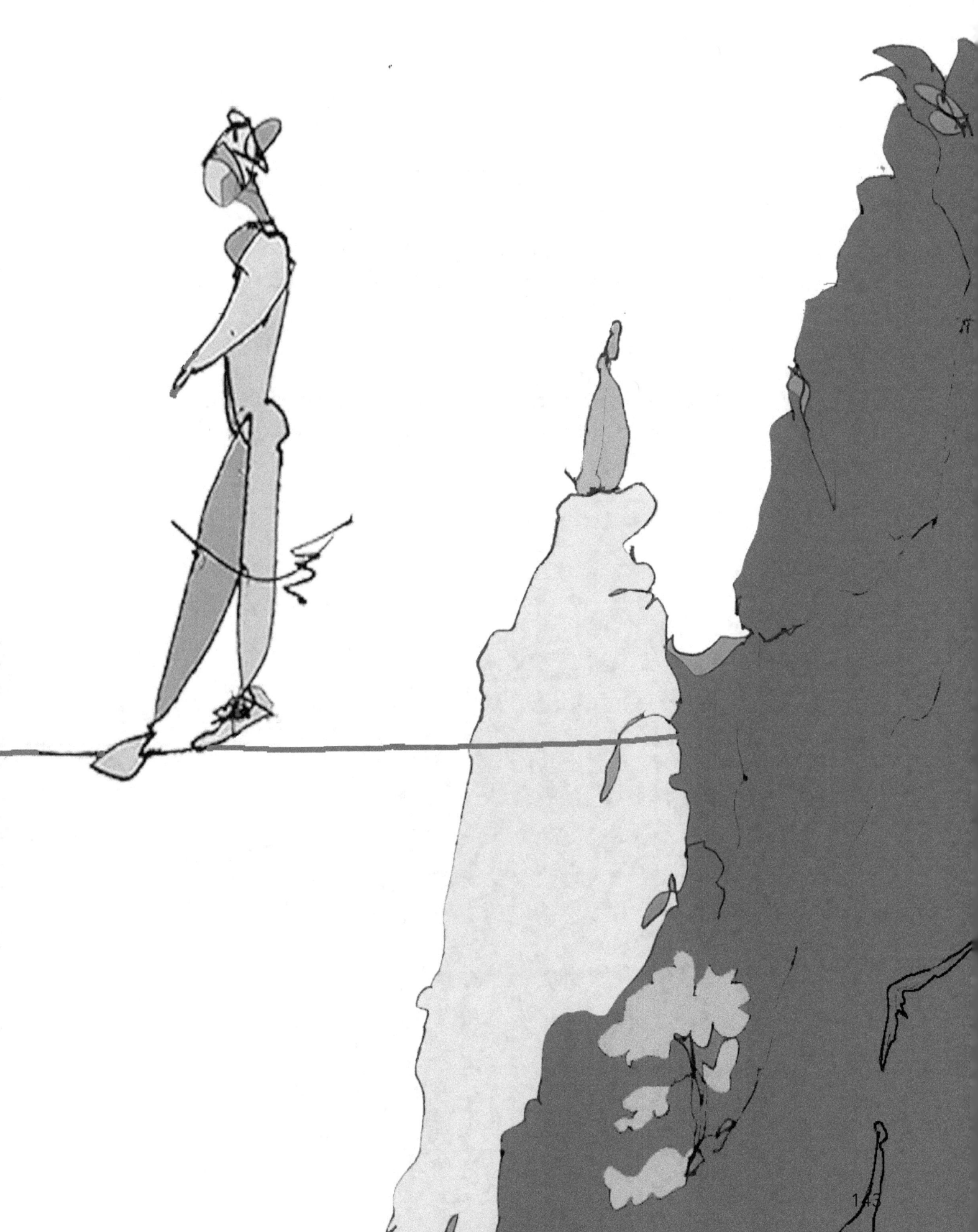

HEARTLINE

Molten ring of gold
Lost to boiling sea of sand and stone
Loss. Loss. Loss.

Gold ring of trust
Fallen amongst sea and silver fish
Restored to the believer.

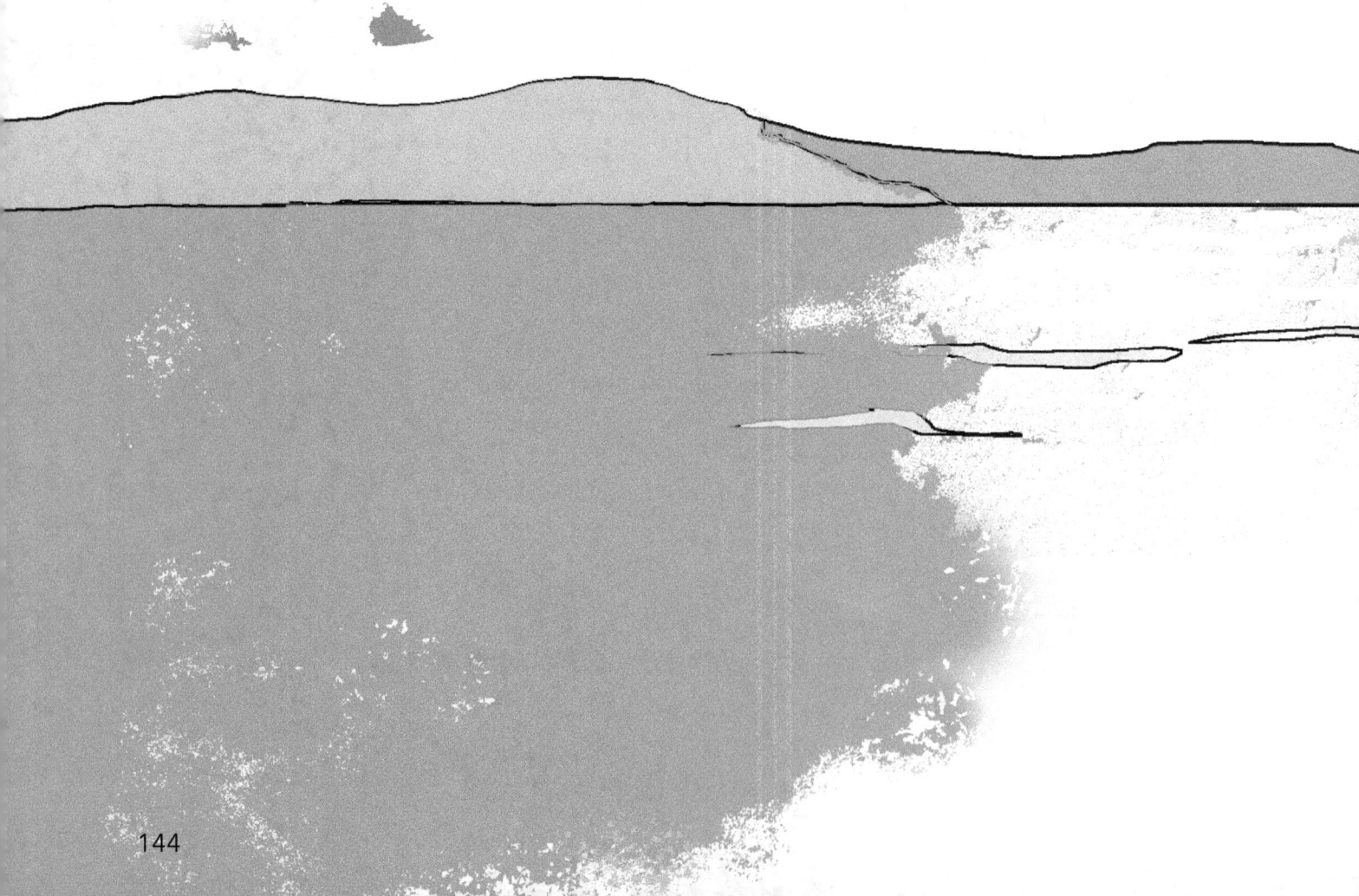

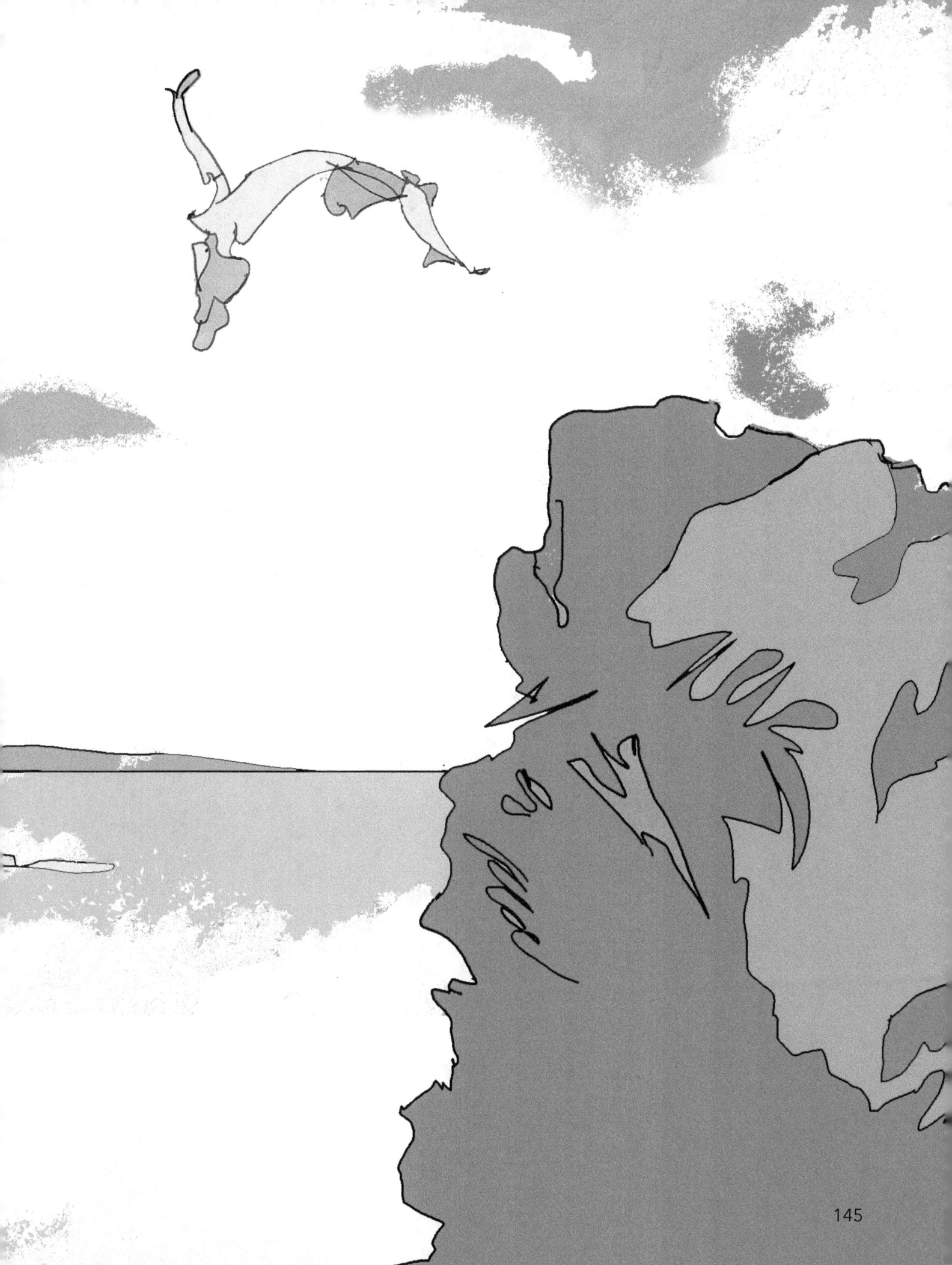

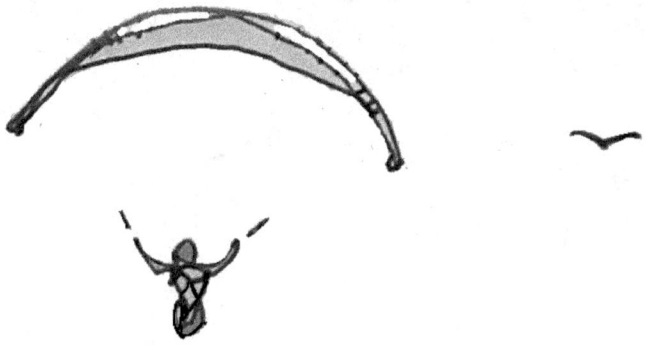

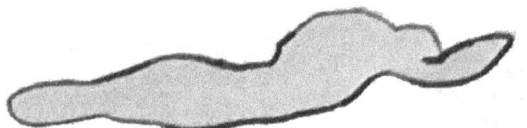

SAPPHIRE BEACH

Sacred oil
Uncovers the art of you and me
Anointed in light.

www.ingramcontent.com/pod-product-compliance
Lightning Source LLC
Chambersburg PA
CBHW062324220526
45469CB00008B/2613